ALASTAIR BUCHAN

PASSAGE MAKING MADE PERFECT

ADLARD COLES NAUTICAL
BLOOMSBURY
LONDON • NEW DELHI • NEW YORK • SYDNEY

Acknowledgements

In helping me write this book I would particularly wish to thank Keith Banks who read and corrected the early drafts of Part One. I also owe a vote of thanks to Bill and George Ross who patiently listened to what I had to say on this subject and corrected my wilder views before they reached paper. Thanks are also due to the many friends and sailing acquaintances who I surreptitiously used as sounding boards who probably wondered why I was forever bringing conversation round to passage making but nevertheless helped me firm up my ideas and how to present them.

Sadly they cannot take the responsibility for any errors and omissions, that remains with me.

As always, a huge thanks goes to my wife who uncomplainingly reads through the text correcting my poor grammar and careless mistakes.

Thanks also to Liz Multon, Jenny Clark and Jenni Davis, my editors, and Mark Silver, the illustrator, a great team who have done a brilliant job of converting a collection of words, figures and pictures into a readable book.

Dedication

This book is dedicated to D J Thurm with the hope that one day he may read it.

CONTENTS

INTRODUCTION

There appears to be no generally accepted definition of passage making, but we use the term assuming everyone knows exactly what we mean by it. The closest definition comes from the website of Taylor Made Systems of Gloversville USA, which says that 'passage making is long-distance cruising'. Its simplicity is then ruined when they go on to describe ocean passage making as 'offshore, either on the ocean or large lake'. In his book *Cruising Boat Sailing*, Bob Bond describes a passage as 'longer than the usual coastal hops and usually involving days and nights at sea', which will disappoint those who happily describe their voyages from our shores to Ireland, France, the Low Countries, Germany and Scandinavia as a 'passage' although these crossings rarely involve 'days and nights at sea'. Elsewhere I discovered that a passage maker is 'a sturdy seagoing vessel, capable of handling large seas, and fitted for voyages to distant ports' (Seatalk Nautical Dictionary: www.seatalk.info) which, depending on your definition of 'distant', could involve ocean voyages.

Running through all these definitions is a sense that passage making is an activity involving sailing further than your usual voyages, whether they be ten miles or a thousand. In fact, passage making is a broad church, offering different activities to different people. Your boat can be a fishing or diving platform, a floating bird-watching hide, the marine equivalent of the garden shed where you escape the travails of everyday life, a floating caravan, or a magic carpet that carries you to new lands and enchanted worlds. Not all of these activities necessarily involve overnight sailing or crossing oceans. No one ever forgets their first entry into a strange port, even if it is only a handful of miles along the coast from home. The first time you lose sight of land or sail at night, even if it is only crossing the bay, loses nothing in the retelling. They are passages that rank, in memory at least, with the greatest of circumnavigations. For me, passage making is going for a sail – *any* sail.

PASSAGE MAKING VERSUS PASSAGE PLANNING

Passage making is often regarded as synonymous with voyage or passage planning, but passage planning is only one part of the story. How you implement your passage plan is a very different, some would say more skilful, activity than planning. The word passage in the term *passage plan* also suggests that your plan only covers the period when you are at sea. In fact, the planning and the preparation for your passage may begin weeks, months or even years before you cast off.

In the words of that old military adage, 'Proper planning and preparation prevent pretty poor performance'. No soldier ever said 'pretty poor performance', but its meaning burns through: if you want a safe, seamanlike passage then think through what you want to achieve and do the hard work ahead of casting off. Another military cliché is 'Sweat saves blood'. Translated into sailor speak, this becomes 'Plan well, prepare thoroughly and sail easy'.

Passage making not only includes all the planning you do before you cast off and your efforts to execute that plan, but it also takes in how you equip and organise your boat, how competently the boat is sailed, the relationship between you and your crew and the general atmosphere on board. Above all else, sailing should be enjoyable for everyone involved and making it so lies heavily on the wise skipper's shoulders. A happy crew means a fair passage.

Even if you are making a passage so familiar you could do it in your sleep, you must still have a passage plan, firstly because you need it and secondly because the law says that you must have one.

SOLAS

Issued under the auspices of the International Maritime Organization (IMO), the International Convention for the Safety of Life at Sea, or SOLAS for short, is probably the most important of all international treaties on safety at sea. The first version was inspired by the sinking of the *Titanic* and came into force in 1914. Since then it has been updated several times. Normally SOLAS only applies to commercial vessels but Regulation 34 of Chapter 5 of the latest version, generally referred to as SOLAS V/34, is a rare exception, applying to leisure and commercial vessels alike.

Dealing with safe navigation and the avoidance of dangerous situations, it requires that 'prior to proceeding to sea, the master shall ensure that the intended voyage has been planned using the appropriate nautical charts and nautical publications for the area concerned, taking into account the guidelines and recommendations developed by the Organization.' Sadly, the SOLAS guidelines and recommendations on passage planning have been developed with commercial vessels in mind. Leisure sailors are left to first work out and then follow their own guidelines and recommendations.

To help, the Maritime and Coastguard Agency (MCA) has produced their own advice for leisure sailors. They recommend that, when planning a boating trip, skippers should take into account factors such as weather, tides, limitations of the vessel, the crew and any navigational dangers; prepare a contingency plan; and leave information about their passage with someone ashore. Remarkably, there is no requirement in the rules or the MCA's advice for the voyage plan to be written down and, most curiously of all, the rules apply only when sailing outside 'categorised waters'. Much of the UK's coastal waters are classed as 'categorised waters'.

MCA ADVICE FOR LEISURE CRAFT ON VOYAGE PLANNING

Regulation V/34 'Safe Navigation and avoidance of dangerous situations' is a new regulation. It concerns prior-planning for your boating trip, more commonly known as voyage or passage planning. Voyage planning is basically common sense. As a pleasure boat user, you should particularly take into account the following points when planning a boating trip:

• WEATHER
Before you go boating, check the weather forecast and get regular updates if you are planning to be out for any length of time.

• TIDES
Check the tidal predictions for your trip and ensure that they fit with what you are planning to do.

• LIMITATIONS OF THE VESSEL
Consider whether your boat is up to the proposed trip and that you have sufficient safety equipment and stores with you.

• CREW
Take into account the experience and physical ability of your crew. Crews suffering from cold, tiredness and seasickness won't be able to do their job properly and could even result in an overburdened skipper.

• NAVIGATIONAL DANGERS
Make sure you are familiar with any navigational dangers you may encounter during your boating trip. This generally means checking an up to date chart and a current pilot book or almanac.

• CONTINGENCY PLAN
Always have a contingency plan should anything go wrong. Before you go, consider bolt holes and places where you can take refuge should conditions deteriorate or if you suffer an incident or injury. Bear in mind that your GPS set is vulnerable and could fail at the most inconvenient time. It is sensible and good practice to make sure you are not over-reliant on your GPS set and that you can navigate yourself to safety without it should it fail you.

• INFORMATION ASHORE
Make sure that someone ashore knows your plans and knows what to do should they become concerned for your well-being. The Coastguard Voluntary Safety Identification Scheme (commonly known as CG66) is free, and easy to join. The scheme aims to help the Coastguard to help you quickly should you get into trouble while boating. It could save your life.

To reinforce advice from the MCA there are hundreds of checklists available on the internet. Written by leisure sailors to lead you through the passage planning process, they all work the same way: tick the boxes, fill in the missing words and you have your passage plan. Checklists have their place. Many of those I have seen were written by those who have been there and done it all. Their checklists have grown out of their own hard-learned experiences in preparing their own boat for their own long, blue water voyages. Their lists have a sound

CATEGORISED WATERS

No vessel is required to have a passage plan when they are sailing in categorised waters. Categorised waters have statutory force under Regulation 2 of the Merchant Shipping (Categorisation of Waters) Regulations 1992 and were meant:

- for the operation of Class IV, V and VI Passenger Ships
- to determine which waters are not regarded as 'sea' for the purposes of regulations made, or treated as made, under Section 85 of the Merchant Shipping Act 1995

There are four classes of categorised water:

1. Category A: Narrow rivers and canals where the depth of water is generally less than 1.5m
2. Category B: Wider rivers and canals where the depth of water is generally 1.5m or more and where the significant wave height could not be expected to exceed 0.6m at any time
3. Category C: Tidal rivers and estuaries and large, deep lakes and lochs where the significant wave height could not be expected to exceed 1.2m at any time
4. Category D: Tidal rivers and estuaries where the significant wave height could not be expected to exceed 2m at any time

Categories C and D include considerable chunks of the UK coastline, much of it very popular with leisure sailors. It would be imprudent to sail in these waters without preparing some sort of passage plan. Meeting short, steep, 1 metre high waves is always uncomfortable. Encountering the same waves when they have grown to 2m is serious, especially if the wind is against the tide.

I suspect that excluding categorised waters from SOLAS V/34 is more for the benefit of commercial vessels, and the implications of the conditions described in Categories C and D for leisure craft were overlooked.

It is worth noting that if you spill diesel then under the Merchant Shipping (Prevention of Oil Pollution) Regulations 1996, 'sea' includes any estuaries or arms of the sea.

empirical base and are frequently prefaced by advice like 'good preparations are essential for a successful voyage'. They contain much worthwhile information that the authors wish to share so that others don't have to reinvent the wheel. But be wary of assuming that one checklist fits all and that you must, for example, prepare for every passage as if you are about to cross an ocean. Nobody can deny that good preparations are crucial to a successful voyage, but they should be appropriate to you, your boat, your crew and your voyage, otherwise you could find yourself behaving inappropriately.

HAVE A GOAL AND KNOW THE FACTS

Confusing passage making with passage planning puts the cart far in front of the horse. Before you begin planning any passage, you need a clear vision of what you are attempting to achieve. In other words, knowing your goal comes first. Not just any goal – *your* goal; or, if you prefer, your aim. They both describe what you wish to achieve.

You cannot plan without information. Once you have an unambiguous goal then you can

GOING TO EXTREMES

We were rafted up alongside another boat on Whitby's Fish Quay. It was a pleasant, sunny, summer's day with a kindly north-westerly wind. Both boats were waiting for the tide to sail south. When the time to cast off arrived, the crew of the other boat appeared on deck dressed in oilskins, seaboots, lifejackets, gloves and harnesses, with fearsome-looking knives, round their waists and, although it was early morning, torches on lanyards round their necks. Only their eyes, sunglasses actually, were visible behind their zipped up hoods. They looked like a SWAT team on a dangerous mission.

As we sailed out of the harbour, the skipper of the other boat told us that they were sailing 16 miles south to Scarborough. He passed this information across in the same tone of voice Columbus used when telling his crew that they were bound for the New World. I felt a little sad. I am sure they enjoyed their sail to Scarborough but I could not help wondering if they had worked out what they were doing for themselves or if they were unquestioningly following some universal passage planning checklist which insisted that on a cloudless summer's day, in a friendly wind and easy sea, they must dress for rounding Cape Horn in a blizzard.

The unthinking ticking of boxes is not confined to clothing. Once clear of the channel when you leave Lymington it is under 3 miles to Yarmouth on the Isle of Wight – less than an hour's sailing. In summer months it is not unusual for a yacht on passage between Lymington and Yarmouth to contact Solent Coastguard and spend ten minutes putting in a transit report, carefully listing details of their yacht, number on board, destination and ETA. Ten minutes later they are back on air advising the coastguard of their arrival in Yarmouth. I am sure that they are only following their passage plan as detailed in their checklist.

Checklists are useful but they are a tool, an aide-memoire, not an instruction or commandment chipped in stone on a distant mountain top. They are not the result of a sudden revelation as you sail down channel towards Damascus. They should grow out of your passage making strategy, be written by you and be unique to your passage.

begin collecting all the relevant information. Only when you have that information can you begin planning how you can best go about achieving your aim: planning without information is to dream.

PLANNING IN STAGES

Everything is easier if it is broken down into small steps. Any strategy for passage making travels through a multi-stage process. Each stage has its own retinue of secondary phases. Going to sea is far down the line.

Passage making falls naturally into two major phases: onshore and at sea. It may seem odd to claim that you do passage making onshore but you do. It is when you do all the hard work.

ONSHORE

The onshore phase begins the instant the idea of the voyage or cruise first occurs to you, which may be some time before you cast off. This is when the bulk of the work happens and when the time available and resources are at their greatest. This is when you have the

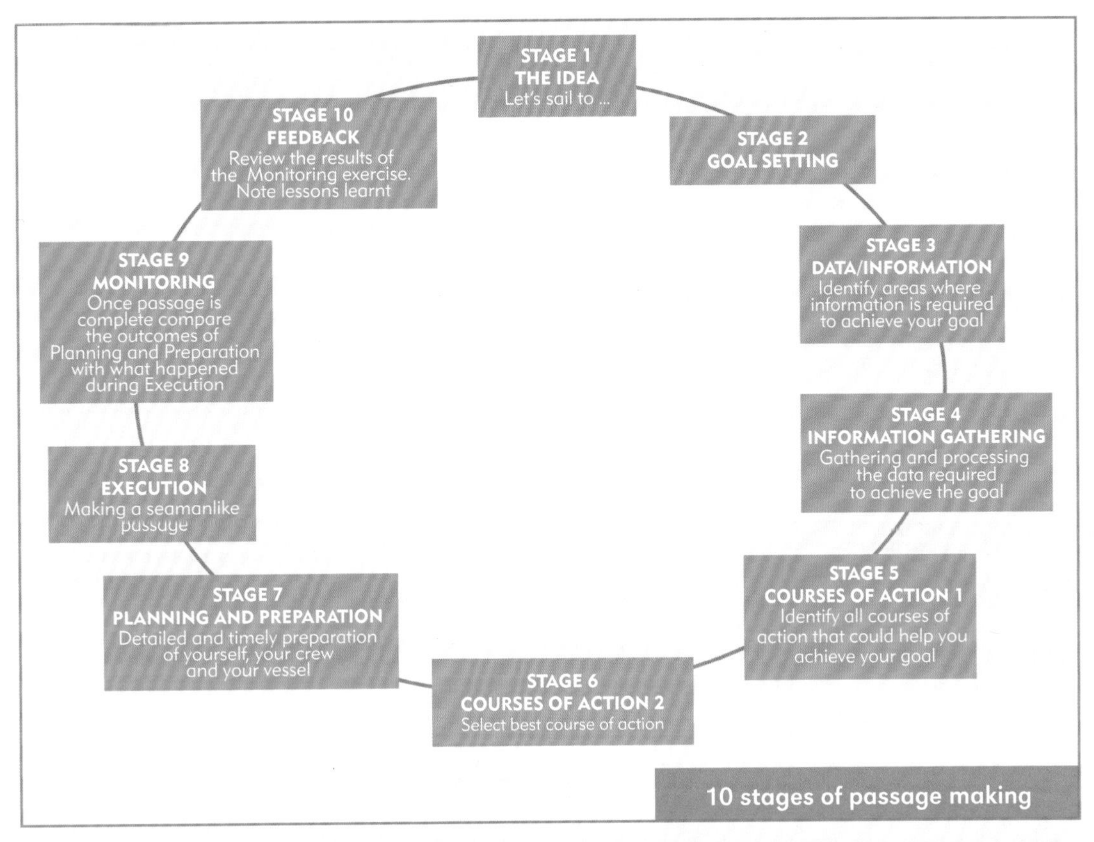

10 stages of passage making

best, and most direct, access to information, suppliers, engineers, electronic engineers, sailmakers, boatyards, riggers and other specialist help. It is when the assets that you can bring to resolving problems and difficulties are at their greatest. It is the time when you have the greatest control over events and the pace at which they happen. You can accept delays or speed the programme up, change the sequence in which work is carried out, or drop or add items to the programme.

It is extremely important to make sure that your work during the onshore phase is fully complete and done to the highest possible standard before you go to sea. Planning and preparation are never again going to be so easy. In his book *Cruises of the Joan*, W E Sinclair tells how in 1927 he planned to cross the Atlantic from Britain via Iceland in his boat *Joan*, a shade over 22 feet overall, in which he had already cruised round Britain and sailed to Madeira and back. As the season wore on, his preparations fell further and further behind schedule until he reached a point where if he didn't sail immediately he might not sail at all that season. It is a temptation to which we have all been exposed and Sinclair, as we all have done, yielded to temptation. He sailed, only to lose his boat south of Greenland. His experience is a salutary warning on the perils of cutting the onshore phase short.

Throughout the onshore phase, lack of cash and time may tempt you to make compromises. Some of these temptations may be trivial and carry no significant penalty. Even so, think carefully before yielding to the blandishments of shortcuts. The sad demise of Donald Crowhurst in the 1968/69 Golden Globe Race was partly due to an evil alliance of lack of cash and pressure of time dominating his preparations. This created problems and difficulties that were unresolved when he sailed, remained unresolved at sea, and ultimately contributed to tragedy.

By comparison, Alec Rose set out on his circumnavigation in *Lively Lady* but returned to harbour after his boat suffered damage in a collision. Faced with further difficulties, he prudently delayed his attempt until the following year rather than set out too late in the season to safely round Cape Horn. Francis Chichester, meanwhile, left later but stole his thunder and sailed *Gipsy Moth IV* into the history books.

AT SEA

At sea, the process of passage making continues through its various phases unbroken, if not uninterrupted, until you have finally achieved your aim and safely berthed. Once you have cast off you are on your own. Fickle gods rule the weather and Poseidon imposes his will on the waves with a rod of iron. Modern communications open up the possibility of seeking advice or information from shoreside contacts, but the bottom line is that setbacks at sea must be resolved using onboard skills and resources. It is impossible to carry bespoke resources for every conceivable situation. All you can reasonably manage is to cover the more obvious and hope that imagination and a talent for make-do and mend provides answers for the rest.

If events don't go according to plan, life doesn't stop while you appraise the situation and work out what to do. It is a truism (not a bad joke) that the situation is fluid and you are always acting under pressure of time using incomplete, possibly inaccurate, information and working with inadequate resources. This is when the time spent shoreside thinking through your goal, gathering information and considering the thousand 'what-ifs' gives you the confidence to trust yourself and your decisions.

SUMMARY

Sailing ought to be fun, not an uncertain and uncomfortable journey from one terrifying incident to another with the crew split into feuding cliques. Having a successful and enjoyable passage is up to you, and this book gives you the tools to do it your way.

Passage making begins with a tailor-made plan for your voyage, your boat and your crew, and writing your own plan involves going back to the first principles of passage making. That is what this book is all about. The first part explains the principles that lie behind creating your own passage making plan. The second part looks at what needs to go into your plan.

To cover as much ground as possible, many of the points discussed in this book are treated as though you are about to make an ocean voyage. This leaves you to pick and choose the factors most relevant to your passage – clearly not every ingredient needs to be considered to the same depth or even be included in every plan. As a general rule, the longer the passage then the more detailed your planning should be.

Once all your planning and preparations are complete, the third section considers how best to put your plan into action and follows up with practical examples of how the principles of passage making can be applied to day, offshore and ocean passages.

The use of the word 'perfect' in this book's title is not an egotistical claim regarding the advice it contains. Any perfection in passage making comes from you, the effort you put into your planning and preparation, the skill with which you execute your plan and the passages that result. Hopefully, this book will help you make it perfect.

THE TEN SECRETS OF PERFECT PASSAGE PLANNING

1 CONSTANCY OF PURPOSE

Create a constancy of purpose by very carefully considering your goal and allocating resources to its long term aims rather than short term objectives.

2 OUT WITH THE OLD

Sailors have traditionally supported time-honoured values and methods. Many of the older generation regret the passing of the old ways. It was ever so. Sometime during the Stone Age, the introduction of sails was ridiculed by traditionalists who reckoned there was nothing wrong with paddling your own canoe. If you do not keep abreast with the latest developments then you will be left behind.

3 USE THE RIGHT EQUIPMENT

Identify the equipment you will use and need aboard your boat and buy, beg or borrow only the best. Second rate equipment often has a short half-life and fails when you need it most. It is a false economy. Buying toys for boys is a waste of money.

4 KEEP RAISING STANDARDS

Aim to constantly improve your passage making skills. Always look for newer and better ways to plan and execute your passages.

5 MAKE TRAINING A PRIORITY

Keeping abreast of new developments includes understanding how they work and taking advantage of them. If you and your crew are not constantly learning new skills then you are on the way to becoming old fogeys.

6 VALUE LEADERSHIP

Develop a style of leadership that helps your crew work better together.

7 BREAK DOWN BARRIERS

There should be no barriers between yourself and your crew. You are a team and you, your mate, watch officers, and crew, especially those with individual areas of responsibility such as the engineer, electrician, purser and bosun, must often come together to resolve a problem. Clinging to the traditional ship's hierarchy and insisting the skipper must always be seen to be in charge can hamper finding a solution. For example, if it is an engineering problem then step back and allow the engineer to take the lead.

8 STEER CLEAR OF EXHORTATIONS

Avoid using slogans, catchphrases and buzzwords to motivate your crew or bond them together. It does not. Jargon soon becomes meaningless and whatever little positive effect it may have is soon lost.

9 ENCOURAGE SELF-RESPECT

Give credit where it is due. When someone does a good job then publicly praise them. If someone has a better idea than you then publicly congratulate them. You feel good, they feel even better and everyone works harder knowing their work will be acknowledged.

10 ALWAYS DO BETTER THAN LAST TIME

Improved performance comes from having the correct equipment, training and practice. Doing better is everyone's job. Your job is to make sure they know this and this time to do better than last time.

UKR
170

PART 1
THE THEORY

ACHIEVING YOUR GOAL

> *Obstacles are things a person sees when he takes his eyes off his goal.*
> **E Joseph Cossman**

A useful tool in passage making is to establish a hierarchy with your aim or goal at the top. Below this are a series of objectives, which – should they be successfully achieved – lead you to your goal. It is rare for objectives to follow one after another in an orderly queue, each waiting their turn. More usually it is a wild dance as they compete for your attention and resources. Under each objective is a series of strategies, which detail how you intend to attain that objective.

It is usual to claim that you can have only one goal; however, there are two complicating factors. Firstly, you may give the responsibility for carrying out some of your objectives to others and, even though they are aware of the bigger picture (ie your goal), what was one of *your* objectives becomes *their* goal. In a further twist, their strategies for achieving their goal (your objective) may be quite different from those you would have chosen. Secondly, goals are not always fixed. Your goal might be to sail from A to B but for all sorts of reasons you may decide to sail to C or D. In other words, you have a new goal.

DEFINING YOUR GOAL

Every passage starts with a light-bulb moment. The instant when the first glimmerings of an idea spark into life is usually preceded with the words 'Let's sail to...'. Many of these unexpected inspirations burn out, like shooting stars, as suddenly as they appeared, dismissed as too fanciful, too ambitious, too costly, too time-consuming, too ridiculous or simply the product of too much ale.

Sometimes one hardy idea, flickering and spluttering, hangs in there, scurrying around your head like a fractious child demanding attention. You give it a second and then a third thought. It has possibilities but you know only too well that in the real world any goal, however modest or ambitious, short- or long-term, comes laden with small print. Goals that do not know their limitations are a fantasy to see you through the boredom of earning a living.

IDENTIFYING THE LIMITATIONS

You must identify the limitations to your goal and work out how best to minimise their effect. Sadly, there is no standard checklist of limitations. Their type and number depend on the passage and person. A useful way to proceed is to write down your goal. This breathes life into your idea, and gives it the energy to spark your imagination. To reveal its limitations, your written goal must be concrete and specific. Bear in mind that every action has its reaction. Your preferred way of solving one limitation, besides tweaking your goal, will also affect how you deal with other limitations.

Identifying every limitation is impossible. No matter how carefully you work to identify the limitations to your goal, some always escape discovery until you are far out at sea.

A THWARTED PLAN

A year or two ago I planned to sail up the east coast of England, through the Caledonian Canal to the west coast of Scotland. There I would play amongst the highlands and islands for a few weeks before dropping through the Crinan Canal into the Clyde estuary and taking the newly restored Forth and Clyde Canal back to the East Coast and home. A pleasant circular route and, since I had previously followed the Leeds to Liverpool Canal from coast to coast, complete my hat trick of traversing Britain's coast to coast waterways.

I knew that before entering the Forth and Clyde Canal I had to lower the mast and checked there were arrangements for this at Bowling where the canal began and also at the other end where I entered the Firth of Forth. I also noted that the locks on the Forth and Clyde take boats 60 feet long and 20 feet wide which was more than adequate for my yacht.

I was in the Clyde and approaching Bowling when I discovered that if I had read further I would have learned that the maximum air-draft of the Forth and Clyde Canal is nine feet. There is a fixed gantry on the stern of my boat. Even with the mast down I was snookered with nobody to blame but myself.

TIME

Most limitations are not self-inflicted. High on most people's list is time. Only a lucky few have sufficient spare time or cash to sail when they like for as long as they like. Fortunately, unlimited time or cash aren't essential for great cruises.

For most of us, our sailing is limited to a two or three week summer cruise, topped and tailed with a long bank holiday weekend sail. In between there is some weekend sailing and perhaps an occasional day or evening sail or a race round the bay. This means that if your boat is based on the south coast and you wish to spend your three week summer holiday exploring Scotland's west coast, then after sailing north you would be lucky to have a week left to discover the Highlands and Islands before beginning the voyage home. A week is barely time for a decent dram, and a day or two of bad weather would see you starting your return journey before you arrived.

There are always options to lessen any limitation – in this case, ways for you to extend your time on Scotland's west coast. Perhaps the most obvious way is to sail your boat north over the long Easter break. Leave it in some suitable harbour and return home by road or rail until it is time for your summer cruise. Once your cruise is complete, you can sail home over the August bank holiday.

This solution insists that you take your summer break between the Easter and August bank holidays. You might consider tagging the August bank holiday on to the end of your three week cruise. This would escape a second long journey north to pick up your boat for the return trip and, since you are simply extending your time at sea, also avoid the need for time-consuming pre-sail checks that would be necessary after a break.

The bank holiday passages are, in effect, delivery passages where you go to sea and keep going until you arrive, regardless of the weather. This is especially true of the Easter passage north, when the chances of meeting heavy weather are fairly high. If you normally sail only with your family, you may require a stronger, more numerous crew to guarantee the necessary manpower to remain at sea continuously. Even so, should the weather prove too much you might find yourself out of time, in a harbour short of your destination. It may not be the end, but it certainly means exploring a new range of alternatives.

Another option is to use three crews. One spends their summer cruise taking your boat north. You then have your three week cruise and finally, around the August bank holiday, another crew brings your boat back to your home port. Placing your boat in the hands of a crew you trust for the delivery passages means you must be confident they will look after her as carefully as you do. This probably rules out complete strangers, certainly as skippers; it also means juggling three sets of holiday dates and possibly discussions with your insurers.

Alternatively, you could spend one summer cruising slowly north and leave your boat in Scottish waters for several seasons while you explore at leisure before spending another summer sailing home. A drawback to this option is that although weekend sailing is just about possible while your boat is kept in Scottish waters, the day and evening sailing you would normally do from your home port is almost certainly out of the question.

Or, you might consider chartering a boat. This becomes the option of choice if your goal is to spend your three-week holiday cruising in the Caribbean, Mediterranean or other distant waters.

AIM: to cruise the west coast of Scotland from home port on the south coast			
Limitation	**Nature**	**Options**	**Consequence**
Time	There are only three weeks available	Sail north as quickly as possible, cruise, and with a week in hand return south	• The trip north is about 550 miles, say 5/6 days at sea. After allowing for the trip home this leaves only 8/9 days for exploring the West Coast • Timetable is very tight. Two or three days poor weather could throw it completely out • Is your normal crew capable of spending 5/6 days continuously at sea? If the answer is 'no' this is not the option for you unless you supplement your crew
		Extend the time available; have one crew deliver the boat north; you cruise for three weeks; have another crew bring the boat home	• Must have absolute faith in delivery skippers and their crews to deliver the boat in a fit and seaworthy condition • Must coordinate timings of your cruise with theirs • Must insist they allow at least 14 days for their passage • Sort out financial arrangements. Do you contribute towards the cost of their cruise or do they chip in to help pay for yours? • Confirm arrangements with insurance company
		Extend the time available; spend one summer sailing north, the next cruising and the third returning home	• Weekend sailing would be topped and tailed by long, tiring road/rail journeys • Day sailing out of the question • Winter refit could be awkward • North/south cruises are splendid opportunities to explore the Irish and Welsh coasts
		Charter	• For a short while you have the expense of running two boats • You could charter a larger boat than needed and invite friends to share the costs

Limitation	Nature	Options	Consequence
			• You escape the hassle of the north/south delivery trips • Weekend and day sailing on your own boat is available as normal outside your summer cruise
		Choose to cruise somewhere within easy reach, say the Channel Islands or Brittany	• Abandon goal. Throw six to start again

THE BOAT

Another limitation to your goal is your boat, but this may not be as great as it might first appear. A belief has grown up that big is best. Twenty or thirty years ago the average yacht was probably around 25 feet overall and there were fleets of pocket cruisers well under 25 feet LOA. Most were excellent sea boats. Classes like Silhouette, Trident, Hurley, Eventide, Corribee and Signet built up enviable reputations and put up some very respectable passages, envied by sailors of bigger boats. Many of these small craft are still going strong today.

Of the five yachts that took part in the first singlehanded transatlantic race in 1960, four were 25 feet LOA or less. The exception was Francis Chichester's *Gipsy Moth III*, which at 40 feet LOA was by far the largest boat in the race. The smallest – *Cap Horn*, sailed by Jean Lacombe – was 6.5m (20.9 feet) LOA.

The first known double Atlantic small boat crossing was made in 1880/81 by Fredrick Norman and George P. Thomas in their 16 foot converted dory *Little Western*. In the 1970s Alan Toone made a very impressive double Atlantic crossing in a 21 foot Corribee, *Corrie Bee*.

In the 1950s to 1980s, boats 30–35 feet overall were thought fit for very serious passages. Alec Rose was only the seventh person to sail solo round Cape Horn. His boat, the *Lively Lady*, was 36 feet LOA. Of the nine yachts competing in the 1968 Golden Globe Race, four were under 35 feet LOA and the winner (and only finisher) was Robin Knox-Johnston's 32 foot LOA *Suhaili*. Joshua Slocum's *Spray* was 37 feet overall.

Nowadays, boats around 35 feet LOA are considered small. The average is about 40 feet LOA and a 50 foot yacht entering a marina barely raises a ripple of interest. Somehow, despite all the evidence, waterline length has become conflated not only with seaworthiness but also with seamanship. The truth that a small, well-equipped yacht is safer and more seaworthy than a much larger, ill-found yacht has been forgotten, along with the history of small boats pioneering ocean cruising.

If your goal is to make an ocean crossing, the size of your boat alone should not be the determining factor whether or not you use your current boat or trade up. If you decide to trade in your present boat for one you believe is more suitable, this will have a knock-on effect on your timescale and budget. There are few, if any, off the shelf, ready to go, ocean-going boats. There are many classes of boats with well earned reputations for making ocean passages and your most likely solution is to buy one of these, new or second-hand, and fit it out for ocean passages. This will probably add at least a year to your timetable.

EQUIPMENT

The longer your passage, the more equipment you will need. The bigger your boat, the more its equipment costs, bringing your boat, equipment and cash into a vicious circle.

If you intend to sail across oceans then you must have some form of absolutely reliable self-steering. My preference is for a windvane but I am not a snob. Electronic autohelms are fine. Compared to windvanes they are cheap, but they require a reliable source of constant power together with the means of generating and storing it. Windvane or autohelm, whatever your choice, you must have one or other or both for long passages.

I once sailed across the Pacific with four others on a yacht with no self-steering. Someone had to be holding the tiller all the time. Having crossed the Atlantic solo, working 9.00am to 5.00pm and only touching the tiller when entering or leaving harbour, I found helming for hours on end under a tropical sun in an unsheltered cockpit an unpleasant, unnecessary and, with some foresight, avoidable slog.

Other equipment you may wish to add for ocean passages includes satellite communications, watermakers, fridges, freezers, generators, solar panels, extra fuel and water tanks and so on. The only limits to this list are your wallet and imagination.

PERSONAL SKILLS

An easily overlooked limitation is whether or not you possess the skills and experience to make the passage safely. Before the introduction of electronic navigation an individual's practical competence in seamanship and navigation more or less kept step with their ambition. If a passage involved sailing out of sight of land, you delayed sailing over the horizon until you were confident that you had the skills to find land again, more or less where expected. Now, have plotter will sail. Plotters and GPS treat sailing across an ocean as navigationally no different or demanding as a trip round the bay and have given people the confidence to boldly sail wherever they want.

It is not uncommon to come across yachtsmen of very limited experience undertaking passages that, if they had to navigate on a paper chart, would be far beyond their reach. Not too long ago, competence in astronavigation was a requirement for any ocean passage. Now, if you went round the yachts in Las Palmas in mid November removing their plotters it would be surprising if the numbers leaving for the Caribbean reached double figures.

Always list what skills and experience are required to achieve your goal, cast an honest eye over yours, and ask whether they fit the bill. There is nothing wrong with being ambitious but is that gap between your ambitions and your abilities a challenge or a yawning chasm waiting to swallow you up? Are you exploring the boundaries of your skills or taking a step too far into the unknown? Can you find some means of bridging that gap?

Before setting out on my first solo Atlantic crossing I had never experienced long periods of solitude. Did I have what it takes to survive weeks of being alone? How would I cope, particularly when the going got tough and there was no one to consult or blame? The only way I could see of finding an answer was to sail and hope.

GOALS ARE BUT MANY SMALL LITTLES

There is a Latin proverb that says: 'Greatness is but many small littles.' Goals are no different. Anything and everything is possible when you dream but when you come face to face with your goal and have to make a start or back down they have a habit of looking bigger and more difficult than you thought. This illusion of size is bolstered by our addiction to hype. The right publicity can make a gentle day sail across the bay appear like an epic voyage into unknown, storm wracked, danger infested waters. Happily, just because a goal is apparently unattainable does not mean it is out of reach. You are simply looking at it the wrong way.

Before setting out on my first Atlantic crossing I spent months in planning and preparation. As the departure date approached I suffered from fits of chronic doubt and my carefully laid plans broke out into a horrible rash. My longest solo passage to date was about 150 miles. Sailing almost 3,000 miles was beyond my ken. At only 20 feet overall, my boat was small for this sort of passage. I knew, in theory, what was required but it is a big ocean. Worrying grew to fill my days and crossing the Atlantic looked increasingly impossible. Finally, my wife, fed up with my constant whining, said, 'Why don't you just go and see how far you can get?' She understood that I had developed a bad case of tunnel vision. I had come to see the crossing as a single, uninterrupted voyage. In fact it was, and still is, made up of a series of relatively short passages.

It is about 500 miles in easy hops between my home port and Falmouth, my departure point for crossing Biscay. I had, almost casually, made that trip the previous year when I had sailed round Britain. A few years before that I had crossed Biscay and cruised along the Iberian coast, albeit with a crew in a larger boat. It was not all unknown waters, and until I left the Canaries no passage was longer than 500–600 miles; but by then I would have the crossing of the dreaded Bay of Biscay under my keel. Even the 3,000 miles between the Canaries and the Caribbean could be taken in two bites by stopping off in the Cape Verde Islands.

For the first time I understood that the uncertainties that dominated my thoughts and loomed over me like a bouncer outside a nightclub were nothing more than a dinner suit on steroids. My goal of crossing the Atlantic remained but I now saw it as a Lego structure made up of a collection of shorter passages, which from a distance presented an imposing, unified construction. An Atlantic crossing is made up of a chain of secondary or minor goals that I could tackle one by one. Some of these shorter passages I had made before. Others I knew were within my experience and capabilities and the rest... well, that was the interesting bit.

As I wandered across the ocean, each day's objective would be my next port, whether it was 20, 200 or 2,000 miles away. I would continue sailing along this chain of mini-goals as long as it remained fun. If, or when, it ceased being enjoyable I would stop, catch my breath and work out whether I wished to continue or return home. In the event I had a great fifteen months making an Atlantic circuit and enjoyed it so much I had to do it again.

TELLING OTHERS

Time spent considering your goal, its limitations and how it breaks down into manageable chunks is never wasted. Once you have all this clearly in mind it is time to sit down and talk it through with your crew.

We all have a natural tendency to see our plan's virtues more clearly than its defects. What we really want is the best plan, not what appears best to us. If you believe in your goal and reckon that your ideas on how you intend to achieve it are sound, there is nothing to lose and much to gain by laying everything out for all to see. You are not seeking accolades. Praise would be welcome but you want constructive criticism. You may have previously considered and dismissed some of the points your crew raise, but other comments they make may give rise to second thoughts. They will see problems from viewpoints different to yours, identify limitations that you missed, and see new, possibly better solutions than those you found.

By incorporating their feedback, your goal comes to meet their needs and expectations as well as your own. It makes your voyage a joint enterprise with everyone pulling in the same direction. Crews who share a well-thought-through common goal, aware of what is expected of them and supplied with the appropriate skills and equipment, perform better than crews who leap aboard, cast off and then look aft, waiting to be told what comes next.

There is a considerable body of evidence that having a shared goal encourages a dogged perseverance. Nothing beats sheer persistence. There will be occasions when it is all that stands between you and failure. Owning a big, glossy boat does not promise success. Marinas are full of boats that leave the pontoon only to go into winter storage. In sailing, qualifications and certificates have an important role to play and are often perceived as carrying a promise of competence – but book knowledge must be backed up with hard won experience to be of real value. Every activity has those who know the theory of everything and the practice of nothing.

In the end, experience, staying power and dogged determination win the day. There is no failure except in no longer trying. The desire to keep going, to keep trying, has solved and will always solve problems and overcome difficulties. Persistence and determination are invincible (not the tunnel vision of mindlessly repeating the same action over and over again). There is nothing in the rules prohibiting the use of intelligence, imagination and good, old-fashioned low cunning. Only losers care how you succeed.

TEN ADVANTAGES OF SHARING YOUR GOAL

1 Goals prioritise. If everyone shares the same goal then time is not wasted on irrelevant activities. The most common reason for failure is doing second things first.

2 Sharing your goal allows you to draw upon the skills, talent and expertise of everyone on board.

3 Sharing a goal means that you and your crew always maintain a positive outlook.

4 Goals reinforce your priorities. Everybody knows what really matters. There is a difference between being busy and being productive.

5 Working to a shared goal means that nobody wastes time on irrelevant activities.

6 A goal focuses everyone's attention, effort and resources where they are required and helps maintain a positive outlook.

7 Goals set standards. Urging crew members to 'do their best' is a waste of breath. What does 'do their best' mean? How do they measure 'their best'? They are probably already working as hard and as well as they can. Besides, doing their best is not enough. Your crew must also know what they have to achieve. Having them rush, albeit very efficiently, every way but in the right direction can be not just counter-productive but fatal.

8 Goals give everyone a clear understanding of the part they are expected to play in achieving a common goal, reducing the possibility of crossed wires or duplicated work.

9 Goals allow the crew to set up self-regulatory mechanisms to check their performance. Skippers cannot constantly monitor how individuals or their crew are carrying out their duties. Giving them a shared goal or delegating work can encourage them to assess their own performance and look for ways to improve.

10 Crews are more likely to pull together and work through problems if pursuing a shared goal. Everybody wants to be on a winning team.

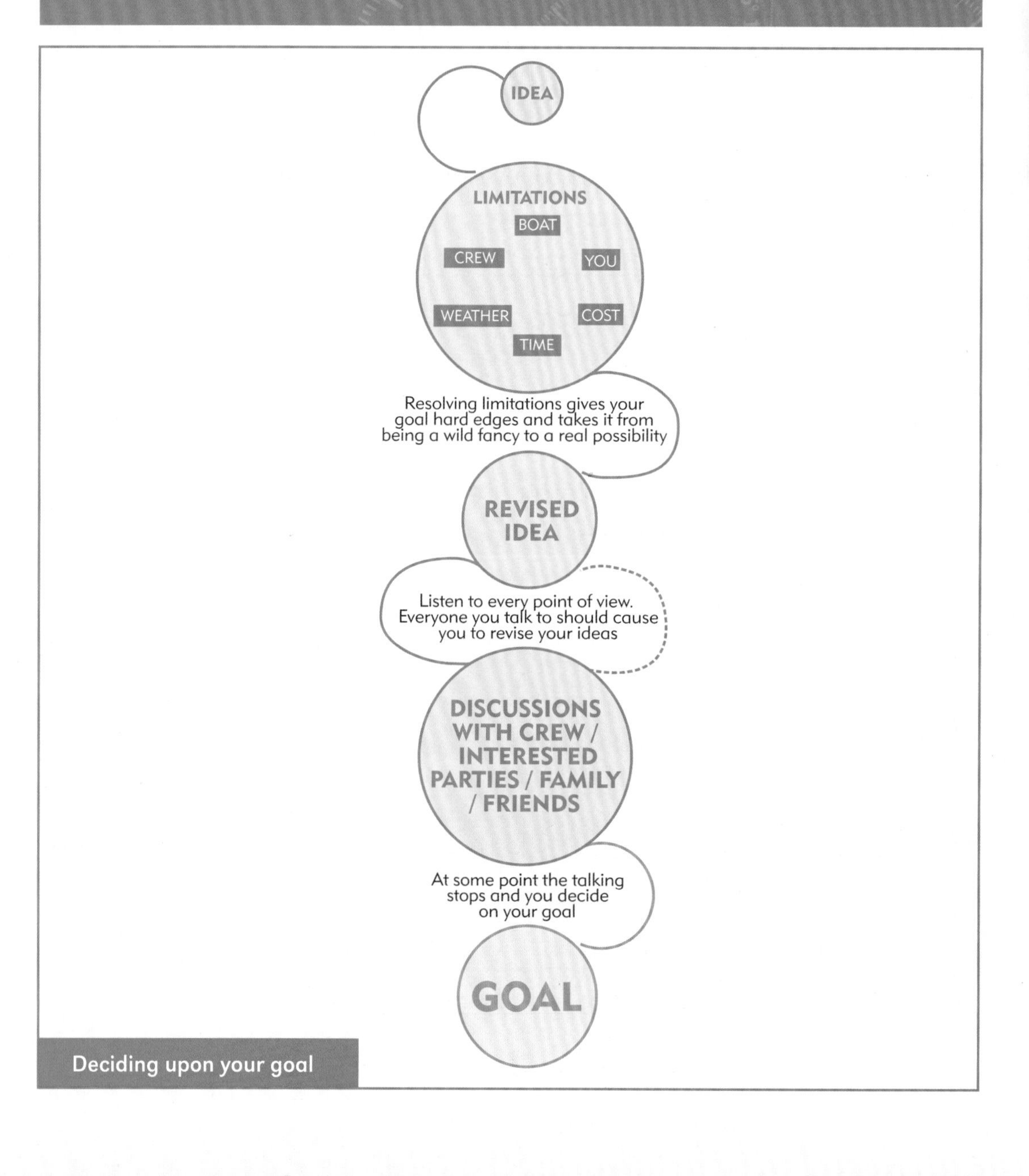

Deciding upon your goal

MAKING A PLAN

> *Life is what happens to you while you're busy making other plans.*
> **John Lennon**

There is no easy formula for preparing a plan. Using a checklist as a guide can create the impression that all you have to do is leave planning and preparations until a day or so before you sail, then tick the boxes and cast off, whether you are about to sail round the bay or round the world. To be effective, however, planning comes before preparations – and preparations can take days, weeks, months or even years.

One plan does not fit all. The elements you include in your plan, and how deeply you go into each element, depend largely upon your proposed passage. Your plan for a day sail round the bay will not be the same as your plan to sail to a harbour 20 or 30 miles along the coast. In its turn, your plan for a short daytime coastal passage differs from your plan for an overnight sail from, say, the Solent to Guernsey or St Peter Port in the Channel Islands. You must also take into account the time of year. You will have one plan for sailing 20 or 30 miles along the coast on a warm summer's day when the sun sets late and another for the same passage in the dead of winter.

Just because two boats make the same passage on the same day does not mean that one plan suits both vessels. To a single-handed sailor, some form of reliable self-steering is important and since they are alone there is a limit to how long they can stay at sea before fatigue becomes a serious problem. Consequently, a single-handed sailor's priorities are different from those of a fully crewed yacht, and these differences are reflected in their passage plans.

Numbers are not everything. A yacht with a crew of fully expert sailors has a different approach to a boat where there is an experienced afterguard of two or three and the remainder of the crew are novices uncertain which end of the boat goes first. If you are sailing as Mum, Dad and the kids you will have different ideas on what to include in a passage plan than a crew of adults racing from one harbour bistro to another. Children are not a limit to how far you plan to sail. Having just arrived in Carlisle Bay, Barbados, I felt pleasantly smug until ten-year-old Henry casually remarked, 'When I made my first Atlantic crossing...'.

Curiously, the size of boat does not matter either. A basic 20 foot yacht intending to cross the Atlantic has to deal with much the same problems as a 50 foot all-mod-cons cruiser, and when their skippers come to deal with these problems they are faced with choosing from a very similar range of options.

You can learn from other people's plans but you cannot claim their plan as your own and use it. Your plan must take into account you, your crew and your boat and you must prepare a new plan for each passage you undertake, even if you have done the same passage before and have kept a copy of the plan in your chart table.

The reason is simple. Each time you make a passage the conditions are different. On one occasion it may be blowing a near gale, another time you have kindly seas and gentle winds. On every passage you learn something new and that must be incorporated in your passage plan on the next occasion you go to sea. It may only be a small snippet of information but each snippet is part of your learning curve. For example, you wish to discover if there is enough water to enter Bridlington Harbour and have had no reply over the VHF. After you have done your sums and crept in, anxiously watching the depth sounder, you learn that the surest way of finding out how much water there is on the entrance is not to call the harbour on the VHF but to ring the watch keeper's mobile telephone number. His radio silence is because he has been carrying out duties that have taken him away from the VHF.

THE PURPOSE OF YOUR PLAN

Any passage plan is, in effect, a statement of how you would go about achieving your aim in an ideal world. In one sense it is a wish list. To succeed, planning alone is not enough. You always have to improvise. Even before you cast off, many of the assumptions used in preparing your plan will have proved if not false then at least over-optimistic, and your timetable a fantasy. Family commitments shanghai your crew, new sails arrive late, lack of cash slows down the work. Preparing to start work on one improvement, for example fitting a wind generator, reveals other work that must be completed before you can begin fitting the wind generator.

When you do cast off, the assumptions you made about the weather and your progress should probably begin with the words 'Once upon a time...'. Even your preferred route or chosen destination (or both) may become impossible. Cynics may say that the principal purpose of any plan is to give doubt and uncertainty an air of respectability. In fact it is a compass that keeps you pointed towards your goal. It is a constant reminder of what you wish to achieve and how you intend to go about it. A good plan has the flexibility to absorb uncertainties and ambiguities as they appear and keep you on course. It accepts that, once it is put into action, its role is one of providing general direction rather than dictating minute to minute or even day to day activity. In military terms, the staff generals write the plan; the fighting generals put it into action.

This distinction may not be readily apparent during the onshore phase when it is possible to stop what you are doing and rewrite your plan to suit changing circumstances, or absorb delays and differences as they arise. Right up until you cast off, you can call a stop to what you are doing or shoot off in an entirely new direction. You can even quit with nothing more than a couple of dents in your pride.

At sea, this is difficult, perhaps impossible. The two most important purposes of any plan are to ensure:

1. That everything possible in terms of preparations, manpower, training, equipment and logistics has been done during your onshore preparations so that you cast off in the best possible order.
2. That you have missed no opportunity to make sure your plan is one that allows you to set sail with a high degree of confidence in achieving your goal.

PUTTING YOUR PLAN TOGETHER

A plan is nothing more complicated than a series of orderly actions that, when followed, lead to your goal. It only takes ten simple steps:

1. Identify all the elements that must be included in your plan to achieve your goal.
2. Consider the individual elements that make up your plan as objectives that lead you to your goal.
3. Gather the information relating to every element.
4. Use that information to identify all the possible courses of action that would allow you to achieve your goal.
5. Select the option that you believe is the best choice. Remember that simple is best and if you cannot find an option you like, then choose one that you can make work. If there is a choice of workable options then choose the easiest.
6. Repeat this process for each element of your plan.
7. By the end of this exercise you have a list of preferred options. Now check these options to ensure they are in the right order and do not clash or contradict each other.
8. Put the options together into a timetable.
9. When you are satisfied that all is well, write it all down. This is your plan.
10. Put your plan into action.

It is a simple process but to do it well demands careful, meticulous work. First you must identify each element of your plan. Deciding what elements to include requires a balancing act between an overly broad-brush approach of lumping everything together, which prevents you making sensible judgements, and a too detailed examination of every element that you may possibly include, losing sight of the bigger picture and unable to see oceans for the waves.

There are no rules where to strike this balance. It is a question of personal judgement. As a guideline, the longer the trip the more detailed your list and the deeper you must go into each element. It seems sensible that the list for a trip round the bay should be short and to the point, looking at no more than a handful of elements. It can be planned over coffee and cakes or a pie and a pint with your crew. Planning for a short coastal passage requires more work and introduces an element of formality. The plan for a Channel crossing would be longer and more detailed than that for a day sail, while the planning for an ocean passage or prolonged blue water cruise would be the most detailed of all, taking several days or more to prepare and running into a fairly weighty book or a decent chunk of your computer's hard drive. Writing it down may appear overly formal, pompous even, but there is much to remember and if you are sharing your plan with your crew without putting it on paper there is scope for confusion and misunderstandings.

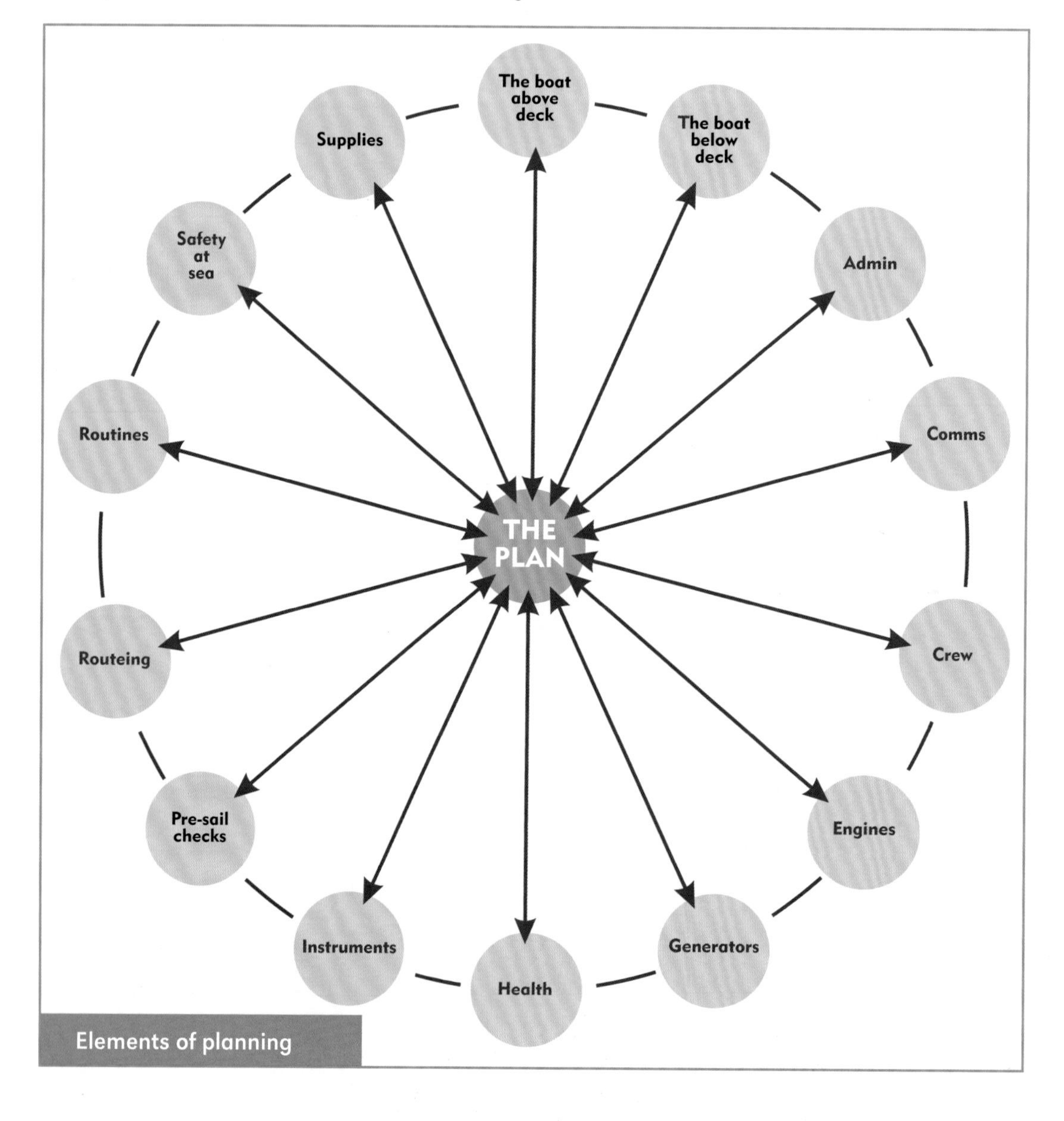

Elements of planning

THE MAGIC QUADRANT

Confidently choosing the best courses of action to fit in with your plan can only be done with hindsight and begins with the words 'If only…'. Until your passage is safely and successfully concluded, every option is possible and rating one above another is a matter of judgement.

Using the Magic Quadrant may help to put options into rank order. The horizontal axis represents the time, effort and resources required to implement an option. The vertical axis measures how much the same option contributes to achieving your aim. The ideal course of action gives you the maximum return for the least effort. The colour coding tells you which options should be considered further.

GREEN QUADRANT: Courses of action from this quadrant carry a high probability of success.

YELLOW QUADRANT: This includes a transitional zone where the increased effort is within acceptable limits.

RED QUADRANT: If you choose an option from this zone then you can expect to work hard from the outset.

BLUE QUADRANT: This is the ditherer's 'wait and see what happens' zone. In the centre is an area where the level of effort and the return on any option is not of any significance. It is the 'no action necessary' zone. If you choose to implement an option from this zone it is probable that you are taking action to be seen to be doing something.

Around the blue and red quadrants is the 'least worst' zone. This is the area where the return on an option does not properly justify the effort it demands but there may be no other choice. If so, then you must choose what you believe to be the 'least worst' option.

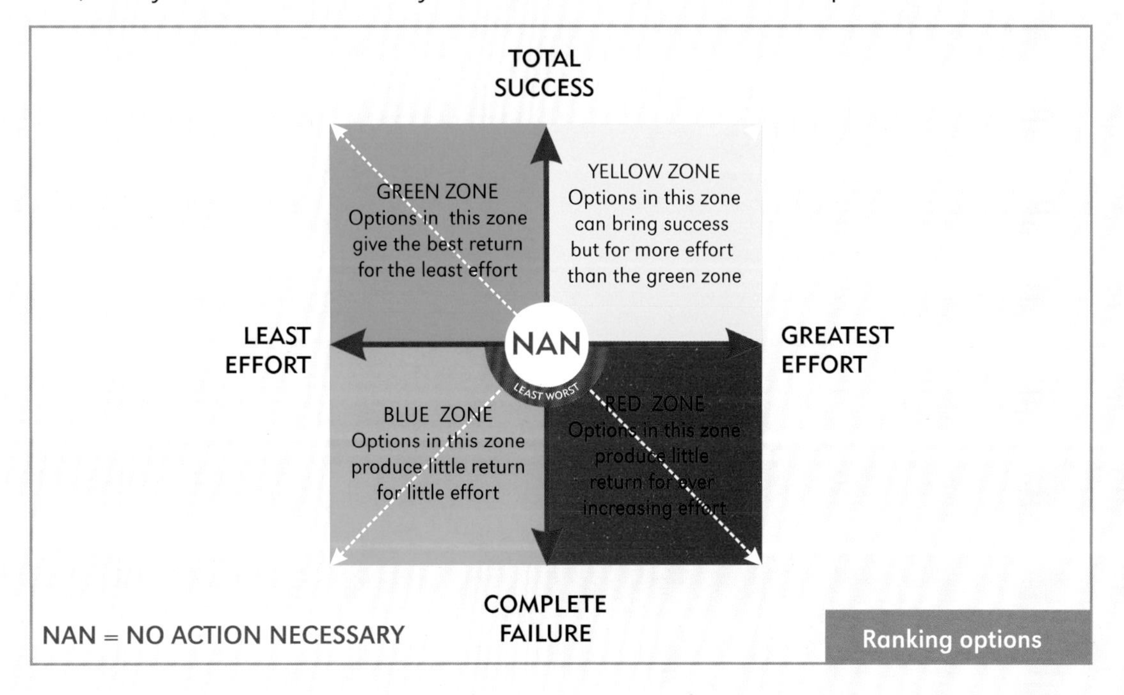

Ranking options

DATA AND INFORMATION

Every plan is built up by reviewing all the options open to you at each stage and then choosing the option you believe offers you the greatest chance of success in taking your plan forward. This requires information, first to construct your list of options and then to make an informed choice as to which option you consider the best. Each plan is only as good as the accuracy and reliability of the information upon which your choice of options is based and your ability to use that information wisely.

Gathering information is an unromantic, time consuming, and occasionally tedious exercise. There is a narrow line between following a blind alley in enormous detail and instantly dismissing a line of research as irrelevant, only to discover later that it held the key to all your problems. What areas to research and how far to follow any line of investigation is a judgement call. Prudence suggests that it is wise to take a quick peek under every stone, just in case there is some gem of wisdom hiding underneath.

When he set out on his circumnavigation in *Gipsy Moth IV*, Francis Chichester wanted to equal or better the times of the nineteenth-century wool clippers. He spent a lot of time researching their passages, although how a fully crewed clipper went about its business may not, at first sight, have appeared relevant to making the same voyage alone in a 54 foot yacht. He had much else to do and was under enormous pressure of time; but the tales of the clippers' voyages, besides clarifying his goal, gave him an insight into the weather and routeing of the passage he was about to undertake.

Preparing for my first Atlantic crossing, I found as many accounts as I could of small boat transatlantic passages. They began around the 1880s and I went up to the 1960s, after which I felt transatlantic racing and the urge to break records made the figures less useful to a cruising yacht. By looking at the routes they followed and the times they took, I could make a fair estimate of the boats' average speed. I was surprised to discover that after nearly a century of improvements in yacht design and equipment their average speed, whether sailing east or west, remained constant at almost exactly half their maximum hull speed.

At sea, a lack of resources and reference books means you frequently have no choice but to accept patchy, incomplete information and use that to make decisions; but, as Chichester was only too aware, during your onshore preparations – with time on your side and enormous research facilities at your fingertips – there is no excuse for not gathering together all the information you can find relating to your goal.

DATA VERSUS INFORMATION

It is easy to confuse data with information and to treat them both the same. They are not. Data is raw, unevaluated facts and figures, lying around, waiting to be found and put to good use. Examples of data are found in tide tables, or the times of sunrise and sunset. You may notice that an important headland you intend to round has a light on it, 62m above sea level. This is data.

A little arithmetic tells you that in good visibility you should pick up the headland and its light at a range of around 18 nautical miles. If the wind is fair, this is around three to five hours' sailing. The almanac tells you that the light has a range of 25 nautical miles, which means that in reasonable conditions at night you could expect to pick up its loom an hour or two earlier than you would see the actual light. This item of data on the height of the light and its range has now become a piece of information or, if you prefer, it is data put into a meaningful and useful context that allows it to be used in decision making, especially if you include the time of sunset.

For example, on passage this information about the light could help you decide if you will arrive off the headland to catch a favourable tide or whether you ought to start considering some other course of action. This is important. The earlier you begin to make modifications to your passage plan, the less dramatic will be the changes you make. You tweak rather than rewrite your plan.

DATA COLLECTION

Not that long ago, researching a voyage meant winnowing through pilots, almanacs, tide tables, tidal atlas, and pilot charts, finding accounts of those who went before. Patient librarians would track down obscure, out of print titles and copies of long forgotten charts. Collecting data was not a task that could be hurried. Happily, sailing has not escaped the digital revolution. Onboard Internet access, at least in harbour, is commonplace. Data and information are instantly available even on the most obscure subjects and mostly for free.

Taiohae Harbour on Nuku Hiva in French Polynesia is pretty remote. If you wish to know what it looks like, use Google Earth. With this facility you can even count the yachts in the anchorage. You can also use Google Earth to check out harbours and anchorages much nearer home, and use what you learn to supplement the information from the pilot books and almanacs you have on board. Google, or your chosen search engine, will easily and quickly point you towards online sources of data on tides, tidal streams, ocean currents, port and harbour facilities, marinas, weather forecasts and weather patterns.

Computers are not just for surfing. For those who wish to practise astronavigation and take star sights, software such as SkyMap Pro, besides giving the times of nautical twilight for any date, also show you the night sky for any date and time and from any aspect; and, with a little effort, you can arrange matters so it shows only the navigational stars and planets appearing in the tables. Using the tables to plot a sight is a separate art to handling a sextant and, if you find thumbing through columns of figures too much trouble, there is a huge range of navigational software where you enter your figures and press a button for the answer.

DATA HANDLING

It would be silly not to take full advantage of this sort of technology and its successors, whatever they may be, especially when it comes to turning data into information. Once, checking the effects of winds and currents on possible routes across the Atlantic meant finding the appropriate monthly pilot chart, pencilling in your route, tediously noting details of the winds and currents from the chart, five degree square by five degree square (data), and then applying them to your boat (information). It took forever to check one possible route in one particular month. Now, software such as Visual Passage Planner allows you simply to enter your start and finish points along with details of your boat, press the return key, and instantly, under fifteen separate headings, you are given everything and more you could want to know about the winds, currents and seas along your optimal route. If that is not enough, there is also a choice of five detailed reports. If you do not like the answers for that month or that particular route, change some or all of the parameters or pick a different month and repeat until you see something you like. Software such as seaPro does the same for boats sailing in tidal waters.

THE COMPASS ROSE

Sailors traditionally describe the direction from which the wind blows using a sixteen-point wind compass rose. This first divides the winds into 'cardinal' winds. Working clockwise, the four cardinal winds are north, east, south and west. Next come the 'ordinal' winds, which are formed by bisecting the angles between each cardinal wind and named by combining the cardinal winds they bisect, eg south-west. Together, the four cardinal and four ordinal winds make up the eight principal or main winds. Each is 45° from its neighbours. The third step is bisecting the angles between the eight principal winds. which gives the eight half winds. Each half wind is named by combining the names of the wind on either side, with the cardinal wind coming first, eg south-south-west. Together the eight principal and eight half winds create a sixteen-point wind compass rose, with each wind 22.5° or two compass points from the next wind.

QUARTER WINDS

Going further, halving the angle between each wind in the sixteen-point wind compass rose creates sixteen quarter winds, making a thirty-two-point wind compass rose where each wind is 11.25° or one compass point from the next.

Curiously, *North by Northwest*, the title of Alfred Hitchcock's famous film, does not appear on any wind compass rose.

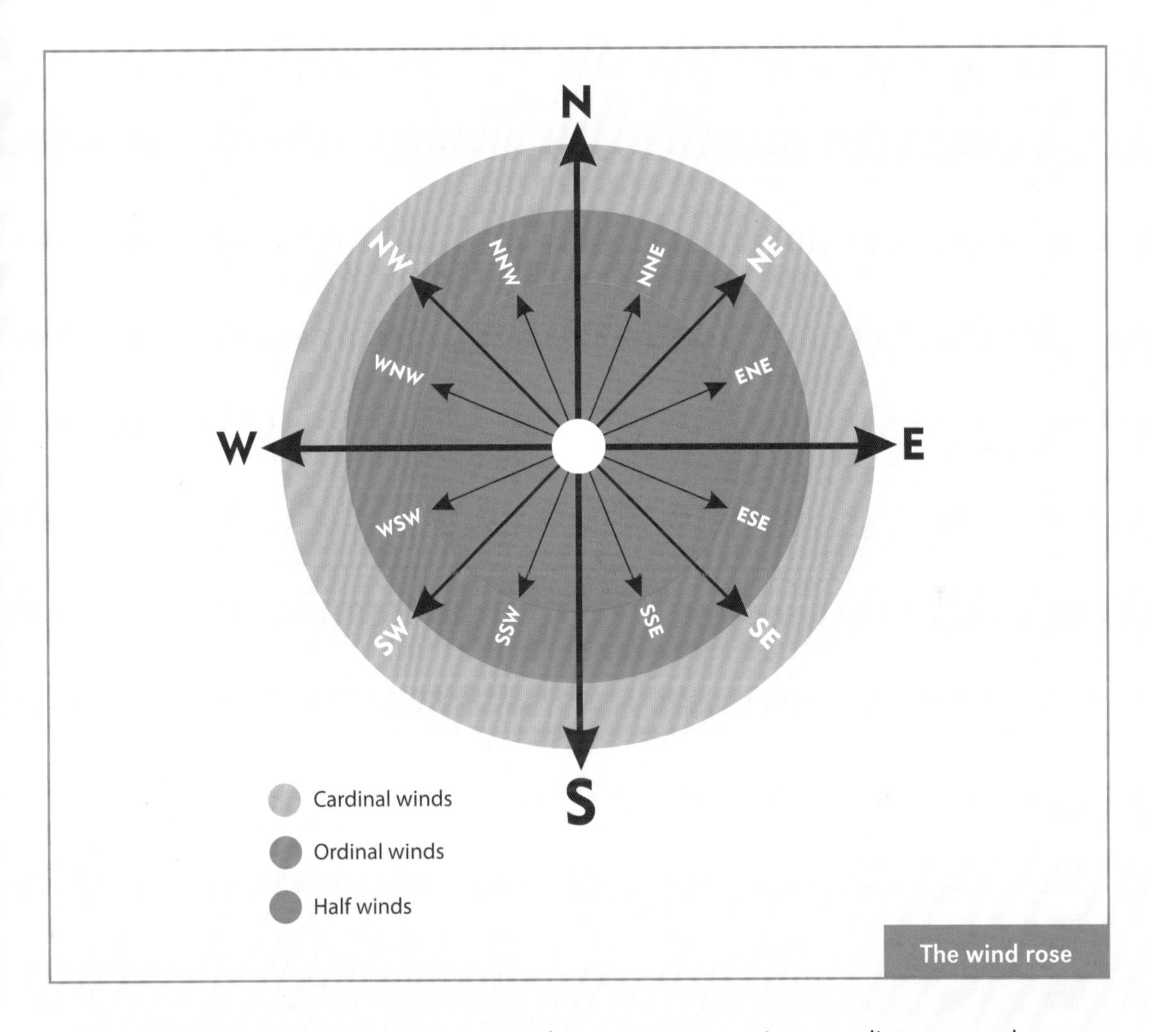

The wind rose

The act of linking the waypoints on your plotter into a route gives you distances and courses to steer between waypoints at the press of a button, quicker and more accurately than you could ever have achieved by drawing them on a paper chart and measuring bearings. You can also easily tweak routes and waypoints to explore alternatives or optimise your chosen route. Interfacing your plotter with an AIS receiver enables your plotter to warn you of an approaching vessel and tells you more about it and how near it will come than you could ever learn from taking compass bearings on it. The risks of a collision or even a close encounter are, in an instant, vastly reduced.

If you are beating upwind towards your destination, what becomes important is not your speed through the water or even speed over the ground but your velocity made good (VMG). If your destination is 15 miles (data) away and you are making just less than 5 knots (data) through the water, it is obvious that you are far more than three hours away from your destination. This is an item of useless information. To find out how long it will actually take you to arrive, you must know your boat's VMG. You can use paper and pencil and do the sums (your plotter or GPS will give you your course and speed over the ground, which you need for the maths); alternatively, some plotters interfaced with the ship's log and compass will give the answer at the press of a button.

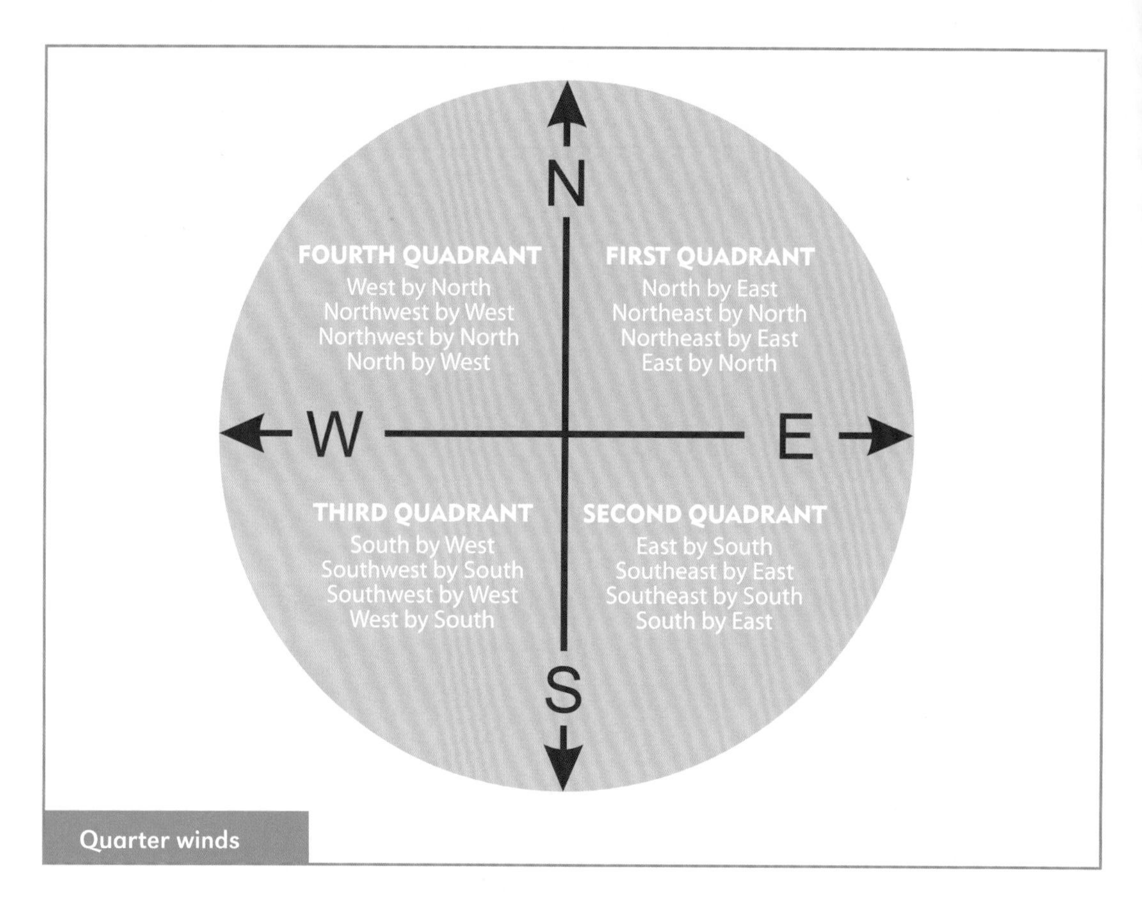

Quarter winds

Curiously, some diehards who insist they can work only on paper charts happily accept the VMG from their instruments and incorporate it into their workings. Nobody is completely resistant to new technology.

Knowing your VMG is 2.5 knots (data), it is then simple arithmetic to discover that unless conditions change you are six hours (information) from your destination. If this estimated time en route (ETE) means that when you arrive the harbour is dry, or you have missed a bridge or lock opening, then you ought to start considering what changes you wish to make to your plan to take this into account.

VELOCITY MADE GOOD

If you race, you will know all about VMG and be forever updating your VMG polar diagrams so you can squeeze the last fraction of a knot out of your boat on any point of sail. Cruising folk take a more relaxed approach and only consider VMG when they are beating upwind or sailing directly downwind. If they are beating upwind, they wish to know their VMG so that they can calculate their revised ETA. On a rocking, rolling run they know that their boat speed equals their VMG. If they then go onto a broad reach, life is more comfortable and the boat speed picks up. The question now is – what has this trade-off done to their VMG?

UPWIND VELOCITY MADE GOOD

Your rhumb line course is the straight line on the chart between your start point and your destination. Imagine you are attempting to sail due south and are close reaching southwards when the wind swings round until it is coming directly out of the south. To continue making progress you must start tacking upwind.

Normally you would draw, or imagine, lay lines on the chart to your destination. These are based on what you reckon is the most favourable angle you can point into the wind. By going about when you reach a lay line, you make your destination in one tack and in the shortest possible time. Sail beyond the lay line and you lose ground and time.

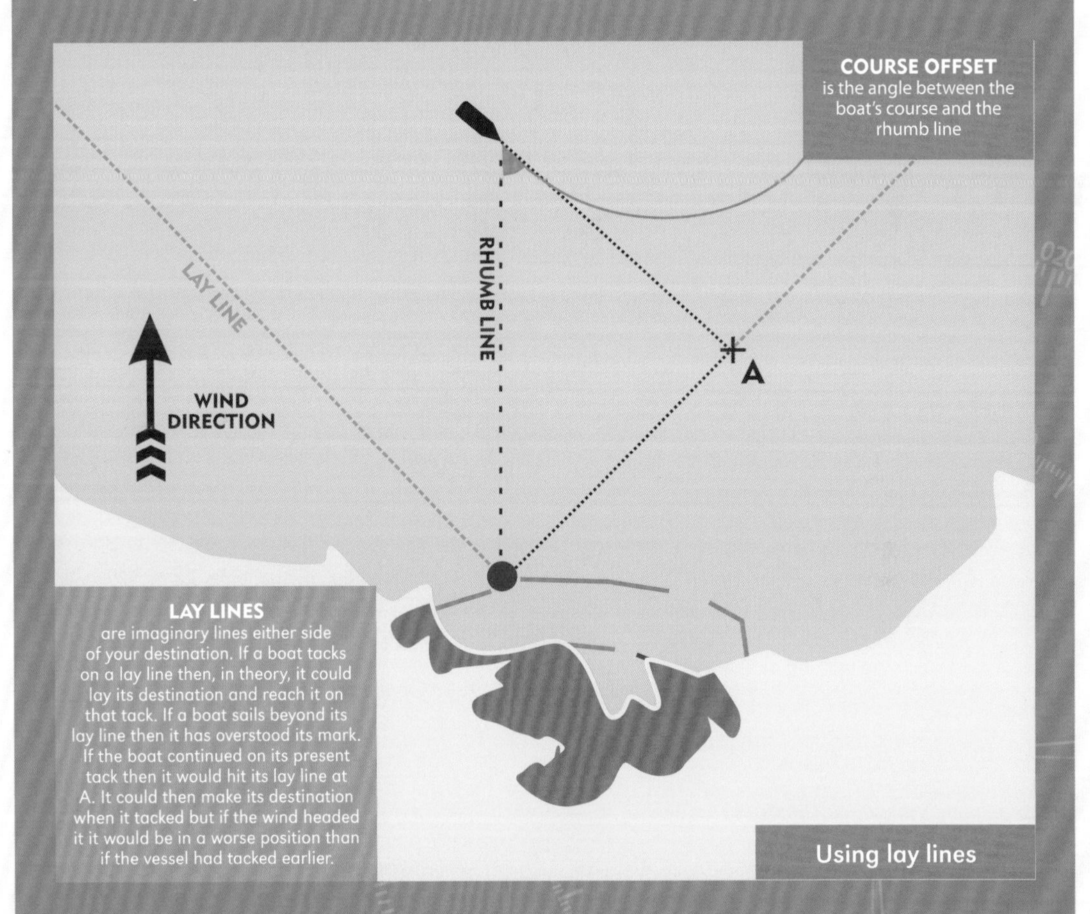

Using lay lines

Sailing to the nearest lay line can take you a long way from your rhumb line course and this is not considered a good idea. A wind shift as you reach the lay line could see you having to throw a six and start all over again. Generally it is better to stay within tack lines, which are imaginary lines 10° to 20° either side of your rhumb line course.

Your boat speed is how fast you are going through the water but to calculate your ETA at your destination you need your speed along the rhumb line. Speed along the rhumb line is your velocity made good (VMG).

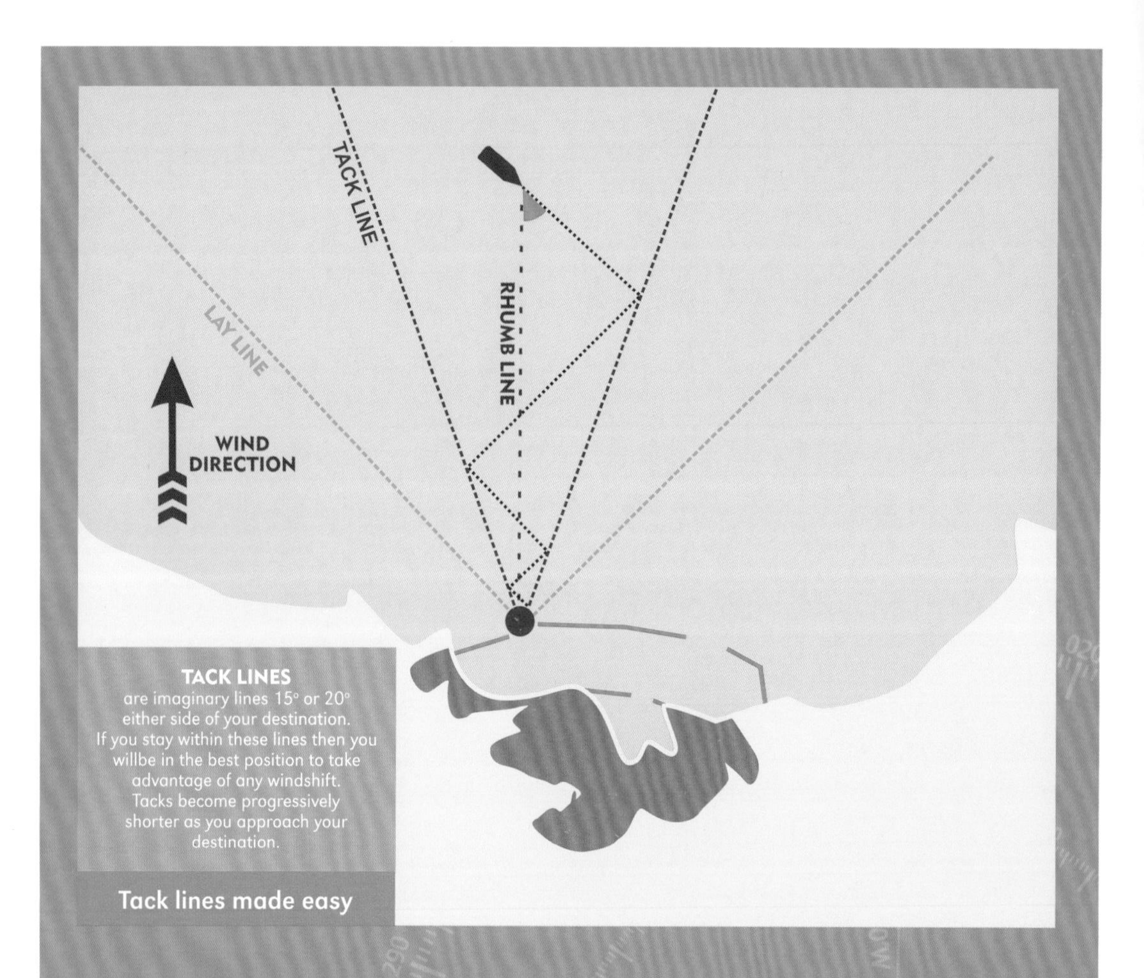

Tack lines made easy

VMG TABLE													
Course Offset	Boat Speed Over Ground												
	2.0	2.5	3.0	3.5	4.0	4.5	5.0	5.5	6.0	6.5	7.0	7.5	8.0
5	2.0	2.5	3.0	3.5	4.0	4.5	5.0	5.5	6.0	6.5	7.0	7.5	8.0
10	2.0	2.5	3.0	3.4	3.9	4.4	4.9	5.4	5.9	6.4	6.9	7.4	7.9
15	1.9	2.4	2.9	3.4	3.9	4.3	4.8	5.3	5.8	6.3	6.8	7.2	7.7
20	1.9	2.3	2.8	3.3	3.8	4.2	4.7	5.2	5.6	6.1	6.6	7.0	7.5
25	1.8	2.3	2.7	3.2	3.6	4.1	4.5	5.0	5.4	5.9	6.3	6.8	7.3
30	1.7	2.2	2.6	3.0	3.5	3.9	4.3	4.8	5.2	5.6	6.1	6.5	6.9
35	1.6	2.0	2.5	2.9	3.3	3.7	4.1	4.5	4.9	5.3	5.7	6.1	6.6
40	1.5	1.9	2.3	2.7	3.1	3.4	3.8	4.2	4.6	5.0	5.4	5.7	6.1
45	1.3	1.6	1.9	2.2	2.6	2.9	3.2	3.5	3.9	4.2	4.5	4.8	5.1
50	1.1	1.4	1.7	2.0	2.3	2.6	2.9	3.2	3.4	3.7	4.0	4.3	4.6

If your rhumb line course is due south and head winds mean on one tack you are steering a course of 045 relative to the rhumb line and making 4.7 knots through the water, then your:

VMG = Cos 45 multiplied by 4.7 = 3.3 knots

When you tack, then provided conditions remain the same so will your VMG.

When you are sailing to destinations that lie other than due south, the angle you use in your calculations is the angle between your course and the rhumb line to your destination.

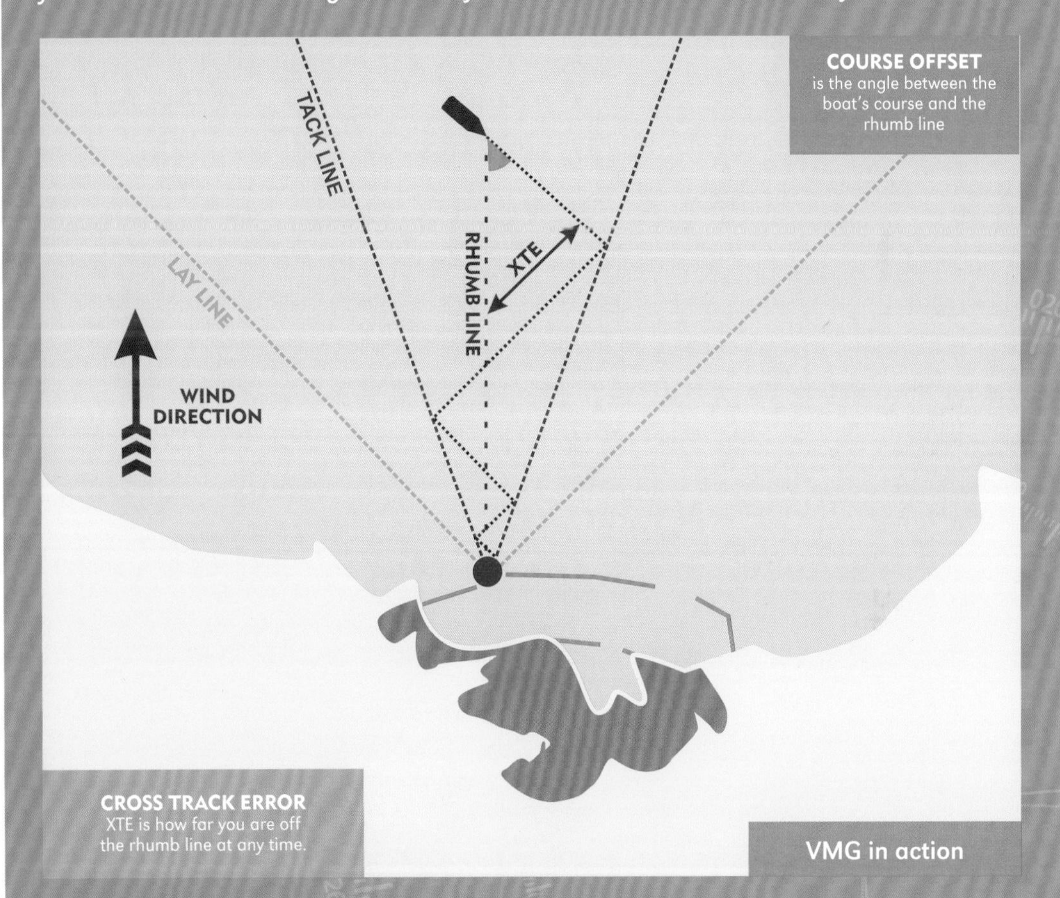

VMG in action

This angle is called the 'course offset'. As a matter of pride, skippers always claim that their boat points as near as makes no difference directly into the wind. Claims of pointing 35° or even 30° into the wind are not uncommon. If you make an honest estimate of how high your boat points into the wind, you can note the cosine of that angle in the navigation logbook and that saves looking it up every time you calculate your VMG. The above formula now becomes:

VMG = Cos (course offset) multiplied by boat speed

The cosine of 45° is 0.707. There used to be a very popular aircraft called the 707. If your close hauled angle is, or is close to, 45° then multiplying your boat speed by 0.707 or even 0.7 gives a good feel for your VMG.

DOWNWIND VELOCITY MADE GOOD

When the wind is dead astern, there is no problem sailing along your rhumb line and your boat speed is your VMG. However, sailing directly downwind is slow, uncomfortable and carries the constant threat of an involuntary gybe. By bearing away, your boat speed and comfort increase and the danger of a gybe is removed. In effect, you tack downwind.

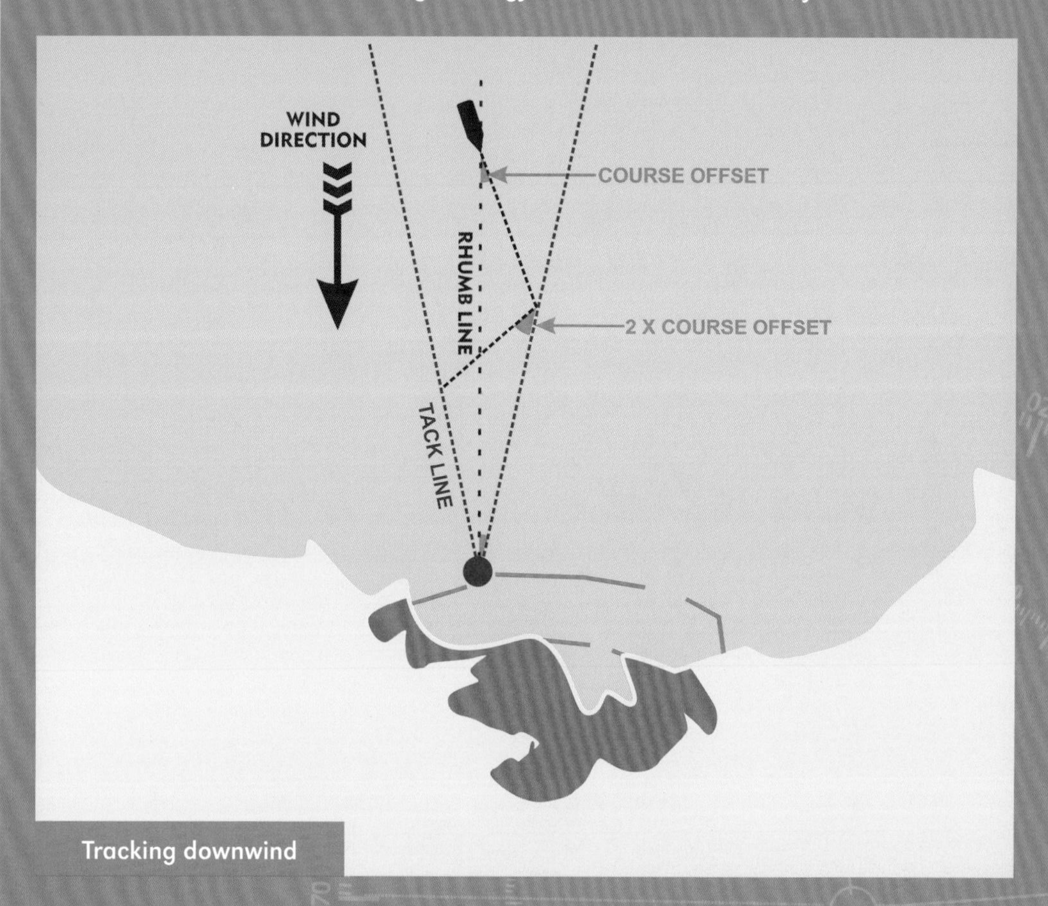

Tracking downwind

As a rule of thumb, the further you bear away, the greater your boat speed until you are going as fast as possible on a beam reach. The cosine of 90° is zero and so is your VMG. What you want to know is whether, as you bear away, your increased boat speed on any particular course gives a VMG equal to or greater than your VMG along your rhumb line course. Put another way, if your increased boat speed gives a VMG less than your rhumb line VMG, you are paying for the increased comfort by arriving later than planned.

To find the best angle, it is usual to bear away in 5° steps and watch your boat speed until you reach optimum.

As you are tacking downwind, it is a good idea to have tack lines. This time the angle of the tack lines to your rhumb line is equal to the course offset and when you come to tack, you tack through twice the course offset.

GOOD INFORMATION

Not all information carries the same weight or needs to be known to the same degree of accuracy. Boat speed is usually taken to one decimal place, but working in the Beaufort Scale for wind speed is fine even though each Beaufort force covers several knots. You should know the course steered to the nearest degree but working in points is best for wind direction.

Always use the best quality information you can find; and when you must use less than accurate information, recognise its shortcomings and the question marks these place over the decisions where it is used. Good information is:

- **Relevant**

The current weather in your home port of Lymington (or wherever) may be very interesting but it is not relevant if you are about to leave Peterhead Bay Marina and round Rattray Head before heading along the Moray Firth. Information on charts in pilot books or ANMs intended for commercial vessels is probably of less interest and not as relevant to leisure craft as yachting pilots.

- **Timely**

Timeliness is having the information to hand in good time to sensibly incorporate it into your course of action. To learn suddenly that there is 3m of water under the keel and it is shoaling fast is not timely information. It is a rush to panic stations. Nor is it timely for the navigator to pop up warning you of an unmarked rock somewhere along your track seconds before you hit it.

- **Accurate**

Accuracy is measured by comparing data to reality. Your log tells you that you are making 6.2 knots through the water, but taking your speed over ground from the plotter and allowing for the tidal stream you come up with an answer of 5.7 knots. This difference is of little importance in the middle of the English Channel but it could be critical if you are making a timed run down a buoyed channel in poor visibility.

Acceptable accuracy can vary depending upon circumstances. Holding a course to within 10 or even 15 degrees is not important mid ocean. In a narrow, rock infested channel, staying on the leading marks to the nearest degree is vital.

Be consistent in the measures you use to judge accuracy. If you have been using the Beaufort Scale when evaluating weather forecasts, you should not judge the accuracy of the forecast wind speed in knots. If it helps, the Meteorological Office reckon a forecast wind is accurate if it is within plus/minus one Beaufort force from the forecast wind.

- **Reliable**

Reliability is a judgement call. Just because yesterday's weather did not arrive as forecast is no reason to ignore today's forecast, but it may place question marks around it. How reliable is that pilot book on entering some port or anchorage? When was it last corrected? Do you have the feeling that the author actually sailed their description of how to enter a particular port or visited by car? In short, reliability is a cocktail made up from equal measures of past performance and gut feeling.

WHAT YOU NEED TO KNOW

Before you begin harvesting data to turn it into information, take the time to identify those areas where you need to gather information. This starts with the usual suspects, such as routeing, weather, the crew, the boat, skills required, training, equipment and supplies.

Each heading breaks down into sub-groups. How far you wish to take this breakdown depends on what level of detail gives you confidence in your plan. As a rule, it is a good idea to keep it simple and work from the general to the detailed. It is unlikely that you will need to take each heading to an equal degree of detail but it is probable that new, previously unconsidered topics, where you require more data and information, will make themselves known as you develop your plan. This is normal. You look at an item of data, ask 'What does this mean?', and find yourself travelling in unexpected directions.

Once you have decided on the list of headings to be included in your plan, the next step is to gather the basic data and information for each heading. This is used to build up an overall picture for what you are trying to achieve. You do not start this task with an empty mind – you should be buzzing with ideas and scraps of information. You may well have previously made this or a similar passage; in this initial data-gathering phase you check out new ideas and information from that previous experience and establish what is required on this occasion to make your dreams reality.

Probably the easiest way to build up a list of sources is to identify where you need, or wish, to know more about the sub-headings on your list of factors and ask:

1 What do I need to know about this topic?
2 Where can I find this information?

Some of the sources of information you need are obvious, others less so; but there is no approved list. Your list will depend upon you, your boat, your crew and the passage you are planning. You must identify the sources most relevant to you. Take weather forecasts. Ashore, the Internet offers a huge range of forecasts regardless of what sort of passage you are undertaking. At sea, the availability of weather information depends on what sort of passage you are making. You do not need to go far out to sea on coastal or offshore passages before losing mobile phone signals along with your Internet access. Relying on these as your sole means of communication or sourcing weather information at sea is unwise.

Most boats are unlikely to have satellite or Single Side Band (SSB) facilities on board, and unless you are carrying Navtex, which has a maximum range of about 400 miles, your weather forecasts are almost certainly limited to the inshore and shipping forecasts from the Met Office broadcast over the VHF or from the BBC on your transistor radio.

Going further afield, after a few days on an ocean passage you lose the Navtex signal and the inshore and shipping forecasts become irrelevant. If you have satellite communications then you can access weather reports like GRIB files from shore-based contacts. If you have an SSB receiver you can listen to the various SSB radio nets covering your sea area. Most include weather information. If you have an SSB transceiver you can join in the discussions on these nets and actively seek forecasts for your position and, with the right equipment, you can link your SSB receiver, or transceiver, to your laptop and download weatherfaxes.

Personal preferences also play a large part in deciding what sources to use. Some are happy to rely on the weather forecasts prepared by the Met Office. Others prefer going online and trawling through a selection of weather sites. Some prefer finding their tidal and port information from the Almanac and yachting pilot books. Others are content to use the data they find on their plotter.

SECOND OPINION

When gathering information, believe nothing and doubt everything. If at all possible, always check the reliability of data you intend to use against some other, independent source. Failure to do this can potentially lead you into all sorts of trouble, as I almost (but not quite) discovered when sailing around the German North Sea coast. There is a drying inshore channel, marked by withies, skirting the island of Neuwerk at the mouth of the Elbe. Follow it, and over two or three tides you can sail from the Elbe to the Weser without going out into the open sea. It sounds a useful alternative for making progress if strong onshore winds make entering or leaving the Elbe impossible.

One pilot book described this passage as 'challenging', which sparked my interest. On closer examination I had doubts. Seeking local information, I wandered round Cuxhaven Yacht Club asking local sailors if they had any information on this route. Nobody admitted having even tried it. Several told me that I might enjoy a visit to Neuwerk but going any further was to enter terra incognita and if I did try it then they would appreciate it if I let them know how I got on.

I trawled through local sailing Internet chat rooms. I discovered this route was popular with canoeists but found nothing relevant to yachts until I came across a query from a sailor whose yacht had a similar draft to my own. Depth under keel is the key to this passage. Could anyone give him details of the route? He received two replies. One said that it was impossible in his boat and the other said that if he must try it he should let the DGzRS, the German equivalent of the RNLI, know of his intentions before he sailed.

It is also a good idea to check carefully the age of the data you acquire. Old data is not necessarily poor data but sometimes it has passed its use-by date. It is not just the obvious items such as weather forecasts or uncorrected charts and pilots. I once cruised the Galician coast using the latest edition of a pilot to that area whose photographs and chartlets long pre-dated great swathes of coastal, harbour and marina development. Trying to reconcile the mental image that I built up in my head through reading the pilot with what was before my eyes became impossible – occasionally misleading and ultimately frustrating.

HOW MUCH DATA AND INFORMATION DO YOU COLLECT?

Thanks to search engines like Google we are a data-rich society; however, this means that collecting data on any subject can become an end in itself. You pick up one thread and follow it as it twists round the topic you are researching. You pick up another thread, comparing it to the first thread, and then another and another, until your head is swimming with data.

Weather forecasts are a good example. There are hundreds of websites offering instant weather forecasts. No two ever promise exactly the same forecast and the differences between them grow the further you look ahead. Reconciling these disparities becomes important if you are looking for a three- or four-day weather window.

In the end, how much data you collect and how far you follow any particular thread is a personal judgement. Researching a passage from Skye to St Kilda, I discovered that the archipelago has a history going back to at least the Bronze Age and found myself collecting data on Bronze Age boats – useless but interesting. Also fascinating, but irrelevant to passage planning, was how the island caught the public's imagination in the nineteenth century when cruise ships began visiting. These visits lessened the islanders' isolation to a point where they began preparing St Kilda craftworks for sale and discovered the cash economy; and increased the islanders' awareness of the outside world to a point where their departure for the mainland became inevitable.

Today the archipelago is owned by the National Trust for Scotland and home to a military base run by civilians. Facilities for visitors are limited and the surest way of visiting at a time of your choosing is by boat. There is, of course, a catch. Visiting an island 50 miles out into the North Atlantic requires settled weather especially as the principal, almost only, anchorage is untenable in some winds. Winds can change quickly and when they do you have no option but to head out into the open sea and take the weather on the chin.

Besides the usual yachting pilots and information from the almanac, there is a huge amount written on St Kilda. Much of it is really no more than background so that you know what you are looking at when you do visit; but that was not why I downloaded a copy of Martin Martin's book *A Late Voyage to St Kilda*, which was published in 1698 and described his voyage to the islands a year earlier. Martin had the idea of writing an account of life in the Highlands, and when he heard that the Reverend Campbell was about to sail for St Kilda he hitched a lift with the aim of gathering material for his book.

The good minister was going to St Kilda to investigate Rhoderic the Imposter. He was an islander claiming to have met St Paul dressed as a Lowland Scot. In Gaelic (the islanders spoke nothing else), St Paul charged him to make sure the islanders lived the good life. For Rhoderic this involved practices nowadays associated with the more extreme religious cults and included private, one to one, sessions for the womenfolk.

Martin's book is probably the first written account of life on St Kilda and certainly the earliest log of a voyage to the island. It is possible to reconstruct his voyage, more or less. He, the minister and a professional crew sailed from Ensay in the Sound of Harris. It is much more likely that they had actually started out from Dunvegan on Skye, where Martin was the tutor to the laird's children, and sought shelter in the anchorage at Ensay either to wait for better weather or because they had lost the tide sailing through the sound. Today Ensay is uninhabited but back then supplies and shelter could be found ashore.

In the evening the wind turned south-easterly and they set out. The minister commented that he did not like the way the seas were pounding on the rocks but the crew dismissed his fears and pressed on. They had barely cleared the Stanton Channel and entered the Atlantic when the wind went southerly and the weather turned stormy.

Conditions made it impossible to return. Instead they dropped the sail and began rowing south, hoping to reach Haskeir Island and find shelter among what is little more than a cluster of rocks. They made extremely slow progress. By morning it was clear that reaching Haskeir was out of the question, as was finding shelter anywhere else along the coast, so they hoisted the sail and, steering a compass course, squared away for St Kilda.

After they had run their distance there was no sign of St Kilda or any of it neighbours. This was a critical time. Beyond St Kilda was only the North Atlantic. Then to the south they saw a flock of birds. Someone mentioned that the islanders used the huge flocks of birds flying out from and returning to their roosts on the archipelago as a navigational aid. Next someone spotted land and claimed it was Boreray.

They were extremely fortunate. If they had been blown a few miles further north then they would have seen nothing. The wind was still foul so they dropped the sail and rowed for their lives, reaching Boreray and managing, with some difficulty, to anchor under its cliffs. They had been at sea for over twenty hours. The next day, before they could continue to St Kilda, another gale arrived and threatened to blow them out to sea; but their anchor held and the following day they finally arrived in Village Bay on St Kilda.

Their hardiness and fortitude demands the highest respect. They were in an open boat, almost certainly under 30 feet LOA, in bad weather for the best part of three days. During that time they had no hot food or drink. We would not trust their foul weather gear in a High Street shower yet Martin, who was an honest observer, does not report any loss of morale, disagreement, fear or even fatigue among the crew, although when they reached the precarious safety of Boreray some of the crew reckoned Rhoderic the Imposter had somehow become aware of the minister's mission and raised the storms to prevent their arrival.

After over three hundred years there is much in Martin's account that is useful to modern sailors. If you miss the tide in the Stanton Channel then you can hide in the anchorage on Ensay. If the weather turns once you are through the channel then the west coast of the Western Isles is not to be lightly approached. Staying at sea is a better option and the birds still fly home to roost at night.

And Rhoderic the Imposter? After staying on the island for three weeks, the minister took a now penitent Rhoderic back to the mainland and into lifelong exile from St Kilda.

TIMINGS AND TIMETABLE

THE ONSHORE PHASE

Timetables for passage making fall into two parts. First comes the onshore planning and preparation phase. This is the time when you prepare your plan and make yourself, your crew and your boat ready for sea. Within limits, this phase is under your control and you can expect tasks to be carried out more or less on schedule. The routeing element of your passage planning automatically gives you some idea how long it will take to sail from A to B; but what is often overlooked is that you must prepare a timetable for the work carried out during the onshore phase – and even then, inevitably there is some slippage. It is a law of sailing that it is impossible for any work to be carried out on a boat without revealing some unexpected complication that must first be resolved before the work you planned can start. Wise sailors multiply their estimates for time by four and costs by five and still include extra time and cost in their schedule for unforeseen problems.

For a day sail there is probably no need to prepare a written timetable; but as passages become longer they also become more complicated. It is important to have a written schedule so that you can keep track of what work has to be done, what work has been done, and what work remains to be done. Your timetable then tells you whether or not it looks as if the remaining work will be completed on time and within budget.

Ensuring that the timetable for the onshore planning and preparation phase is correct is crucial to a successful passage. If it is wrong then you will:

- sail ill-prepared on schedule with work hurriedly done or left undone, or;
- sail late, or;
- abandon your passage.

THE OFFSHORE PHASE

The second phase is when you go to sea, and when you attempt to put all your planning and preparation into practice. At sea you have far less control over your timetable. Your planned timings were drawn up using assumptions made weeks or months earlier about, for example, the weather and the performance of your boat in the conditions you imagined you might encounter. They are, at best, informed guesswork.

LIMITATIONS AND DEADLINES

Like goals, every timetable comes with its baggage of limitations. If during the onshore preparations you plan to attend training courses then, once you have signed up, their dates appear as fixed limitations in your timetable and other work must be planned around them. Some fixed dates see you planning backwards from that date to establish the start date for your shore-based work, so that everything is ready on time. If you intend to take part in a race, everything done during your preparations is dominated by the need to have your boat on the start line on time. This means that the completion date for Phase One is determined by the date and time the race starts. If the race is not at your home port, you must factor travel to the race venue into your timetable.

If you are taking part in a rally, your start date is also fixed. If the start of the rally is spread over several days, as a fair number of rallies are, this offers a little flexibility. Even when a rally has a fixed start date it is possible to create some breathing space to complete unfinished work. It has been known for yachts taking part in the Atlantic Rally for Cruisers (ARC) to cross the start line with the rest of the fleet at Las Palmas on the appointed day so that they are officially part of the rally and then to return immediately to the harbour to complete their preparations before beginning their crossing proper.

Independent cruisers also have their deadlines. The start and finish dates of any summer cruise are normally fixed by the time that has been booked off work. Delay the start and you are eating into scarce holiday and if you extend your cruise by postponing your return to work then you do so at your own risk. Many years ago, late on a Sunday evening and through no fault of mine, I ended up on the mud in front of the lock gates at Hull Marina. Transport was waiting to take me home to be ready for work the next morning but there was no way I could start for home until my boat was safe inside the marina. That meant waiting for Monday morning's high tide and that required another day's leave. My boss, who believed holidays were a privilege that should always start on a Friday evening and never exceed two days, including weekends, saw no humour in my tale of nautical misfortune. He simply could not understand my decision to take another day's holiday or accept that anything could take priority over work.

Some passages impose their own timetable. If you are sailing towards Europe from the Caribbean or the Eastern seaboard of the USA, the weather window for this opens around the end of April and closes early in June. If you are not tucked up in the Azores by the end of June, then – although you may not encounter a full-blown hurricane – there is a real risk of meeting an extra-tropical storm on your way to the Azores.

THE TO-DO LIST

The first step in creating any timetable is to identify a list of all the work that must be done to make your boat ready for sea. This includes items such as training courses, modifications to your boat above and below deck, victualling, and installing and learning how to use new equipment. This is your basic To-Do list. It is worth taking the time to make sure it is as complete as possible. Once you have compiled your basic list, make your best estimate of the time each task on the list will take to complete. Be generous, if only to make some allowance for the optimism we all display at this stage.

It is useful to place an estimated cost, together with details of possible suppliers, opposite each task on your To-Do list. This will give you some idea of the total budget and also possible pause for thought. If it looks like you are heading for a budget overrun, you can go through the list item by item and ask:

- Is this item absolutely necessary or merely desirable? If the latter, it can be deleted from your list.
- Is there a cheaper alternative that will do the same job just as well? For example, consider bulk-buying stainless steel nuts and bolts instead of buying in ones and twos from the local chandler. Or investigate buying rope by the reel from a wholesaler.
- Are there alternative suppliers on the Internet? Your local supplier may be willing to meet any better price you find on the net.
- Is there a suitable second-hand version?
- If you plan to sail beyond the EU, is there any possibility of buying equipment duty-free? If that is not practicable, can you delay its purchase until you reach a duty-free port?

This produces your revised To-Do list.

The next step is to create groups of tasks where one task naturally follows on from another. For example, you cannot anti-foul until you have cleaned the hull. If you intend to spray paint the hull, this cannot be done until you have tented the hull to prevent the wind blowing paint over other boats or grit and dirt on to your fresh paint. To tent the hull, you must first find scaffolding and tarpaulins. Stand-alone tasks, or singletons, which do not fit neatly into any group, can be slotted into the timetable wherever it is most convenient.

If you are doing all the work yourself, since you cannot do two tasks at once you will naturally have one long list where every group of tasks follows on one from another. Even so, it is worth the effort to draw up groups of tasks. This allows you to prioritise the work and see what is involved in completing any one group and how long you expect the work to take.

If you have a crew, you can press-gang them or, in the absence of crew, family and friends can be encouraged to help. It may be necessary to contract specialist work out to boatyards, sailmakers and the like. If you do contract out work either to individuals or companies, another task for you is to monitor the timely completion of that work. There is nothing so frustrating as being unable to make a start on some other work because you are waiting for a contractor, who daily promises 'Tomorrow, for sure' to finish their work. It is not unknown for contractors to take on more work than they can handle and resort to spending a day with each customer. Depending on the number of customers they are trying to keep happy, you may only see them once a week.

All else being equal, the start date for the work on your timetable is the day after you finish drawing it up. How long this is before you go to sea depends on the passage you intend to make. If you are building a boat to make a circumnavigation, going to sea may be some years in the future. For a sail round the bay it may be the evening before you cast off. The end date for the onshore planning and preparation phase gives you the date when you go to sea. It also tells you how long you have to complete your To-Do list. If it looks like you have too much work to do and insufficient time to do it in, and since you have already reduced your To-Do list to its essentials, then you must:

- Accelerate the rate at which work is carried out. This normally involves working longer or requires bringing in more people so that work on two or more task groups can be carried out simultaneously, or by contracting more work out to boatyards and the like.
- Accept a lower quality of workmanship if this results in a worthwhile saving in time without involving any risk to the seaworthiness of your boat.
- Delay going to sea. If that is impossible, then abandon your passage.

The earlier you identify any time overrun, the easier it will be to deal with this problem. If, for example, you reckon you are going to be six weeks late on an eight-month timetable, the chances of making up that time if you start doing so in the first month are good. If you wait until a week before you are due to sail, you must abandon hope and face up to reality.

THE WORK SCHEDULE

Your next step is to produce a work schedule. For years I kept track of preparing for my summer cruise in a small, hard-backed notebook. For simple cruises this worked well; but as my ambitions grew it became less helpful. Instead of haphazardly filling the notebook with points as they occurred to me, I tried dividing it into sections, one for each group of tasks. I even went as far as marking the sections with coloured tabs, but it didn't work. Firstly my handwriting, at best a scribble, is normally illegible to me after a few days. Secondly, taking an overview was almost impossible. Thirdly, on those occasions when I did not have the notebook with me I would make notes on any scrap of handy paper and then forget to transcribe them into the notebook.

If you wish to work on paper, to prepare a timetable take a sheet of paper and rule seven columns. Working from left to right, head them:

Task	Start date	Duration	End date	Current date	Days completed	Days remaining

In the column headed TASK, enter the tasks by group. Opposite each task write down the date on which you expect to start work on that particular task. This is the START DATE for that particular task. Under DURATION enter the time, in days, you expect that task to take. Do your sums, or consult a calendar, and note the END DATE for that task. These columns can be completed in ink. You may wish to complete the rest in pencil.

Any time you wish to see how work is progressing, you enter that day's date under CURRENT DATE. Some more counting on fingers tells you how many days you have been working on that task. Enter this under DAYS COMPLETED. Subtracting that answer from the figure you entered under DURATION gives you the DAYS REMAINING and you can now see whether or not the work is on schedule.

Every time you update your timetable you seem to end up doing this for every task so that you have a complete overview of progress. It can be tedious. Then I discovered Microsoft Excel and spreadsheets. Spreadsheets handle dates as easily as they do numbers. Although explaining how to create a timetable in Excel looks horribly complicated, in reality it is quite simple to create a timetable covering the whole of your cruise and taking into account every task involved. Better still, it is a doddle to update and if you wish to brief your crew on the latest position you can print everyone their own copy rather than have them crowd round trying to make sense of your scribbled list. Best of all, you can update your timetable whenever you wish with almost no effort.

By taking the duration, days completed and days remaining for each group of tasks, you can use this information to produce a poor man's Gantt chart.

WORK SCHEDULE BY MICROSOFT EXCEL

Much of the hard work in preparing and updating your work schedule can be avoided by using a spreadsheet such as Microsoft Excel. Spreadsheets take the pain out of playing with numbers and dates. For anyone unfamiliar with using a spreadsheet, here is a step-by-step account of how to prepare a work schedule.

STEP ONE

Open up a new spreadsheet.

STEP TWO

In cell A1 type the word TASK, B1 type the words START DATE, C1 type the word DURATION, D1 type the words COMPLETION DATE, E1 type the words CURRENT DATE, F1 type the words DAYS COMPLETED, G1 type the words DAYS REMAINING

STEP THREE

Using the task list you have written down:
In cell A2 type in the name of the task.
In cell B2 type in the start date you have allocated to this task. In Microsoft Excel, dates are entered DAY/MONTH/YEAR so 3 December 2011 would be typed in as 03/12/11 or 03/12/2011.
In cell C2 type in the number of days you reckon it will take to complete this task.
In cell D2 you wish to know the date on which this task will be completed. Microsoft Excel does this for you. In Cell D2, type in the following formula =B2+C2 and press return and the completion date will appear. All you are doing is telling the spreadsheet to add, say, 50 days to the start date. It is that easy.

The remainder of the spreadsheet is concerned with how work is progressing once you have made a start.

Cell E2: Every time you wish to update your work schedule and establish the current position, enter in Cell E2 the current date in exactly the same format as you entered the date in Cell B2.
Cell F2: tells you how many days you have been working on this task. Enter the formula =DAYS360(B2,E2,TRUE), press return and the number of days will appear in Cell F2.
Cell G2: tells you how many days you have left to complete the work on schedule. Type the formula =C2-F2, press return and the answer appears.

STEP FOUR

You now repeat the above for each separate task. This could be tedious since there can be over a hundred entries on the list and the potential for mistyping and entering formulae incorrectly is fairly high. The lazy method is to highlight from Cell B2 to Cell G2 and down to the last task on your list, hold down the control key, press the D key and your spreadsheet completes itself. Note, do not highlight the list of tasks or headings, just the columns where you have entered or would have to enter formulae.

UPDATING YOUR TIMETABLE

When you come to update your work schedule, first enter the current date in Cell E2 then highlight that and the rest of the dates in Column E. Press Control and D and the spreadsheet will update itself. This is so simple that preparing weekly or monthly updates becomes a habit.

ARRANGING THE INFORMATION

Using the sort and filter button, a spreadsheet allows you to sort the tasks in each group by date, cost or any other factor you wish. This can be very useful if you are pondering how to bring work back onto the timetable or keep it within budget.

GANTT CHARTS

If you wish, though it may be an option too far, the stacked bar graph option of Microsoft Excel allows you to draw a simple Gantt chart. Gantt charts show graphically the duration of any task against time and allow you to see what should have been achieved at any point.

Gantt charts were developed by H L Gantt around 1910 and used to monitor the building of the Hoover Dam and the US state highway system. Today's Gantt charts are drawn using sophisticated software that automatically shows the order in which tasks should be done, important milestones, and features that allow you to estimate the effect of any remedial action to bring the timetable back onto schedule or budget.

POOR MAN'S GANTT CHART

Gantt charts are useful for scheduling work and critical path analysis. Project managers use very sophisticated Gantt chart computer programmes to manage major projects. This simplified version, using Excel's bar graph function, shows you the countdown of days remaining against duration allocated to a particular task. This can be a useful reminder when time becomes critical. When you run out of time, the green bar disappears.

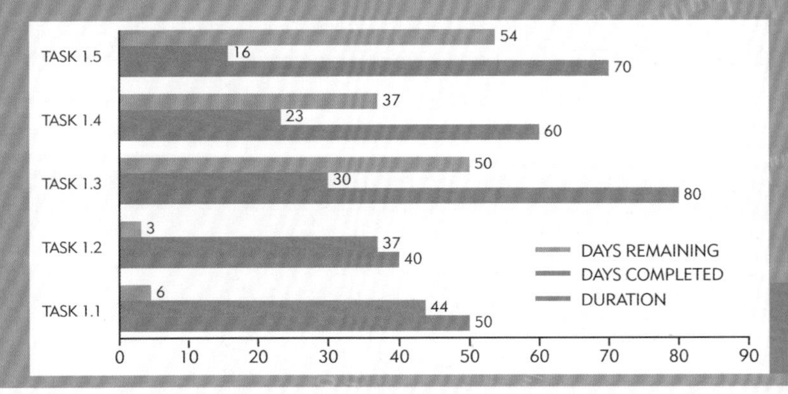

Poor Man's Gantt chart

TIMETABLE SPREADSHEET

TASK	START DATE	DURATION	COMPLETION	CURRENT	DAYS	DAYS	WORK	COST	EXPENDITURE	BALANCE
		IN DAYS	DATE	DATE	COMPLETED	REMAINING	DONE BY			
Formula	*Enter Date*	*Enter Duration*	*Enter =B4+C4*	*Enter Date*	*Enter =DYS360 (B4,E4,TRUE)*	*Enter =C4–F4*				
GROUP 1										
Task 1.1	03/12/11	50	22/01/2012	17/01/2012	44	6				
Task 1.2	10/12/11	40	19/01/2012	17/01/2012	37	3				
Task 1.3	17/12/11	80	06/03/2012	17/01/2012	30	50				
Task 1.4	24/12/11	60	22/02/2012	17/01/2012	23	37				
Task 1.5	01/01/12	70	11/03/2012	17/01/2012	16	54				
GROUP 2										
Task 2.1	10/12/11	15	25/12/2011	17/01/2012	37	–22				
Task 2.2	15/12/11	35	19/01/2012	17/01/2012	32	3				
Task 2.3	04/01/12	80	24/03/2012	17/01/2012	13	67				
Task 2.4	24/01/12	60	24/03/2012	17/01/2012	–7	67				
Task 2.5	03/02/12	70	13/04/2012	17/01/2012	–16	86				

Normally it is easier to group related tasks together. Grouping can be tasks of a similar type or tasks that naturally follow on one from another.

You can finish the spreadsheet at the days remaining column but it might be helpful to include columns on who does what and how much it costs.

06 DECISION MAKING

St Matthew was right. 'No man can serve two masters' (Matthew 6:24). No ship can have two skippers. Doubt over who is in charge and who decides what happens invariably leads to confusion. Even worse is a crew of eager, expert sailors, each one wearing their skipper's hat, full of their own ideas about what should be done, each absolutely determined that their opinion is the one that should be put into action. This is as close as you can have to a guarantee of disorder, disagreement and disputes.

Boats are democracies only in the sense that at sea there has long been a custom of one man, one vote – and as skipper that solitary vote is yours. By all means talk situations through with your crew. Listen carefully to their views. Seek out their advice, especially in areas where they have a particular expertise; but on board ship, decisions are never made by counting a show of hands. At sea, democracy is one man, one vote and the skipper has it. You make the decisions because as skipper you are responsible for the safety of your vessel and your crew. This is an awesome responsibility. Your prime task is ensuring that everyone aboard your boat is returned safe and healthy to shore. You can never delegate this responsibility. It lives with you twenty-four hours a day. If you do choose to hand it over to someone else, it is just your way of declaring that matters have reached a point where it is 'Everyone for him/herself'.

Once you have worked out how you are going to put your strategy into action, you can tell everyone what they have to do, and when they have to do it. Lastly you cry, 'Let's go!' and implement your plan.

GIVING WORK TO OTHERS

Just because you cannot escape your responsibilities as skipper does not preclude delegating the tasks to other crew members. Nor does it mean that once you have delegated the work you must micromanage, hovering over their shoulder and hissing advice in their ear while they try to carry out the task you have given them. Every skipper knows that the dangers of micromanaging are waiting to pounce. It is an insidious infection. It begins with mild, well-meant outbreaks of showing novice crew members how to carry out some work with which they are unfamiliar, but quickly reaches a point where the skipper cannot delegate even the simplest of chores without first showing how it should be done and then subsequently blaming someone else for the poor workmanship. Such pettifogging, cheap behaviour really does wonders for crew morale.

Generally, it is good practice to leave the individuals you have charged with the various tasks to carry them out as best they think fit. The key word here is 'leave'. If they need to be closely supervised, they should not have been given the task in the first place. Either way, if they are successful, *they* win the credit – and *you* carry the blame if they fail. By leaving them alone to carry out their allocated tasks, crew members appreciate the confidence and trust you show in them and while they do the work you are free to carry on with your job of leading the crew and sailing the ship.

GIVING ORDERS

There are skippers who see any opinion other than their own as challenging their authority and firmly believe that initiative in others, if not smothered at birth, should be derided and ridiculed. Nothing could be more out of place on a yacht being sailed for fun. The skipper who behaves like this may command the boat but is unlikely to command the respect or willing commitment of their crew.

On small yachts, the wise skipper discusses their plans with their crew. Normally they delegate as much of the action as they can to others, leaving them, within agreed limits, to decide how that task is to be carried out. So, saying to the mate 'I'd like a reef in the main if the wind goes above force 5' gives responsibility for that task to the mate. Should the wind rise above force 5, the mate issues the orders to reef and supervises the work without seeking any further authorisation from his skipper. Hopefully he would let you know what is happening.

Sensible skippers issue as few direct orders as possible. Instead, they frame them as a request. When they do give a command, they think it through before opening their mouth and make sure it is clear, unambiguous and issued in a calm, unaggressive manner. The old military parade ground advice of CLAP (Clear, Loud And with Pauses) for giving orders has its place at sea. Behaving like a bully-boy clipper skipper and surrounding your orders with colourful language will only convince your crew that you are unsure about what should be done.

Every order has four essential components:

1. It clearly identifies who is to carry out the order. This may be 'all hands' or 'port watch' or even 'John and Mike'.

2 It specifies the work to be done. This may be 'weigh anchor', 'hoist the mainsail' or 'inflate the dinghy and put it over the starboard side'.
3 It says when the work is to be carried out. This may be 'at 6pm' or 'after lunch'. If no time is specified, the order should be carried out immediately.
4 The recipient(s) of an order acknowledges receiving and understanding it. It is possible, particularly in heavy weather, for orders to be lost among the noise of wind and sea but if the crew are in the habit of not acknowledging an order, the skipper does not know whether their order has been heard or not.

An order like 'Let's get the mainsail up' is a poor command, leaving the crew wondering just who is to do what and when, while the impatient skipper, dancing from foot to foot, demands to know why nothing is being done.

LEAPS IN THE DARK

When deciding on a course of action, try, if at all possible, to avoid jumping to conclusions. Very occasionally, lack of time and a sense of urgency may drive you towards off-the-cuff decisions based upon nothing more than an overwhelming desire to be taking action; but this should happen every other blue moon. Some use this as their preferred decision-making strategy. They believe reacting before knowing what they are doing is proof that they are on top of the job. They exist in a world of snap decisions, hunches and arbitrary guesses. In trivial cases the consequences, good or bad, do not matter; but a surfeit of instant decisiveness has much the same effect as a glut of constant indecision: total and complete chaos. On most occasions, however imperative it may appear to take action, it is usually wiser to give some thought before making a decision. The Duke of Wellington was right when he said, 'No situation is as good or as bad as first reported.' There is always time to assess a situation and review your options before taking action. It is a lesson I learned the hard way.

Many years ago, crossing from Padstow to Milford Haven, it began blowing a near gale and the mast broke when we were about mid-channel. I began hauling in the raffle of gear that was hanging over the side. It was a struggle and my wife asked if she could help. Eager to give her something to do (busy crew do not have time to be scared) I told her to start the engine and hold the boat into the seas, which would make it easier for me to pull the tangle of rigging, lines and mast aboard. She demurred. I told her to do it. Just before she put the engine into gear she questioned again what I had asked her to do and again I told her to get on with it. Seconds later the lines in the water fouled the prop and the engine stopped. It was almost thirty hours later when we got out of that mess.

It was not one of my better moments or brighter decisions. I have since sometimes wondered whether, having made a poor decision in haste, my pride could not let me review it and made me deaf to any other, wiser suggestions. Whatever, the lesson that I should think before opening my mouth and leaping into action was well learned and never forgotten.

CHECK THE FACTS

Before making a decision, it is a good idea to review the facts available to you and, if possible, check them out. Once, heading along the Moray Firth for Inverness, we were caught in a north-westerly blow and driven into Spey Bay. The obvious decision of choice was to head for

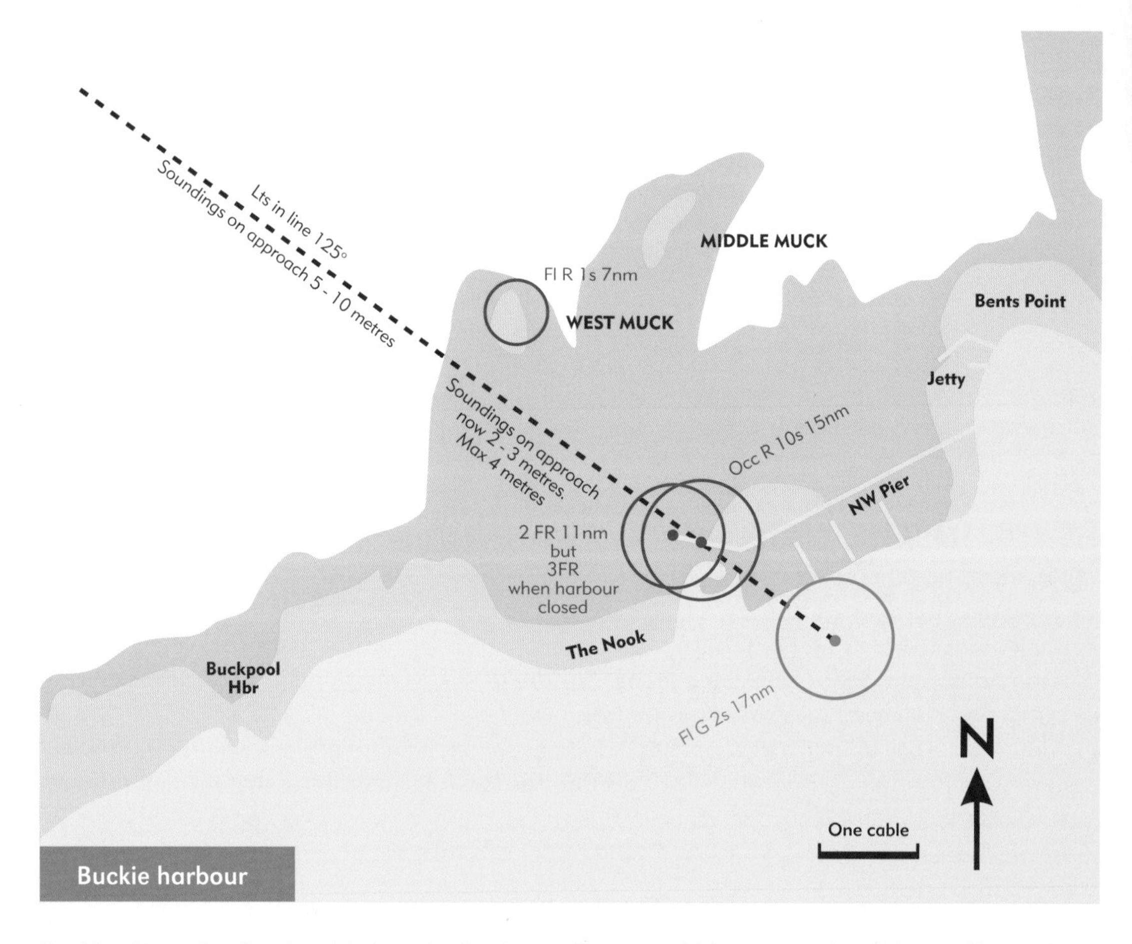

Buckie harbour

Buckie. Our pilot book said that the harbour there *could be entered safely in all weathers.* But, from the chart, the approach looked very committing. First, in a north-westerly wind we were running onto a lee shore. Second, we would have to slide past the reefs of West and Middle Muck (which would be kicking up a horrid sea) and then make a hard turn to port in the middle of the backwash of the seas hitting the beach before finding the shelter behind the breakwater. I have a natural reluctance to approach a lee shore in poor weather, but it was the turn into the harbour that really concerned me. In the horrendously confused sea I expected to find by the harbour entrance, safety lay in brute power and I doubted if our engine – even with the help of the sails – had enough.

We tried calling the harbourmaster on the VHF to seek his advice but received no reply. Instead we got Aberdeen Coastguard. We explained our situation and after a few moments they came back, reporting that they had telephoned the harbourmaster who said we were welcome to come in – but added that we were to be told that the fishing boats were not going out. We took the hint.

INTUITIVE DECISIONS

There is a distinction between a snap judgement and an intuitive decision. Although no two people agree on the nature of intuition, it is generally accepted that intuitive thinking allows you almost instantly and without conscious effort to draw upon all those useless items of information stored in your brain and come to a workable solution to a problem without going through the usual analytical processes. Intuition can also give you that pricking in your thumbs that warns of something unwelcome approaching. This is not a sixth sense but merely that you have, without being aware of it, picked up signals that are fluttering around on the edge of your consciousness.

Perhaps the most important attributes of an intuitive decision maker are experience, whether their own or learned from others, and an ability to focus on the relevant issues. If you reckon you are an intuitive thinker, it is useful to remember that the best intuitive decision makers also find the time to check their answers using more analytical methods.

RIGHT AND WRONG DECISIONS

Sometimes there is no obviously right or wrong option and you are unsure what action to take. In such circumstances you have no choice but to go with your gut feelings. Some years ago I was anchored in company with three other boats in a beautiful bay on the north coast of Isla Tortuga off the Venezuelan coast when word came that Lenny, one of the season's more eccentric hurricanes, was about to pass nearby.

We all agreed we must do something but disagreed over the best course of action. In truth we were novices. None of us had ever experienced a close encounter with a hurricane. All we had was book knowledge and no one's opinion carried more weight than any other.

In the end, one boat headed for the hurricane hole on the south side of the island; one boat stayed put; one disappeared westwards towards a collection of reefs called Los Roques; I hid deep in a mangrove-lined inlet to the south of Cabo Codera on the Venezuelan mainland. This was about as far inland as I could go without wheels. Four boats, four very different options – and when we met up in Curaçao weeks later, we learned that we had all escaped Lenny's fury and were all convinced we had made the right decision. I suppose we had.

THE HALF FULL GLASS

Another way of looking at decision making is to decide what sort of person you are. Do you always look on the bright side? This is the way of the optimistic decision maker who considers the most favourable outcomes for each course of action and then chooses the option they believe promises the best of all possible outcomes.

THE HALF EMPTY GLASS

On the other hand, you may reckon that disaster lurks in every shadow. This is the approach of choice for the pessimistic decision maker, who considers events are always going to end badly. For them it is important to minimise the consequences of failure rather than reap the benefits of success, and the best decision they can make is to choose what they believe to be the option that comes with the least worst consequences.

PLANNING FOR THE WORST

Pessimistic decision makers are first cousins to those who claim they always plan for the worst and hope for the best. There is nothing wrong with considering various eventualities and how you may deal with them and, if you wish, you are free always to look on the dark side – but to make this the foundation of your plan is madness. The only certainty is that, should disaster strike, it will not be among those catastrophes you considered and planned for; and skill, talent, initiative and sheer hard work are more likely to produce a successful outcome than waiting for hope to appear over the horizon.

MIXED DECISIONS

In practice, most of us avoid extremes and follow the white line in the middle of the road. There are few courses of action that carry the promise of either complete disaster or total success. Instead, we try to balance the possible gains against probable losses and look to make our choice from options whose advantages outnumber its disadvantages. It is important to remember that you are not making a crude count of advantages and disadvantages. You also have to take into account the consequences of each advantage and disadvantage. A host of advantages, all with small positive consequences, could easily be outweighed by a single disadvantage with one extremely negative consequence. There is no mechanical or formulaic answer. It is a question of judgement.

It is dusk. You have just picked up the loom of a light on a headland you have to round to reach your destination. Your sums tell you that it is 15 miles away and in the present conditions you will not reach it for another four hours, by which time the tide will have turned foul.

The courses of action open to you include:

1. Do nothing. Carry on sailing and pushing through the foul tide. The downside to this option is that it is spring tides, and the wind blowing over the tide could create conditions that stop you in your tracks until the tide turns in your favour. You will almost certainly arrive well behind your ETA. The question is, have you and your crew the reserves of energy to take a battering lasting several hours and spend longer at sea?
2. Change course to pass the headland further out to sea, out of the worst of the tide, and once round the headland angle back in towards your destination. Looking at the chart, this would add 15 miles to your passage or about four or five hours' sailing. Throw in a couple of hours to allow for the effect of the foul tide and you will arrive up to six hours after your original ETA. The next point to consider is: have you and your crew the reserves to spend another six hours at sea, albeit in more reasonable conditions?
3. Slow the boat down so you arrive off the headland just as the tide turns fair or, alternatively, sail up to the headland and then heave-to until the tide turns. This course of action depends on whether or not your boat will happily heave-to. Some modern hull designs are reluctant to park at sea. Whether you heave-to or slow down, you will spend longer at sea and face the same questions about crew endurance. At least in this option, whether hove-to or jogging along, there is a chance to prepare a hot meal and for those off watch to have a decent rest.
4. Finally, just before you reach the headland is a harbour. You have never visited it before but the pilot book says it is available at all states of tide and weather. Your ETA for arriving there is about the same as for being off the headland. If instead of heaving-to off the headland you entered harbour, everyone could rest for a few hours before the tide turned in your favour, when you could hurry back to sea and round the headland. The question is, are you happy making a night entry into an unfamiliar port and then finding a berth in what may be a crowded harbour? And having done all this, will there be time left to rest and make the effort worthwhile?

None of the above options about rounding that headland are wrong; they could all be made to work. Once you have weighed them up, one may appeal more than others because you reckon its disadvantages are outweighed by its advantages and carry the highest probability of success. If you cannot decide which option that is, take into account such factors as the skills and strengths of you and your crew, and the condition and capabilities of your yacht, then select an option you believe you can make work. This choice is no more the 'right' choice than the other options are 'wrong'. What is wrong is making no decision at all.

DOING NOTHING

Doing nothing is not the same as not making a decision. Doing nothing is an option in its own right. Perhaps the one you prefer. Fine. Do nothing but be idle for good reasons. But doing nothing while gabbling, 'I don't know what to do' is being indecisive to a point where you are a danger to navigation.

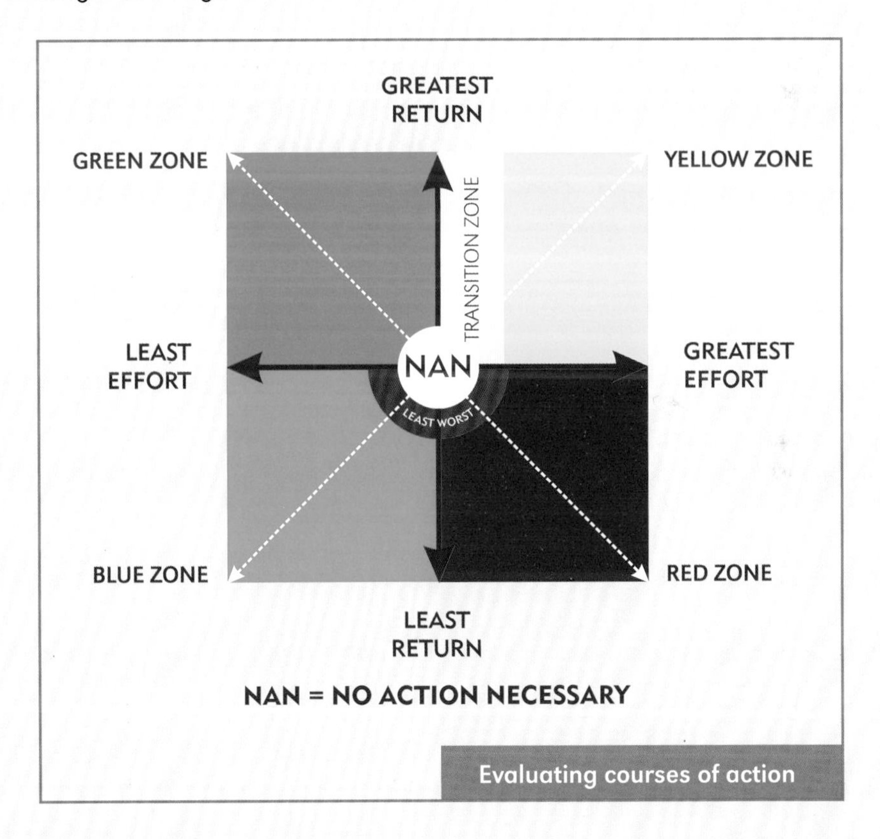

Evaluating courses of action

DECISION TREES

At sea, decisions are normally made without putting anything on paper. Ashore, when you have more time, you may find drawing up a decision tree a helpful tool to keep track of your options and possible outcomes. A decision tree is nothing more than laying out your options so you can see them all, and their outcomes, at a glance. It can help you see links between options and suggest advantages and disadvantages that have not yet occurred to you. It can draw attention to when you must commit yourself to a decision once and for all.

In the above example, you might decide to sail up to the headland and heave-to, waiting for the tide to turn. There is a lot going for this option. You are well placed to resume sailing the instant the tide turns and will probably lose the least time. Hove-to, only one person need suffer the weather in the cockpit. This maximises the amount of rest everyone can take and it is possible to make hot drinks and warm food. Right up until the moment you heave-to, and

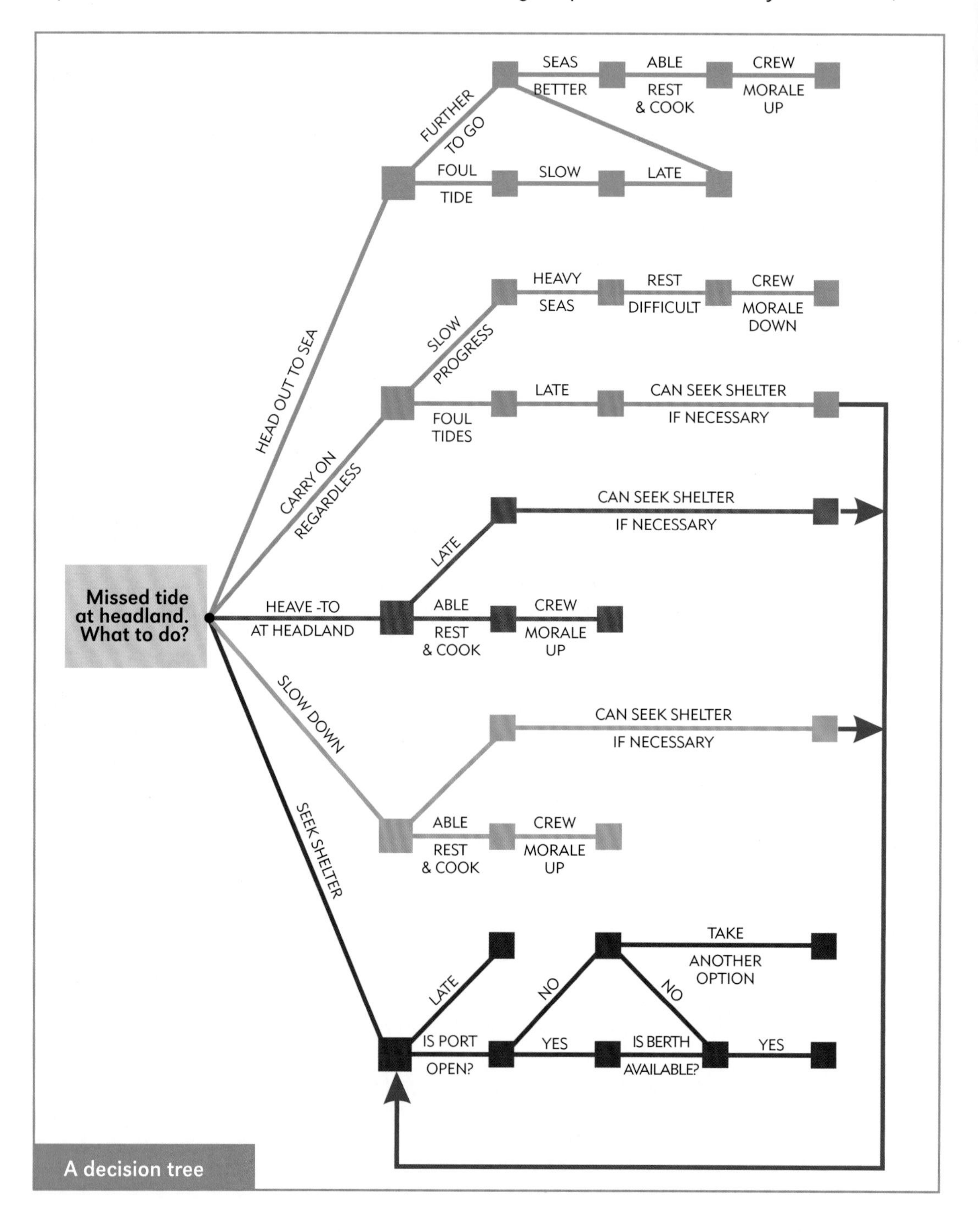

A decision tree

possibly even later, you can change your mind and choose one of the other options – so if the weather suddenly worsens, or there is a gear failure, it is a simple matter to change course and head for the shelter of the harbour. Changing your mind is not being indecisive or weak. You are prudently reacting to shifting circumstances. A cunning skipper will already know the course to steer to reach the harbour.

To draw a decision tree, take a sheet of paper and on the right-hand side draw a square. This represents the decision you wish to make. From this square draw out lines, each line representing one of the options open to you. Label each line and keep them as far apart as you can so that you have space to add detail later. Draw a square at the end of each line and from each of these squares draw out lines each representing an issue, good or bad, that you must take into account when weighing up that decision.

Going through your decision tree with your crew can be a useful way of making sure everyone is working for the same end. As you work through your decision tree, they can see that their individual ideas have been noted and considered and they have an opportunity to understand the reasoning behind your chosen course of action – that is, if your crew can understand your drawing. Decision trees are visual aids to help you. Even prepared in the best of conditions they can look like a demented web of randomly drawn lines. Drawn on a bouncing boat with a pencil between your teeth and dripping water over the chart table, the end product may mean much to you but others may be so confused that they doubt your sanity.

THE ONLY CHOICE

One point that decision trees highlight is that a decision is a choice between options. If there is no choice, there is only one course of action open to you. At this point you are no longer in charge of the situation. The safety of your vessel and the well-being of you and your crew now depend on your skill in executing a course of action not of your choosing in circumstances that you have not foreseen. Hindsight will probably reveal a long chain of earlier decisions that unobtrusively reduced the options open to you until only a forlorn hope remained. When selecting a course of action it is always wise to ask: if this course of action is followed, what other options are closed in future? If the answer is 'all of them', it is time for second thoughts about your choice of option.

PART 2
ELEMENTS OF PLANNING

INTRODUCTION

It is never easy deciding what elements to include in your plan. Too few and your plan is inadequate; too many and it is a labour of Sisyphus. Fixing on how deeply you wish, or need, to go into each element places you on the horns of a dilemma. Too little information on any element can mean missing important points; too much and you sink under the weight of detail.

The topics discussed in this section are comprehensive but not definitive. The detail for each topic tends to reflect the needs of an extended blue water passage with the hope that, from it, you can pick and mix to reflect the needs of another cruise.

If deciding what to include is difficult, then it is harder working out the relative importance of one element to another. If you are starting by building your own boat, it is obvious that routeing is not yet a priority – but it is rarely that simple. Attempts at creating some sort of hierarchy only serve to underline that every element is somehow related to every other element and what happens in one area will, in some way, affect the rest.

Any starting point is arbitrary. It seemed reasonable to begin with the boat. Without some sort of craft, you cannot sail; but thereafter the list works through the principal headings in my usual haphazard fashion. You may be happier working through them in a completely different order that suits you. Some elements you will rightly dismiss as irrelevant to your passage. Others, like routeing or supplies, are mandatory. Every passage involves some navigation and we all need to eat, even if it is only a sandwich and a flask of coffee.

Most topics deal with work that should be carried out before casting off. Even though you anti-fouled the hull at the start of the season, you may wish to haul out for a scrub and brush up before setting out on your annual cruise; a sail needs repairs, or some running rigging may need replacing. For longer passages you might consider fitting a more powerful alternator to your engine, or installing a wind generator or solar panels. Fitting a windvane self-steering system may appeal, as may additional water or fuel tanks, cockpit awnings or an SSB transceiver.

Before you rush out and buy any new equipment, you must first discover which type and model is best suited to your boat. This means doing your homework and, when you have discovered which is best for you, finding the best source for buying it.

If you are going foreign for the first time and have not registered your boat, you must investigate how this is done. It would also be prudent to speak to your insurance company to confirm that your cover extends to foreign seas and check that your passport is in date.

When considering crew training, you may decide it would be wise to go on a first aid course or – if you are like me, a mechanical illiterate – attend an engine maintenance course.

When you have worked through your chosen topics, you will discover that you have gone a long way towards creating your own personalised checklist for the particular passage you have in mind. You will also have discovered that there is a surprising amount of work to be done before you are ready to go to sea. The next task is to place that work into some sort of sensible order and prepare a timetable for carrying it out. The next shock is the realisation that if you do not make a start on the work tomorrow and stick to schedule, you will never cast off on time.

Sanding off anti-fouling is perhaps one of the nastiest tasks you have to undertake at the start of the season, before you can sail

THE BOAT ABOVE DECKS

The term 'above decks' covers everywhere outside of the cabin, including the exterior of the hull, keel, rudder and propeller. As it is your principal working area, it makes good sense to ensure that everywhere above decks is a safe and comfortable workplace, regardless of the length or type of voyage you propose to undertake.

NON-SLIP

Working on the pitching deck of a small boat is extremely precarious. It is not just the risk of falling overboard – slips and falls cause bruises and sprains whose effects linger for days and ruin your cruise.

A good non-slip deck minimises the risk of this happening. Traditional teak-laid decks give a good non-slip surface and, as a modern substitute, many GRP boats have teak veneer laid on top of their GRP deck. Many more GRP boats have a non-slip pattern cast into their GRP deck, usually in strips or squares broken by areas of smooth gelcoat. The gelcoat areas, when wet, act as a skidpan. This is not so important when you can be sure of placing your feet on the patterned areas but it is very dangerous in the dark or when you are lugging a sailbag. Possibly the easiest and quickest answer is to fit additional adhesive non-slip pads to the areas of smooth gelcoat. Another solution is to cover these areas with non-slip paint. Normal deck paint can be made non-slip by the addition of special granules that you can buy and add to any tin of suitable deck paint, or you can purchase ready to use non-slip deck paint. There is a choice between a not too aggressive yacht version, which aims to strike a balance between providing a non-slip surface and not spoiling the appearance of your boat, and commercial non-slip paints. A good example of the latter is called flight deck paint, which is intended for use in areas such as flight decks and external walkways on commercial ships and oil platforms. It may not be pretty but it does what it says on the tin. If you slip on a deck coated with this paint, you leave your shoes behind.

Probably the best way to reduce the risk of slipping when you are on deck is not to go out on deck or, at least, reduce the need to work on deck to a minimum. This involves looking to your sail handling and making arrangements for as much as possible to be done from the security of the cockpit.

SIDEDECKS

The sidedeck is the area between the coachroof and the toe rail. On yachts above 32–35 feet LOA they are normally wide enough to provide a comfortable walkway. Below that size, the designer's dilemma of maximising cabin space by making the coachroof as wide as possible and providing a decent walkway often comes down in favour of cabin space.

Some boats have no sidedeck; others, for appearances' sake, have a very narrow sidedeck, and by the time you add chain plates, stanchion bases and sheeting track it is so cluttered that movement along it is all but impossible. If you are going from the cockpit to the foredeck it is easier to climb out of the cockpit, shuffle forward outside of the guardrails, and climb back over the guardrail when you reach the foredeck, where the motion of your boat can be at its most violent. It is not the safest of activities and there is a good argument for removing the guardrails forward of the cockpit to avoid the danger of climbing over them to reach the foredeck. The disadvantage of this solution is that you must now work on the foredeck without the protection of the guardrails. One slip and you could be over the wall. Reducing this danger leads back to having a good non-slip deck.

DECK HARDWARE

All deck hardware such as:

- guardrails
- grab rails
- jackstay anchor points
- tether anchor points
- winches
- jammers
- chain plates
- cleats
- stanchions
- stanchion bases
- bow roller
- fairleads
- sheet tracks

must be in good condition and bolted through the deck onto substantial backing pads. Chain plates are an exception. They should be attached to the hull in such a manner that the loadings they impose are spread throughout the hull. This normally means tying them into some major structural feature, such as bulkheads.

It is important that all hardware stays in place, not just those you clip in your safety tether. This requires no special skill. It relies upon the work being done to the right standard in the first place and then regular checks to confirm that it is in good order. I once watched a winch pull out of the deck and fly forward like it had been launched from a catapult. It narrowly missed one of the crew working at the mast before punching a hole in the spinnaker and disappearing. On another occasion, on a boat under tow, a cleat snapped, flew aft and smashed into the skipper. He was taken to hospital by helicopter to have his hip rebuilt.

GUARDRAILS

Attached to the pushpit and pulpit, wire lines called lifelines, but also known as guardrails, run through the stanchions to form a continuous loop around the deck. Their purpose is to prevent anyone falling overboard, or at least help reduce the possibility of that happening. Except on the very smallest of vessels there are two guardrails, one above the other. The upper lifeline should be not less than 24 inches (600mm) above the deck. The lower lifeline should be not less than 8 inches (200mm) above the deck. On vessels less than 40ft (12m) LOA the lifeline wire has a minimum diameter of 4mm. On vessels over 40ft LOA the wire should have a diameter of at least 5mm.

Guardrail wires should not be covered in plastic and they should be tight. It should be difficult to move them more than 2 or 3 inches (50–75mm) vertically. Less is preferable. The guardrail wires must not be kinked or have any broken strands, both of which seriously weaken the wire and are caused by either the wire kinking or from physical damage. The terminals on the ends of the wires must be in good condition and any split pins should be turned to prevent them slipping out. The ends of split pins can be very sharp. Taping the entire split pin with a turn or two of electrical insulation tape or self-amalgamating tape removes any risk of it cutting hands or clothing. If using lanyards to secure wires to the pushpit, check that they are in good condition without any evidence of chafe or UV degradation through aging. It is an RORC/ORC requirement that lashings are less than 4 inches (100mm) long.

It is poor practice to hang fenders from guardrails or allow the stanchions to be used as handholds either to fend off from other boats or to haul yourself on board. The leverage this usage imposes can bend the stanchions or loosen their bases. Bending weakens stanchions and loose stanchion bases are a promise of leaks, not on a scale that threatens to sink the boat but enough to weaken the backing pad and, if they are inside a locker, flood it and ruin everything stowed in it.

GRAB RAILS

I am not a fan of the traditional wooden grab rail. They look pretty but I can never forget that they are held onto the deck by small screws coming up through the deck into a piece of wood 30–35mm wide. These screws do not normally come with backing pads. I wonder how this arrangement would perform if I was hanging on for dear life while winds and seas tried to fling me overboard. For me, a grab rail is something you can slap your hand onto and wrap your fingers around, knowing that if it fails you take half the deck overboard with you. Grab rails like this do not come as standard.

JACKSTAYS

Jackstays run along the deck, port and starboard, outside of everything so that anyone leaving the cockpit should be able to clip into the jackstay before leaving the cockpit and remain clipped in until they have safely returned to the cockpit. Their anchor points are through bolted to substantial backing pads from positions abeam the cockpit to the bow.

Jackstays may be either of wire or webbing tape. If they are of tape, then the older they are the more UV degradation they have suffered and the greater the loss of their original colour. Replace faded jackstays. If there are any localised colour changes this can be a sign of chafe. The source of this chafing must be discovered and the jackstay replaced. If the jackstays are of wire, they should be of 5mm 1x19 wire. Check that there are no kinks or damage to the wire. Do not use plastic-covered wire. The slight movement of wire jackstays across the sidedeck may appear silent to those on deck. To anyone in the cabin it sounds like being inside a snare drum.

Check that the lashings or attachments to anchor points to both webbing and wire jackstays are in good condition. Lashings should have at least four or five complete turns.

BOW ROLLER

It is a sign of how far anchoring has fallen out of fashion that some yachts now come without a bow roller to take the anchor rode but instead rely on small port and starboard bow fairleads. These are fine for anchoring for lunch but are unsatisfactory for prolonged use.

Is the bow roller taking the anchor rode of sufficient size and strength to hold the boat safely? Is it through bolted with adequate backing pads? Would it perform well in heavy seas that caused the bows to pitch and roll violently? Can you prevent chafe or the anchor rode jumping out of the bow roller? If your answer to these questions is 'No' then give some thought to how any deficiencies can be made good on your boat. No single answer fits every case but ultimately your anchoring system may be all that stands between riding out some bad weather and being driven ashore.

Once, I was chatting to the harbour master in Las Palmas. It was a calm, peaceful day and the sea was so flat that the hydrofoil drove round at full speed to create a wash that would lift it onto its foils. Standing by the marina, we watched a mini tidal wave of wash roll in. Pontoons and boats rocked violently and several boats lost fairleads. Imagine what would have happened if they had been at anchor in a gale. The loadings imposed by the anchor rode can be very considerable. In a gale in Stonehaven Harbour I watched a small yacht moored fore and aft tear its bow roller out of the deck as it surged back and forward.

A bow roller for all seasons

SHELTER

At least half of every passage is spent on deck taking the worst that the weather can throw at you. It is good sense to give yourself and your crew as much protection as possible. No one is at their best if they are cold, wet and tired. Modern foul weather gear is excellent but it should be the last line of defence against the weather, not the first.

A wheelhouse is good. A wheelhouse with a heater is even better. Then you can stand in shirt-sleeved comfort and watch the weather do its worst. Next best is a doghouse and last of all a pram hood. In terms of the shelter they offer, there is not much to choose between a doghouse and pram hood but a doghouse wins because it also provides a good home for those instruments such as plotters, compasses and echo sounders that you need to hand in the cockpit.

Dodgers between the cockpit and the pushpit, besides carrying the vessel's name, provide those in the cockpit with protection against flank attacks by rogue waves.

WORKING LAYOUT

The three principal on-deck working areas are the foredeck, around the mast and the cockpit.

Thanks to roller reefing, the need to go forward to work on the foredeck is much reduced. The days of crawling forward with a sailbag clenched between your teeth, hauling down and hanking on sails are all but over – but at least that taught you that foredeck safety came from keeping your weight low and doing as much of the work as possible sitting down. Now you only have to go forward to fly a spinnaker or cruising chute, to anchor or handle the berthing warps; but the principle of keeping your weight low still holds good.

This is not always possible when working at the mast, where you must stand up to handle halyards, jammers and winches properly. On some boats there is sufficient free space around the mast to fit granny bars; otherwise, look for ways of providing anchor points for short tethers so that those working at the mast can clip in and brace themselves against the tether while they are working. If that is not possible, it may be time to consider fitting in-mast or in-boom mainsail reefing systems that can handle the mainsail from the cockpit so that the need to work at the mast is much reduced.

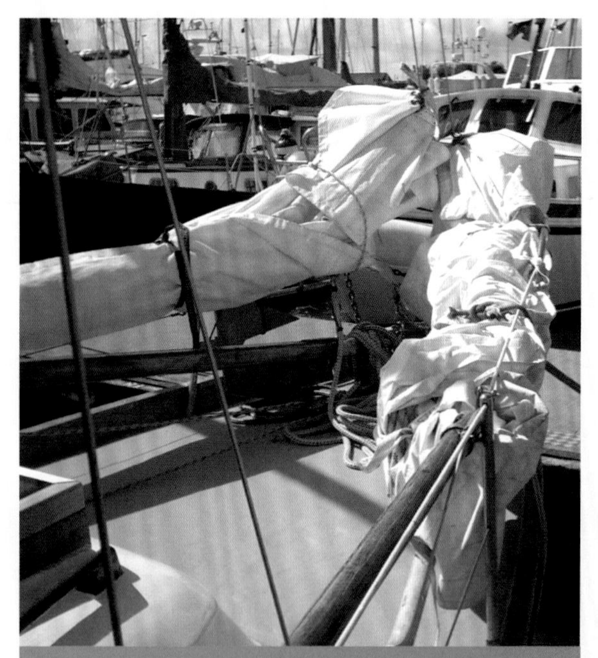

Traditional headsails are hanked on, changed or reefed for different wind speeds. They occupy valuable cabin space when not being used or suffer ultra-violet damage tied to the guardrails. One of these headsails is boomed, making life easier when tacking

Every yacht cockpit is a compromise between providing enough space and being as small as possible. There are two reasons for keeping cockpits small. Firstly, if it does fill with water then there is less to drain away. Secondly, it maximises living room below decks. Without major surgery there is nothing that can be done about cockpit size or helming position but carefully rearranging winches and cleats can improve the working layout.

ABOVE DECK STOWAGE

Normally, the items stowed above deck are those that are needed for use on deck such as spare fuel in cans, fenders, ready to use warps, buckets and the like. All need to be stowed securely and in such a manner that does not hinder their intended use.

Both the dinghy and the liferaft must be stowed in such a manner that they are absolutely secure and cannot come free to skitter around the deck. The catch with the liferaft is that it must be stowed so that one person can release it and throw it over the side in seconds. This is a tall order. I once sailed on a yacht where the liferafts (it had two) were stowed standing on their sides at the bottom of a narrow, deep locker. I was never convinced that, had we needed them, they could have been launched in time.

Lifebuoys and danbuoys must be held securely in place, within reach of the helm and able to be thrown instantly overboard. This is another tall order but it is worth resolving this conundrum. You may be the person in the water. Dinghy paddles and boathooks may be tied to grab rails. Make arrangements for stowing spinnaker poles on the mast, on the sidedeck or along the guardrail.

The growing fashion for stern cabins has tended to reduce both the number and size of deck and cockpit lockers. Lazerettes or stern lockers are often sacrificed to create a stern cabin. It is useful to give some thought as to what goes into each deck and cockpit locker and how it is stowed so that what you need comes easily to hand rather than having to sort through a lucky dip. One deck or cockpit locker should be dedicated to stowing the cooking gas bottles. If you are in the habit of locking cockpit lockers when you go ashore, be sure that they are open and ready to use before going to sea.

ENTERING/LEAVING DECK

Movement between the deck and cabin takes place mostly via the companionway and less frequently though a deck hatch. The companionway is normally an arrangement of a sliding hatch and washboards or, less commonly, small doors. Access should be wide enough so that major items of equipment can be passed through. Like every hatch, the companionway should be capable of being opened from above and below decks; and if washboards are used to close off its vertical face, there should be some arrangement that still allows access from above or below decks but which also ensures that in the event of an inversion the washboards remain in place. It is a good idea to have grab rails port and starboard, immediately inside and outside of the companionway. People climbing in and out of the cabin are vulnerable if the boat gives an unexpected lurch, and a well-placed grab rail may save them from injury.

Many vessels have several deck hatches but there is usually only one large enough to allow someone to climb through; the remainder are for ventilation. The man-sized hatch is usually on the foredeck – hence its name, the forehatch – and was once the principal means of passing sails between the deck and the forepeak; it was this, more than the need to allow a body through, that determined its size. On most yachts, using this hatch to leave or enter the cabin requires some agility. It is frequently awash, particularly in heavy weather when it may leak and make the forepeak a damp, unwelcome hole. If that is the case, and if it is not much used, then consider sealing up the forehatch.

OPENINGS IN DECK

Hatches apart, probably the only other openings in the deck are the cable glands carrying wiring from the mast, which should be waterproof, and ventilators, which should be able to be closed off when water is being thrown over the deck.

If your boat has small cave lockers let into the cockpit coaming, either make sure they are provided with drain holes (and remember to store nothing in them that cannot take a soaking) or provide them with waterproof hatches so their contents remain dry.

ABOVE DECK LIGHTING

The principal above deck lighting includes:

- Navigation lights: On yachts there can be a masthead tricolour to be used when under sail as well as sidelights, steaming and stern lights for use when under power or if the masthead's tricolour fails.
- Spreader lights: These are intended to provide light for those working on deck at night. If they are used, always remember that it is difficult for the lookout to see beyond the area of light, and when the spreader lights are switched off it will take several minutes for them to regain their night vision. This is usually of no great matter out at sea, but it is not such a good idea to switch the spreader lights on to help the crew stow the sails as you wriggle up a tight channel.

This is a transom hung skeg rudder. The skeg runs the full length of the rudder and, since it is transom hung, the rudder stock does not occupy valuable space in the cockpit

UNDERWATER FITTINGS

If you are going on a protracted voyage, it is important to check all underwater fittings before you sail since they are difficult to inspect and impossible to replace when you are afloat.

SKEG, SPADE AND TRANSOM HUNG RUDDERS

Originally, skeg hung rudders came from a desire to reduce the wetted area. This saw the keel nibbled away so that, aft, the rudder was left hanging onto a stub of keel, which became the skeg. Skeg hung rudders have their advantages and disadvantages. They give the rudder some protection and improve lateral stability, which is useful on a boat that may be on the one tack for days, but unless they are well made they may tend to flex when the rudder is under load and be prone to damage in the event of a grounding.

Eventually the skeg disappeared to create the spade hung rudder, which needs to be enormously strongly built or it will suffer from the skeg's drawbacks without its advantages.

With a volunteer going over the side wearing a face mask and snorkel, both skeg and spade rudders can, with care, be removed to replace bearings or effect repairs when afloat. In contrast, a transom hung rudder can be lifted directly up out of the water; but hanging off the stern it is more exposed to the risk of damage than either the skeg or spade rudder.

TILLERS

Tillers make for the simple life but if you have a wheel then check the quadrant and steering cables or hydraulics, and the other bits and pieces of the steering system.

PROPELLER

Carefully check the propeller for corrosion or electrolysis. Make a note of its size and pitch as well as the prop shaft length, diameter and taper. Repack the prop shaft gland and carry a spare cutlass bearing and zincs. If you are on a really long passage, you may wish to consider carrying a spare propeller and key.

OTHER UNDERWATER FITTINGS

Other underwater fittings, such as seacocks, transducers and speed log impellers, can be inspected by a snorkeller when the boat is afloat. It may be possible to carry out simple maintenance, such as removing marine growth, but their servicing or replacement often requires the boat being hauled out.

For long passages, some form of self-steering is essential. This is an example of a Monitor servo-pendulum system

A traditional two bladed propeller: the lower blade is badly chipped and needs to be repaired or replaced before this boat goes back into the water. Used in its present unbalanced state, it could damage the engine

DINGHY

If you are only out for the day, there is little point in carrying a dinghy unless you intend to anchor or pick up a buoy and go ashore for lunch. The same is true if you plan a cruise that carries you from one marina berth to another. By all means take a dinghy along, but the chances of it being used are slim. It is very different if you plan to cruise somewhere like the west coast of Scotland or go on an extended cruise. Now the dinghy becomes your principal link to shore. It must be strong, durable, stable and seaworthy. It must carry not just you and the crew but also supplies, including cans of diesel and water. Since rowing a dinghy upwind is hard work, it helps if it can take an outboard motor.

Dinghies may be inflatable: a small semi-rigid inflatable or, less commonly, rigid. Give some thought as to how best to stow the dinghy when under way and how to launch and recover it from on deck. Think carefully before deciding to tow the dinghy. On short day trips this can avoid the bother of inflating and deflating the dinghy, but in a good sailing wind inflatables have a tendency to kiting, and all dinghies, unless they have a good cover, have been known to fill and sink.

The yacht *Elektra* entering Peterhead: power comes from an outboard engine mounted on the transom. The lack of remote engine controls has the helmsman awkwardly crouched on the lazarette to handle the throttle and gears

THE BOAT BELOW DECKS

If you do no more than day sail in and out of your home port, the cabin and everywhere else below decks is somewhere to stow sails and gear and eat your sandwiches out of the rain. If your summer is spent day sailing from port to port then during the day, when you are sailing, the cabin can be treated as if it is a large locker for sails, oilskins and the like, and at night rearranged to become home. Your cruise is the maritime equivalent of a camping holiday and it can be magnificent fun.

If you are in an open boat the parallel with camping is even more marked, with boom covers providing five-star accommodation. It is worth remembering that small open boats have made some remarkable voyages.

For longer voyages, the cabin serves as both an office for the boat's administration and home. As computers and plotters continue their unstoppable rise, the need for a dedicated office/navigation area diminishes and what you need is a space where you can have all the comforts and facilities of home, whether you are at sea or in harbour. Few yachts come set up for this lifestyle and if it is what you want then modifying an existing boat is probably the easiest way of providing the facilities you require.

MAST STEP

The heel of a keel-stepped mast should be securely attached to the mast step or some other nearby suitable structure. If you have a deck-stepped mast, it must be adequately supported in such a manner that the mast thrust is taken down to the keel.

This was a problem for the mizzen mast on one 40 foot yacht I saw in Portugal. The mizzen was on a pedestal in the cockpit, which also carried the wheel. This arrangement was directly above the propeller shaft so it was impossible to carry the thrust directly to the keel. Perhaps an arrangement of partial bulkheads and strong cross beams might have worked, but the builders had chosen the simple option and relied on the inherent strength of the GRP deck which had bowed under expectations and created a shallow dip where rainwater collected.

GRAB RAILS

Grab rails are fitted as a matter of course above decks and around the companionway but below decks they tend to be conspicuous by their absence. This is surprising. True, it is difficult to be thrown overboard from below decks but cabins are full of sharp corners. If you are thrown against them with any force the result would be bumps, sprains and broken bones.

It is sensible to fix sturdy grab rails and arrange them so that when moving around below decks you do not have to let go of one grab rail before you take hold of another. The bigger the boat, the more important this rule.

CABIN SOLE

The cabin sole should be strong enough to withstand anyone leaping onto it from the cockpit. The floors and bearers supporting the cabin sole should be in good condition, firmly attached to the hull and not showing any signs of damp.

ACCOMMODATION

On vessels under 35 feet LOA, bunk spaces tend to be dual purpose and the number of bunks that boats of this size claim to provide are probably true within the advertising code of standards. However, it is only possible for everyone to take to their bunk at the same time in harbour, and only then after completely reorganising the boat. This is no hardship if you are day sailing between ports with perhaps the occasional overnight passage, but on longer voyages you should give some thought to how many people your boat will comfortably accommodate without rebuilding the interior accommodation. If, for example, your boat claims to have bunks for four or five, then on a long passage it will probably provide a comfortable living space for a crew of two.

You may think that working watch and watch, and with hot bunking, this number could be doubled – but there are problems. The forepeak will almost certainly be used for sail stowage and the other bunks are probably settee berths. This means that if the watch on deck come below for any reason there is nowhere for them to sit, and almost everything they do, from making a cup of tea to navigating, disturbs those off watch. Finally, in really heavy weather off-soundings, when progress is impossible, the safest place for everyone on board is in their bed – and this is why on long passages it is important that everyone has their own bunk space.

The below decks layout of some larger boats is meant to accommodate two couples. Aft, there is a master cabin with its double bed and en-suite bathroom. Midships there is a large social area with a galley and all mod cons. Forward is another cabin with its double bunk and its own en-suite facilities. Technically, everyone has their own berth and this arrangement is ideal for sailing during the day and stopping in harbour or at some anchorage every night; but the lack of sea berths makes it unsuitable for long passages.

GALLEY

For day trips, it is quite easy to survive on a fixed stove for cooking when in harbour and to prepare a flask of coffee and sandwiches for when you are at sea. For longer trips a gimballed stove is preferable. The usual two-burner stove with a grill takes up more space than a comparable fixed stove and is more difficult to install; but they do allow cooking in a seaway, even though the pots may need to be clamped to hold them over the flame. A stove with an oven requires yet more space but greatly extends your possible menu, although it is essential that the oven door can be secured, otherwise it may fly open and deposit your supper on the cabin sole.

The cooking fuel of preference nowadays is LPG with all its well-known dangers aboard boats. The fitting of a gas alarm is prudent and being able to turn the gas supply off at the stove essential. The gas bottles must be in their own locker, which drains outboard so that, should there be a leak, the gas flows over the side and not into the bilges.

Nowadays, most boats have a pressurised or pumped water supply where water comes out of a tap when it is turned on. Some also have a separate hot water supply where water is heated either by the engine cooling water or its own heating element. Automatic water supplies are convenient when you have generous water tanks and are never far from a means of refilling them. This may be from a shoreside hosepipe or a watermaker. If the latter, then on a long voyage it will probably need to be run every day or so to ensure that the water tanks are always close to full capacity because, should the watermaker fail, then with care there will be enough water to see you through the passage.

It is also common to find refrigerators on board. Some boats even have freezers. It is even possible to install a 12- or 24-volt microwave oven, which might be a useful way of preparing a hot meal when you are cold and wet. All these appliances may come built in or be retro-fitted and, like a pressurised water supply, increase the demand on your domestic power supply.

Regular hot meals are a boon but if you are going to cook at sea it is important to ensure that the galley is a safe place to work. The cook must be able to use both hands. This means that they must either be sitting down and able to brace themselves in that position or held in place by a safety strap and able to brace themselves against it. The risk of scolds and burns is always present and if the boat is particularly lively it is a good idea for the cook to wear oilskins so that spills run off.

SINKS

Until boats reach about 40 feet LOA, sinks tend to be on or close to the centreline. If it were to port or starboard then on one tack or the other the sink drain would be below the waterline with the risk of seawater back siphoning into the boat. On smaller boats, even with the sink on the centreline it is so close to the waterline that the merest roll has seawater gurgling into the sink. If this is the case on your boat, it is worth investigating installing a pump so that, rather than relying on gravity, any water in the sink has to be pumped out. This reduces the risk of seawater back siphoning into the boat, but the only way to be certain this cannot happen is to turn off the sink outlet at its seacock.

HEADS

Nowadays, pumping raw sewage, euphemistically called 'black water', directly overboard is generally frowned upon and, in some waters, illegal. Many boats have installed a foul water holding tank and can switch between that and pumping directly overboard. It is important that the seacocks used when waste is pumped directly overboard are open only when waste is being pumped. If they are left open it is possible for seawater to back siphon into the boat and I know of at least one yacht that sank at its moorings when the heads seacocks were left open.

Smaller craft may find a chemical toilet perfectly adequate and far less exciting.

STOWAGE

It is a fundamental law of sailing that the demand for stowage space always exceeds the number of lockers available. Stowage comes in three forms:

1. the ubiquitous under bunk locker, which provides the majority of the stowage on most craft
2. cave lockers, with or without doors, running around cabins above the bunks
3. hanging lockers, one of which may be the wet locker for oilskins

The need for stowage takes four forms:

1. deep stowage for items that are needed very infrequently. Bringing these items into the light of day normally involves unpacking every other locker in the cabin and then stumbling over the rubble clutching whatever you are looking for in triumph.
2. day to day stowage, which is for items such as tools, supplies and spares to which frequent, though not necessarily daily, access is required.
3. ready to hand stowage, which is all those items you need to put your hand on at any moment. This includes pilots, charts and almanacs as well as the day's food and the makings for sandwiches, snacks, coffee and tea.
4. personal stowage: everyone needs one locker where they can stow some, if not all, of their belongings. If they are expected to live out of their sea bag, it should be stowed somewhere other than their bunk space.

It is important that lockers stay dry. There is little more dispiriting than opening a locker and discovering everything inside is a sodden mass. This is a particular danger of under bunk lockers. On one boat I had, every under bunk locker had a limber hole into the bilge as well as the lockers on either side. An early task was to glass these holes shut.

Cave lockers under the sidedecks run the risk of filling up from leaking windows. It is unlikely to be life threatening but cave lockers are often home to cameras, iPods and similar equipment, which do not take kindly to seawater baths.

The wet locker is for oilskins and sea boots. Ideally it should be close to the companionway where oilskins can be put on and taken off and so minimise the need to walk, dripping, through the cabin. This is not always possible. Its next most popular location is around midships, close to the heads. No matter. What is important is having a wet locker, otherwise damp oilskins will either clutter the cabin sole or soak bunks and bedding. Unlike other lockers, the wet locker should be allowed to drain into the bilge. Ideally its limber hole will have a plug. This will allow you to pick the moment to let out the water that has drained off the oilskins and stop bilge water backing up into the wet locker.

Before casting off, develop the habit of checking that everything below deck is properly stowed and secure and that nothing is likely to start flying round the cabin.

ELECTRICS

If your boat has a wiring diagram (boat builders often provide one with a new boat), is it up to date? Usually it is only of historic interest and it is safest to treat it as such. Wiring is usually hidden behind the headliner, which reduces clutter but makes adding new circuits and equipment difficult. Unless you are very meticulous, after a while it is anyone's guess which item of electrical apparatus is on which circuit.

There are two classes of below deck electrics – domestic and instrumentation.

DOMESTIC ELECTRICS

These include:

- cabin lighting – the lights that illuminate the whole cabin
- individual lighting – the less powerful lighting over bunks that allows their occupants to read or write without disturbing others who may wish to sleep
- red lights – some boats have red lights, used to protect the night vision of crew below decks
- sockets – a generous supply of suitable 12-volt sockets scattered throughout the boat for the ever-growing list of equipment that needs charging, including handheld VHFs, computers, rechargeable batteries for flashlights and other apparatus, mobile telephones, cameras and iPods
- domestic radios, televisions and DVD players
- galley equipment – fridges, freezers and, if fitted, microwave ovens
- air conditioning and heating

It is good practice for all these items to be on their own fused circuit, clearly identified on the main electrical switchboard. All fuses should be easily accessible for quick replacement.

INSTRUMENTATION

Instrumentation covers all the ship's electronic instruments and radios as well as all electric pumps, whether automatic or switchable. Like the domestic electrics, it is good practice to put everything on its own fused circuit.

BATTERIES

There should be at least two batteries – an engine start battery, which only starts the engine, and a domestic battery, designed for long life and deep discharge, for everything else. The total power demands on the domestic battery, which also includes the navigation lights, is normally so great it is usual to have a bank of two or more batteries to provide enough capacity for normal day-to-day use.

Both the engine and domestic battery banks can be charged from some combination of:

- the engine alternator
- shore power

- a separate diesel or petrol generator
- solar panels
- wind generators

Most boats rely upon the engine alternator and plugging into mains voltage shore supply for battery charging and domestic use when in harbour.

PUMPS AND SKIN FITTINGS

All bilge pumps, both manual and electric, should have an easily accessible strum box that can be quickly cleared if blocked. The handles of all manual bilge pumps, whether in the cockpit or below decks, should be on a line securely attached to the boat so they cannot go overboard or become lost.

Skin fittings below the waterline should be made of phosphor bronze and the hoses to them should be attached by two jubilee clips. Taped to the hose, close to the skin fitting, there should be a tapering soft wooden plug that can be hammered into the fitting should it, or the hose, fail.

ENGINES

The main engine on most boats is a diesel powered inboard engine. Other boats use saildrives and outboard motors, which may be diesel or petrol powered.

For inboard engines check that the:

- engine mounts
- fuel lines
- fuel cut-off switches
- drive train/prop shaft and stern glands
- engine exhaust blowers and engine room ventilation
- exhaust

are all in good working order. In addition, the seals round saildrives should be examined to confirm that they are in good condition.

For boats using an outboard engine as their main propulsion, check that whoever is on the helm can reach the controls without having to perform gymnastic contortions. If this is the case, it is worthwhile examining some means of fitting a remote control to the outboard's throttle and gearbox.

ADMINISTRATION

Administration is the lifeblood of any well-organised setup and there is no escaping paperwork just because you have gone to sea. Administration falls into two parts. There are formalities of the various bureaucracies you meet on your travels and there are the routines and procedures that keep your boat running smoothly with the minimum of effort.

BUREAUCRATIC PAPERWORK

SHIP'S PAPERS: THE LOG BOOK

If you sail only in UK waters, the only bureaucracy you must observe is the ship's log. This is a legal document and should provide a full, accurate and contemporaneous record of the voyage. It is not a poetic narrative of events. That is for your personal log or diary. It is nothing more than a factual record of who is on board, courses steered, sail carried, weather encountered and actions taken. Although logs should be written up as events occur, this can be a chore. All too often they are written up after the voyage from half forgotten memories and scribbled notes on the back of envelopes. This could be a problem. If there is an incident then, depending on its severity, the authorities could ask to see the ship's log and it will do your case no good if all you can produce is a tattered sheet of paper covered in illegible doodles.

The authorities may also examine your plotter. Most plotters act like a black box and hold a record of recent courses steered and speed made good. This would enable the authorities to reconstruct course and speed over the ground but not tell them anything about the course steered, sails carried, winds, visibility, or sea state. The most powerful reason of all for keeping the log up to date is that, should the plotter fail, the information in your log book allows you to work up a DR, from which you can begin navigating by paper and pencil.

The log book is also a useful place to keep a note of:

- your vessel's dimensions
- the policy and your insurer's contact telephone numbers
- weather forecast terminology

WHAT IF ...

I once made a long cruise on a yacht where I discovered by chance that I was the only person on board entering any details in the log. Curious what would happen if I stopped, I did – and found that days went by without a single log entry.

SHIP'S PAPERS: INSURANCE POLICY

Many marinas insist that boats carry third party insurance of several million pounds but few seem to ask for a visitor's insurance certificate, so it is tempting to leave this document at home where it will be safe. However, make sure you have a note of your policy number and contact details of your insurer in case you do need to make a claim when you are away. I once had to phone home for this information.

Even though it is not a legal requirement, most yachts are comprehensively insured. Most policies exclude personal possessions. Often these are defined as anything not bolted or permanently installed on the boat. This can mean that items such as hand-held radios and plotters and the binoculars you may believe are part of your boat's equipment are not covered by the ship's insurance. It is worth checking the position with your insurer and, if necessary, taking out a policy to cover all your personal equipment.

On some blue water passages, insurance companies insist, before they offer insurance cover, that vessels are of a certain minimum size and carry a minimum number of crew who hold recognised qualifications appropriate to the passage being made.

SHIP'S PAPERS: GOING FOREIGN

If you do go foreign, you may have to clear out of the UK (see chapter 28) and then deal with customs and immigration services on arrival.

- They will ask for the ship's Registration Document. If your vessel is not already registered, then before you go foreign you will either have to put it on Part 1 of the shipping register – which is costly and, in the case of a vessel that has passed through several hands, time consuming – or, if your boat is under 24m (79ft) LOA, not owned by a company, not used for fishing and not a submersible, you can put it on the cheap and cheerful Part 3 of the shipping register. Details on how to do this can be found at www.dft.gov.uk/mca/shipsandcargoes/mcga_ukshipregister.
- They will almost certainly ask for the papers you were given when clearing out from the last country visited. Their reaction on learning that you do not have this documentation

can vary, but there is a good chance you may be refused entry.
- They will check the crew list together with the passports and, where appropriate, visas of all those on board.
- In EU countries, they may wish to inspect the sale agreement from when you bought the vessel, together with the VAT receipt showing that the VAT due has been paid.
- They will also check personal certificates of competence such as the ICC and, if on inland waters, whether they are CEVNI endorsed (see Chapters 27 and 30).

In some countries, when checking in you may be asked how long you intend to stay in that country and which other ports you wish to visit. Always indicate that you wish to stay for as long as possible and to visit everywhere. Otherwise there is a good chance that you will find yourself trying to extend the length of your stay. This is usually difficult, expensive or both. If, subsequently, you unilaterally vary your agreed list of ports, the penalties for visiting ports not on your list range from a reprimand to fines.

It helps if you keep all the ship's papers in a folder inside a waterproof bag so that, when dealing with officialdom, you can pull out whichever piece of paper they wish to see. If they come aboard and notice that you have, for example, an SSB transceiver, they may ask to check your radio licences. They may become excited when they see that your first aid kit carries some high-powered painkillers and other drugs. First aid certificates can reassure them you have no intentions of competing with the local drug barons. They will become very excited if you are carrying weapons.

Clearing in and out can involve contacting the port authorities, customs, immigration, police and health authorities. They may or may not visit your boat. All will have forms that must be completed. Sometimes there will be fees to be paid. Some countries require a visa, which must be obtained before your arrival.

PERSONAL PAPERS

For convenience, you may keep everyone's passport with the ship's papers. If a crew member's passport is out of date or they have no visa or the wrong visa, the authorities will hold you, as skipper, responsible. This is a responsibility that extends to paying all the costs of resolving the matter, including the costs of flying them home if they are declared persona non grata. It is therefore prudent before you sail to make each individual crew member aware that it is their responsibility to make sure all their personal paperwork is in order. They should prove this to you before casting off.

Should anyone fall ill abroad, the vessel's skipper is responsible for any medical fees, so it is sensible to extend the definition of 'personal paperwork' to include proof that each crew member has adequate medical insurance. Should you be sailing to places where nasty diseases are commonplace, this should also include the certificates showing that they have had jabs protecting them against illnesses such as yellow fever and hepatitis B.

COMMAND STRUCTURE

One of the first steps in the ship's administration is to decide on its command structure. The purpose of a command structure is not to create a pecking order but to make arrangements so that all the tasks required to make a safe passage are carried out by the right people in a timely and seamanlike manner.

There are probably as many different command structures as there are boats. Some may be extremely formal and others so laid back as to be invisible, but that reflects more upon the style in which you exercise command than your command structure. All command structures are about finding a balance between the skipper delegating work to others and behaving like a feudal lord surrounded by his serfs. Once you have settled on a command structure, stick with it. Changes only bring confusion.

COMMAND STRUCTURE: MATE

This is an important position and careful thought should be given to the candidate/s for mate. When you are day sailing it is no hardship always to be around to offer advice, make decisions and make sure your boat is sailed safely. There is no need for a mate. The instant you set out on a passage that requires a watch keeping system, there must be someone aboard who is competent to take over your duties when you are off watch and ensure that the boat continues to be sailed as you would wish. This person is the mate. Sadly your mate cannot take over your responsibilities. As skipper you remain responsible for everything that happens on your boat when you are sound asleep or even ashore.

It goes without saying that you must have the utmost faith in your mate and their judgement. You must allow them to do the job in their own way. Otherwise you will spend your off-watch time in a state of continuous anxiety. If you are working a watch and watch system, you will head one watch and your mate the other.

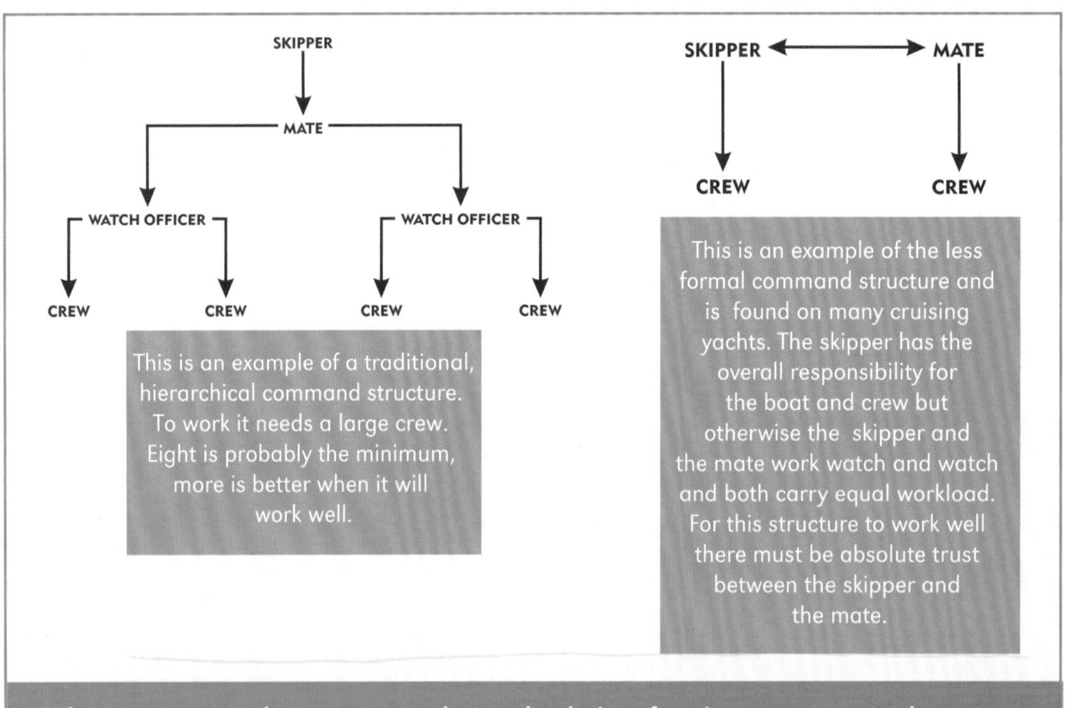

Whatever command structure you choose the duties of navigator, purser, cook, engineer, bosun and first aider must be shared amongst the crew. The fewer in the crew the more these duties are doubled up

In addition to acting as your deputy, the mate has the traditional role of making sure the day to day routines are carried out, such as the daily checks, the preparation of meals, and cleaning above and below decks. Obviously some of this type of work is more popular among the crew than others. It is the mate's job to share out the work fairly and, as skipper, it is your job to keep well out of the way until you are brought in to adjudicate in some dispute when you will, naturally, support your mate.

It goes without saying that you and your mate should have sailed together before, and know each other well. In the same way as you trust the mate to do their job, the mate must be confident that you can do yours. As Captain Bligh discovered, there is nothing more dangerous than a falling out between the skipper and his mate. If your mate begins muttering to the crew 'I wouldn't do it this way' as he passes on your orders, unrest will surely follow.

COMMAND STRUCTURE: OTHER APPOINTMENTS

Other appointments include watch officers, purser, navigator, bosun, engineer and cook. On most yachts it would be unusual to formally spell out the duties of each post but at the same time every post holder must clearly understand what is expected of them, and everyone should be aware not only of their own duties but of those of other post holders.

Lack of numbers also means it is usual for most posts to be doubled up. Frequently the skipper is also the purser as well as the navigator and everyone takes their turn at cooking and washing up. On one boat I know, the skipper is also the engineer because he once owned a garage and there was a presumption he knew all about engines and mechanical devices. Playing to a person's interests and strengths when handing out duties is a characteristic of a good command structure.

CREW DUTIES

- **THE MATE**, as the second in command, takes over command should you become incapacitated. He also:
  - acts as the link between the skipper and the crew. This is a traditional role but on a yacht this is probably less important than formerly
  - organises the day to day running of the boat
  - checks all equipment is properly maintained
  - allocates daily work
  - makes sure the watch system runs smoothly
  - ensures everything is stowed properly
  - checks that the ship's routines are followed
- **WATCH OFFICERS** remain on watch until they are properly relieved and are responsible for:
  - the safe navigation of the vessel during their watch even when the skipper is on deck, unless the skipper tells them they are taking over the watch
  - complying with the skipper's standing orders and any additional night orders that may be issued
  - keeping a proper lookout at all times

- THE PURSER is responsible for:
  - all provisioning
  - the ship's accounts
  - the interior inventory
  - assisting the skipper with the ship's paperwork

- THE NAVIGATOR is responsible for navigating the vessel. The navigator's duties include:
  - all voyage planning
  - when underway, being aware of the vessel's position at all times
  - always being able to advise the skipper on timing en route
  - maintaining all charts and nautical publications up to date
  - keeping weather reports and forecasts up to date

- THE BOSUN or boatswain is responsible for:
  - cables
  - ropes
  - anchors
  - dinghy
  - sails
  - all marlinspike seamanship
  - the exterior inventory

  The term 'boatswain' comes from a mixture of the old English 'bats' and the old Norse 'svien', meaning a young retainer or follower. If you wish to be unkind, this translates as 'silly boy'. Until 1990 it was the oldest active rank in the Royal Navy and is still one of the oldest US Navy rates in continuous existence.

- THE ENGINEER is responsible for and maintains the ship's mechanical and electrical systems including:
  - the engine
  - heating
  - air-conditioning
  - refrigerators
  - freezers
  - electrical systems
  - plumbing

- THE COOK is responsible for preparing all meals on time and advising the purser what provisions are required. If the job of cook is rotated among the crew, the purser would take on the task of keeping a record of provisions required.

STANDING ORDERS

It is unwise to interfere with how the watch officers and others with delegated duties do their job, but neither do you wish them to sail into situations beyond their abilities or experience. Your standing orders provide the trigger points where you want to be told what is happening. This is not the same as saying that the instant you are told that one of these trigger points has been reached you will leap onto the deck and start shouting orders. The purpose of standing orders is to make sure you are aware of the situation so that you can assess it for yourself. Having made your assessment, you may be perfectly happy with how the situation is being handled and leave your crew to carry on.

Standing orders should begin, 'You will call me immediately if...'. Be specific as to what action you expect to be taken and leave no room for doubt. They cover topics such as:

- man overboard
- fire
- collision or stranding
- damage to hull, rigging or any equipment
- rules for wearing harnesses and clipping into strong points
- wind speed – for example, call me if the wind increases above 20 knots
- wind direction – for example, call me if the wind direction changes so you can no longer steer the given course
- changing sail
- visibility – for example, call me if visibility falls below 2 nautical miles
- other vessels – for example, call me if any other vessel approaches within 2 nautical miles
- sighting land or lights

Most standing orders end with the catch-all captain's cloak, which says something like 'call me immediately if you require any advice or are in any doubt as to the situation or what action to take'.

Night orders are written to cover specific events. If you are on passage and expect to pick up Start Point light by 1.00am, you might put in your night orders that you are to be called:

- when Start Point light is picked up, or;
- at 1.30am if Start Point light has not been picked up.

WATCH KEEPING

The surest way of making everyone miserable and ruining a passage is to make them tired. If you can add making them wet and cold you do not just have a better quality of misery, but have succeeded in creating a dangerous situation. When people are tired their judgement suffers and they make mistakes.

On overnight and longer passages, there must be a watch keeping system. The purpose of all watch keeping systems is to make sure that everyone aboard has regular and adequate rest. There are many different systems to choose from. Some skippers vary watches from, say, four hours on watch during the day to three hours at night. Some opt for watch and watch. Others have watch systems with dog watches to rotate watches so that everyone has their fair share of the miserable midnight to four o'clock watch.

The minimum sensible off watch time is three hours. Less, and it is impossible to have a proper sleep. It is reckoned that the average sleep cycle essential to proper rest is about 90 minutes. Allowing for topping and tailing the time off watch by struggling in and out of clothing and coming and going on watch, two hours off watch is not enough for proper rest.

Avoid systems that run watches only during the night hours, leaving the crew to fill the daylight hours as they feel best. By 8.00am, those who came on watch at 4.00am are ready to come off watch; but now dawn has broken, those off watch, believing that the need to stand watches is over, remain 'asleep' in their bunks until approached in a threatening manner.

PRE-SAIL CHECKS

It is unseamanlike to cast off without first checking that your boat is ready to go to sea. The only way to be sure is to carry out pre-sail checks of the boat and its systems. For a sail round the bay, when you rely heavily upon your winter refit, this check can be short, sweet and ticked off on your fingers from a mental checklist.

As passages grow longer, so does the checklist. For an ocean passage it will be several pages long. Examples of a checklist appear as an appendix in this book. It is not really meant to be used as a checklist but is intended to give you ideas as to what points you may wish to include when preparing checklists tailored to you, your boat, your crew and your passage.

DAILY CHECKS

On passages longer than a couple of days, daily checks are a feature of shipboard life. The intention behind them is to pick up on gear suffering from wear and tear before it becomes worn and torn and to carry out routine maintenance on schedule. If a couple of inches of stitching on a sail becomes unravelled, take the sail down and mend it. Leave it and Murphy's Law says the sail will blow out when you need to haul yourself off a lee shore. If a rope is chafing, replace it, or at least turn it end for end. If it is time to change the engine oil and fuel filters, then change them.

The daily checks are hardly onerous but every defect and deficiency they reveal must go into the defects book.

DEFECTS BOOK

The defects book is a to-do list of outstanding work. It is made up from the faults, breakages, defects and deficiencies revealed by the daily checks plus any shortages and ideas for improvements that occur to the crew. It has five columns. If you sail as a couple, the NOTED BY and DONE BY columns are probably unnecessary; but if you have a large crew or regularly change crews then you may wish to discuss the defect with whoever entered it in the book.

DEFECTS BOOK LAYOUT

DATE	DEFECT	NOTED BY	DONE	DONE BY	DATE
the date on which the defect is noted in the book	brief details of the defect	the name of the individual who noted the defect	the defect has been made good and ticked off	the name of the individual who made good the defect	the date on which the defect has been made good

The rule should be that anyone can enter anything in the defects book. It is far better to have levant items entered than for some inconspicuous but important flaw to go unnoticed.

v defects can be made good on passage. For others, only temporary, get-you-home possible and these form the basis of your in-port refit when you reach port – thus d deficiencies book is a valuable document. Modern yachts are complicated beasts and it is impossible to carry details of all outstanding work in your head. If you try, then something, perhaps several items, will be missed and return to bite you when you are back at sea.

The defects book has escaped digitisation. If you put it on the computer, people are less likely to enter defects because they find it too much trouble. A notebook with a pencil tied to it and kept by the chart table or on a bookshelf works far better. Also, notebooks are immune to computer gremlins and power failures and by flicking through a notebook you can quickly establish what repairs remain undone.

INVENTORIES

If you are going for a day sail, you may only need to check that the coffee and sandwiches have not been forgotten, the sails are hanked on, and there is enough fuel in the tank should you need to motor. As passages grow longer, so does the need to know what is aboard, where it is stowed, and in what quantity. On long passages you also need to monitor consumption during the voyage, especially of food, water and fuel. On passage, updating the inventories is part of the daily checks, for an out of date inventory is not just worthless – it can be misleading.

You may believe that you know your boat and carry details of every inventory in your head. If you write down all that is on board you quickly realise this would be a great feat of memory. Factor in that the quantities of some inventories vary daily and it becomes impossible to be sure of remembering everything.

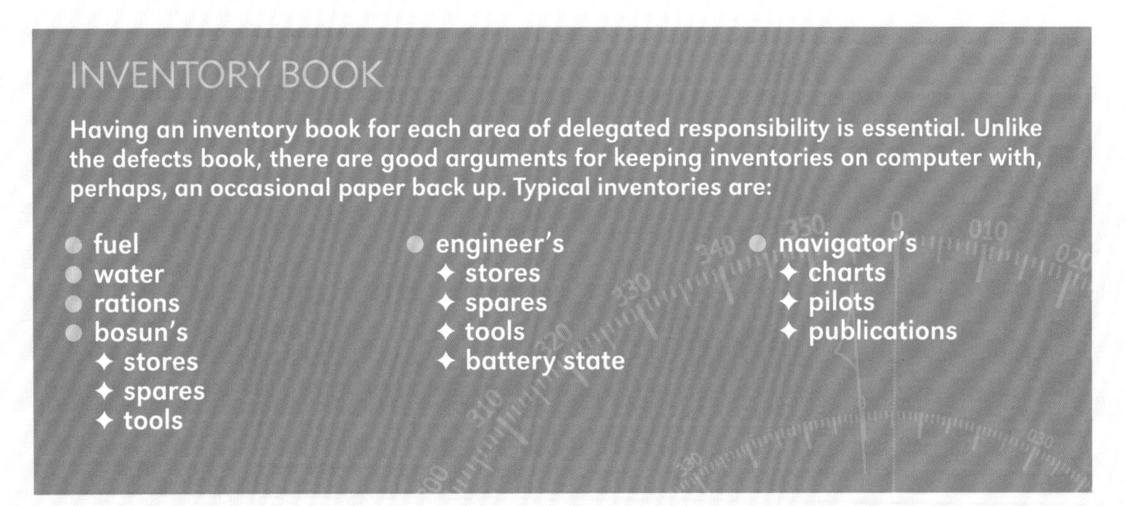

INVENTORY BOOK

Having an inventory book for each area of delegated responsibility is essential. Unlike the defects book, there are good arguments for keeping inventories on computer with, perhaps, an occasional paper back up. Typical inventories are:

- fuel
- water
- rations
- bosun's
  - stores
  - spares
  - tools
- engineer's
  - stores
  - spares
  - tools
  - battery state
- navigator's
  - charts
  - pilots
  - publications

COMMUNICATIONS

Good radio communications are essential to safety. Forget flares. Radios are how you attract attention when you are in trouble. More prosaically, radios allow you to chat with other ships, contact marinas and port authorities and receive weather forecasts.

At sea there are five ways of communicating with the shore or other ships:

1. visual signals
2. sound signals
3. VHF radios
4. cellphones
5. long range communications:
   a) single sideband radios
   b) satellite communications

VISUAL SIGNALS

Visual communications are out of fashion. It would be a surprise to see a storm cone hoisted on the pier end as you left port. These were introduced in 1860 by Vice-Admiral Robert FitzRoy, six years after his appointment as superintendent to the meteorological department of the Board of Trade. Nowadays, the only place you could be sure of seeing one is on his gravestone in All Saints church in Croydon. Light signals too are becoming unfashionable. The number of people who can send or receive Morse code by either sound or light is probably about the same as those who can read hieroglyphics. Most of us could understand SOS if it were sent slowly but after that we are blind, deaf and dumb. Honest.

FLAT BATTERY

I had left Penzance three weeks into a weekend cruise (don't ask) and was now faced with returning home. I was reluctant to retrace my track along the south coast and that left the choice of either sailing along the north coast of France or up the Irish Sea towards the Caledonian Canal.

In a fit of indecision I let the wind have the casting vote and it pointed the bows towards Milford Haven and the Irish Sea. I had rounded Gwennap Head and was about to creep past Land's End when a large RIB roared to stop alongside. Would I tell the coastguard that they had lost a diver? Of course, but why did they not inform the coastguard themselves? The battery on their handheld VHF was flat.

They sped off to quarter the sea for their diver and I put out a Mayday relay. I hung around, drifting with the tide, with one eye open for a tired diver. After around an hour the coastguard asked me to tell the RIB their diver had been found safe and well. It took another half an hour to attract the RIB's attention and pass on the message before resuming course for Milford Haven.

Sailors in the crowded shoreside bar in Spanish Harbour on Curaçao had their revels interrupted when one of the anchored yachts let loose a near continuous series of squawks on its fog horn, accompanied by its deck lights flashing on and off. The general consensus among this group of very experienced sailors was that those on that boat, lucky souls, were having a better time than everyone else. Drinking continued with greater vigour. Next day it was learned that the couple on this yacht had been robbed and were signalling for help.

Beyond raising your arms slowly up and down to indicate distress, semaphore has become a mystery, and flag signals other than Alpha (I have a diver down), Bravo (I am taking on or discharging explosives) and November Charlie (I am in distress) are a closed book. It is still possible to buy sets of flags but only for decoration.

About the only visual signals leisure sailors carry and would recognise are the day signals for a yacht under power or at anchor.

INTERNATIONAL MARITIME SIGNAL FLAGS

If used in combinations, like NC, then a further meaning, completely different from simply combining the meanings of the individual flags, is created. RY together means 'Pass by my station slowly and with caution' and is sometimes seen on ships when they are in harbour. It does not mean 'The way is off my vessel and you may feel your way past me and I am also carrying mails'.

The meaning of the alphabetical flags can be communicated by sound or light. This is probably their greatest value to yachts, which rarely carry flags. If they do carry flags big enough to be seen and read at a distance, then for most the greatest difficulty is finding a suitable position to fly the flag, bearing in mind that if the intended recipient of the message is directly up- or downwind, it is impossible for them to see the flag.

A 1 I have a diver down. Often painted onto a board and carried on a flagstaff or hung in the rigging 2 If on a vessel underway, it means: I am undergoing a speed trial. Often seen painted on a board on small craft like RIBs	**B** I am taking on or discharging explosives. Sometimes seen on vessels like oil tankers	**C** Affirmative
D Keep clear of me, I am manoeuvring with difficulty	**E** I am altering my course to starboard	**F** I am disabled, communicate with me
G I require a pilot	**H** I have a pilot on board. Seen on all pilot vessels whether or not they have a pilot on board	**I** I am altering my course to port
J I am going to send a message by semaphore	**K** You should stop your vessel instantly	**L** You should stop, I have something important to communicate
M I have a doctor on board	**N** No (negative)	**O** Man overboard
P 1 In port – all aboard, vessel is about to proceed to sea. This is the Blue Peter 2 At sea – your lights are out or burning badly	**Q** My vessel is healthy and I request free practique. In the first port you enter of a foreign country you fly this flag until you have finished clearing in	**R** The way is off my ship. You may feel your way past me

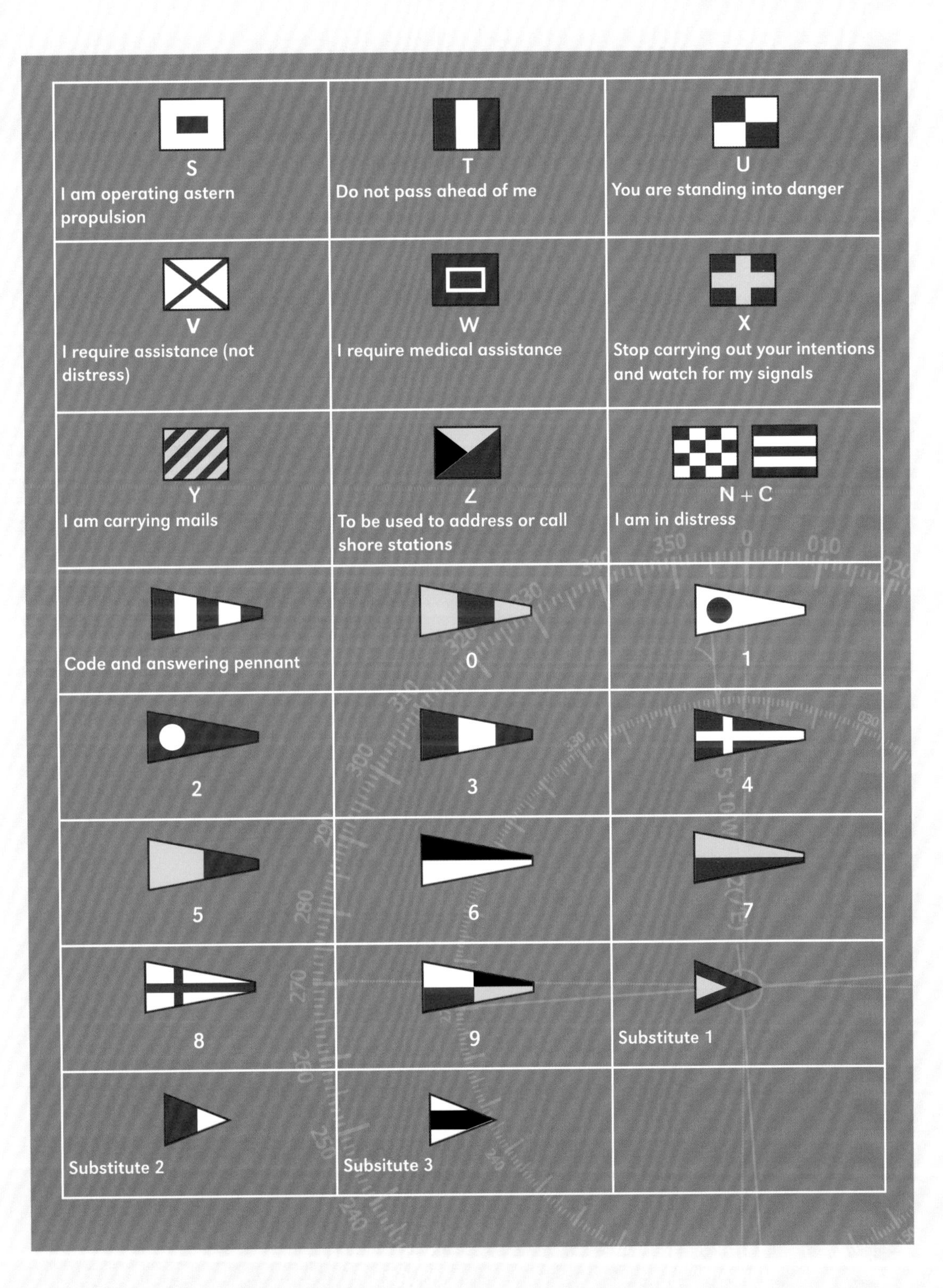
S
I am operating astern propulsion
T
Do not pass ahead of me
U
You are standing into danger
V
I require assistance (not distress)
W
I require medical assistance
X
Stop carrying out your intentions and watch for my signals
Y
I am carrying mails
Z
To be used to address or call shore stations
N + C
I am in distress
Code and answering pennant
0
1
2
3
4
5
6
7
8
9
Substitute 1
Substitute 2
Subsitute 3

SOUND SIGNALS

I had sailed up from the Azores and was making my landfall off the Lizard in poor visibility when the radio squawked and a VLCC warned that he and a small craft 6 miles away in position 49° 50.8N 05° 25.2W were on a collision course. As near as I could make out, the small craft was me. I was about to reply, asking what I should do to avoid a close encounter, when another vessel popped up on the airwaves claiming to be the vessel in question. I was absorbing the fact that another yacht was on top of me when a second boat came on the air, saying that they were the vessel in question. I crept quietly away.

I had heard not a single toot on a foghorn. At best, and this incident was not in that number, sound signals made by small craft in poor visibility are only likely to be heard by other small vessels. The idea that a commercial vessel with its watch keeper in his air-conditioned bridge would hear our pathetic hooting is laughable.

About the only sound signals small craft would recognise are the three toots: one for 'I am altering course to starboard', two for 'I am altering course to port', and three for 'I am operating astern propulsion'.

VHF RADIOS

The principal means of communicating between ships and to the shore is the VHF radio. These may be fixed installations or handheld. As the range of a VHF is limited by a combination of transmitting power and line of sight, the higher the antenna the better – which gives a fixed installation with a masthead antenna the edge. If you have a fixed installation, you should also carry a handheld VHF as a back-up should the fixed VHF or the ship's battery fail, or if you are dismasted. If you have only a handheld VHF, you should carry a spare. It is also a good idea to keep a fully charged handheld VHF in the grab bag. Should you ever have to abandon ship it is a more certain means of attracting the attention of passing ships than firing flares.

CELLPHONES

Mobile telephones are only of limited value at sea. Normally the signal is lost between 3 and 5 miles offshore, sometimes less. In some areas there is not a signal to lose. They should not be relied upon as a means of contacting the emergency services. Their principal use when in range of a mast is telephoning shore contacts and speaking to marina or harbour authorities who are out of VHF range.

LONG RANGE COMMUNICATIONS

The further afield you sail, the longer range communications you need if you wish to stay in touch. Lack of long range communications while on passage between the Canaries and Barbados meant I diverted into the Cape Verde Islands to ring home and tell them that my passage was taking longer than planned. For yachts, there are two principal onboard long-range communication systems.

MARINE SINGLE SIDE BAND RADIO

Many blue water cruisers use a marine Single Side Band (SSB) transceiver as a means of communication, especially in the Mediterranean, Caribbean and Pacific. It is worth considering it among your options if you are planning a cruise in these waters.

INSTALLATING AN SSB TRANSCEIVER

Installing an SSB radio is more complicated than fitting a VHF radio. First you need a marine SSB transceiver. This is a single sideband radio set up to receive and transmit on the frequencies allocated for marine use. You can receive on other frequencies but you cannot transmit on them. If you wish to work the ham (amateur) bands, you will also require a second transceiver set up for the ham bands. Cunning ham operators have been known to modify their transceiver so that they can work marine and ham bands on the one transceiver, but this is frowned upon.

Secondly, you need a separate aerial tuner. The length of the antenna should vary according to the frequency you are using. Since most yachts use their backstay as their SSB antenna, varying its length is not possible, and the aerial tuner is tasked with fooling the transceiver that the backstay is the correct length of antenna for transmitting whatever frequency you are using. The aerial tuner needs to be as close as possible to the backstay, or whatever stay you are using as an antenna. This normally means finding a dry space in the lazarette to house the antenna tuner. Using a stay as an antenna means that if you lose your mast you also lose your SSB antenna. This could be troublesome if you need to seek help. The solution is to make provision for an SSB whip antenna and carry it disassembled until it is needed.

Thirdly you need a good earth. The sea is a splendid earth and an SSB earth is usually a special copper plate fixed to the outside of the hull below the waterline. Some cruisers simply attach the earth cable to a skin fitting or even just throw it over the side when transmitting.

Putting all this together is a skilled task. If you are paying someone to do it for you, it is good advice not to part with cash until you have watched them actually contact one or two distant stations and spoken to them. Often the strength of the transmitted signal is measured using a dummy load. This is essentially a tin full of sand. It can show a perfectly adequate signal is going out from the transmitter but it is not the same as actually speaking to somebody.

CRUISER NETS

SSB radios have a range of several thousand miles. Calls between yachts are free. Many yachts join one or more of the many cruiser radio nets, which have regular daily schedules where you can keep up to date on the latest news and gossip. The best time of day to listen out for these nets is between 6 and 9 o'clock in the morning and 6 and 9 o'clock in the evening. This is local time and when radio conditions should be at their best.

SOME CRUISER NETS		
CRUISER NET	**FREQUENCY KhZ**	**TIMES**
Mediterranean Net	8122	0530 UT
Caribbean Calling and Safety Net	8104	0815 AST
Bahamas Weather Net	4003	0700 AST
Caribbean Weather Net	4045 8104 8137	0700 AST

You can also, for free, receive weatherfaxes and there are cheap SSB email services to keep in touch with friends and family who do not have an SSB radio.

If you ignore the fairly high cost of buying and fitting an SSB radio and the fact that it is power greedy (it is often necessary to run the engine to be sure of having enough power to transmit), then compared to satellite communications it is much cheaper.

SSB LICENCES

To use a marine SSB radio on board ship you need to hold a GMDSS Long Range Radio Certificate. This usually requires attending a four-day course and then taking and passing an exam covering:

- Safety of Life at Sea (SOLAS) examination paper (eleven questions with a 75 per cent pass mark)
- Regulations Paper (ten multiple choice questions, of which six must be answered correctly)
- Radiotelephone Communications (R/T) exercise simulating a Distress situation (simulation of using SSB at sea; pass mark is 75 per cent)
- Operation of Equipment (demonstrating practical skills in using the equipment; pass mark is 70 per cent)

There is an optional satellite module covering more on SOLAS and Inmarsat C Terminal operation. The pass mark is 70 per cent.

SSB EMAIL

Sending an SSB email is as simple as sending any other email. To set up an SSB email system you need a suitable SSB radio and a radio modem that links the radio to your computer running on Microsoft Windows. You also need an SSB email provider.

SSB email service providers such as SailMail (www.sailmail.com) charge an annual subscription for unlimited use, unlike cell or satellite telephone messaging services, which normally charge on a combination of the amount of data sent and each occasion the service is used. If you are going to use SSB email, it is best to set this service up before you sail.

Some SSB email providers, such as SailMail, use a mixture of private and marine frequencies and your transceiver will need to be modified to cover these additional frequencies. It is possible that some transceivers will not be capable of being modified.

SATELLITE TELEPHONES

A satellite telephone is a mobile telephone that operates through satellites instead of land-based cell masts. Like an ordinary mobile telephone, the latest generation of satellite telephones allow you to make calls, send text messages (SMS) and email from anywhere on the planet. High speed satellite Internet and data services now offer mobile office capability anywhere in the world.

GEOSYNCHRONOUS SATELLITES

Some satellite telephone systems use geosynchronous satellites. These are satellites in geostationary orbit, remaining in a fixed position at the magic altitude of 22,236 miles (35,785km) where the satellite's orbital period matches the earth's rotation. This keeps the satellite over the same area of the earth and allows global coverage with only three or four satellites. At present the bandwidth available from geosynchronous satellites is much greater than that available from Low Earth Orbit (LEO) systems but due to the huge transmission distances there can be some delay (about 0.25 seconds) between transmitting and receiving signals.

On board ships, a geostationary satellite system normally has a gyroscopically stabilised antenna inside a dome – the larger the dome, the bigger and more powerful the antenna and the more data it can transmit per second. The antenna is linked to a controller, which is then connected to a telephone or laptop, and as long as line of sight is maintained to the geostationary satellite, connectivity is maintained even in heavy seas.

Inmarsat, founded in 1979, is the oldest operator of commercial satellite communications and is, at present, the only provider to offer (polar regions excepted) worldwide coverage.

LOW EARTH ORBIT SYSTEMS

A Low Earth Orbit system (LEO) uses a network of satellites orbiting the earth at an altitude of between 400 and 700 miles. Each satellite has an orbital time of around 70–100 minutes and makes around fifteen orbits a day. A network of satellites is required to provide continuous coverage. Depending on the relative position between the satellite and your telephone, a typical useable pass of an LEO satellite will last between 4 and 15 minutes, after which another satellite from the network must come over your horizon and pick up your call to maintain continuity.

Iridium and Globalstar, both American companies, began operating in the 1990s but lack of subscribers meant they could not cover the launch costs and were forced into bankruptcy. New owners bought the assets and restarted the companies around 2001. Iridium claims worldwide coverage, including the polar regions, and uses radio cross links between satellites to relay messages to the nearest satellite with a connection to an earth station. It also offers a pager and call alert service. Globalstar does not cover the polar regions and the satellite you are using must also be in range of an earth station to relay your call.

Satellite telephones are custom built for one particular network and, unlike terrestrial mobile telephones, cannot be switched from network to network. Early satellite telephones were similar in size to the first mobile telephones and came with a large retractable antenna. Current satellite telephones are about the same size and appearance as a regular mobile telephone and doubtless continuing technological advances will soon make them indistinguishable. Second-hand handsets for LEO systems can be relatively cheap but the latest handsets are expensive.

Compared to SSB radio, calls from a satellite telephone are costly. At present they vary from around $0.90 to $3.00 (approx £0.55 to £1.88) per minute and calling a satellite telephone from a landline is much more expensive. Data transmission costs are higher still. The cost of calls between satellite telephones is frightening. Most satellite telephone providers offer prepaid plans for various sums.

Unlike SSB radios and geostationary satellite systems, should you be forced to abandon ship you can take an LEO satellite telephone with you and use that to contact shore-based emergency services and help coordinate your rescue.

THE CREW

Most of us take on the role as skipper because it is our boat and we hope that among the privileges of ownership are the skills and experience necessary for managing the crew and making a safe and seamanlike passage. Only you know if this is true of yourself. Wise skippers are aware that besides sailing within their own performance envelope they must also sail within their crew's capabilities. It is a balancing act. If you have a strong crew, you can push your limits. If you have a weak crew, you can stretch their boundaries. Asking too much of both yourself and your crew usually brings problems.

Before you begin planning your voyage it is prudent to ask yourself if you have the skills to make it. It is important to be honest. Make two lists. The first is the skills you know you have and the second is the skills you reckon you need for your intended passage. Put the two lists together and highlight the skills you lack. Training courses may fill some gaps, as may support from organised rallies. Your reservations may not be about a lack of a particular skill but rather questions over personal capabilities and character. Resolving these has to wait until you are on passage. These are the bits that tend to be referred to as a 'challenge' and are probably the reason you want to make this particular passage. They are part of the fun.

CHOOSING THE CREW

If you are a family sailor, you have no choice over your crew. If you have sailed for years with the same gang of friends, it is difficult to maroon them ashore while you head off towards new horizons. This works both ways. Perhaps your family, or friends, do not want to go on this particular voyage but they may be reluctant to let you down. They may feel obliged to come along even though they believe that for them (or you) it is a voyage too far. At some point along the way their concerns may prove too much and they quit, leaving you short of crew, destroying your friendship, and leaving everyone wishing they had spoken up much earlier. I have seen it happen.

The wrong crew ruin a passage. They may well be experienced, competent sailors but if the personal chemistry between those on board is not right then the friction this causes can rapidly spiral into guerrilla warfare. There are countless examples of this happening. You will have heard of instances and may have experienced it. The longer the passage, the greater the risk. Happy, long-married couples have crossed the Atlantic and the instant they reach port they rush to the nearest divorce lawyer. Yachts crewed by friends who have sailed happily round the coast together arrive with the skipper issuing orders through his solicitor.

When relations between crew members go bad, cliques form and onboard feuds break out whose violence puts the Clintons and the McCoys to shame. At times it appears that warring tribes are manning the boat. There is no single cause for this social unrest. It is not as simple as blaming the generation gap. You may expect a mixed crew of old and young to fail to see each other's point of view and, fuelled by an inexhaustible supply of mutual misunderstanding, to squabble continuously. In truth they are just as likely to sail happily together as they are to argue.

Perhaps trouble breaks out because most of us are unaccustomed to working and living together in cramped conditions. Once at sea, a yacht is isolated in a way that is beyond the ken of those who have not been there. Once you have sailed 10 miles offshore, unless you have the cash for unlimited satellite communications there is no Facebook, no texting, no Twitter, no blogs. Even private space may be scarce. You are part of a community that is thrown upon its own resources in a way that is unfamiliar today. If you have an everyday disagreement with another crew member, once it is over there is not the physical space to avoid them until the cause is forgotten and your irritation evaporated. They are an arm's length away, glaring at you as you glare at them. It is little wonder that minor disagreements fester and grow.

Ashore, we are a society in a hurry. We expect results now or even sooner. Speed is good. Governments dig up the countryside and spend billions saving a few minutes on a train journey. Journeys of several hundred miles in a day are unremarkable. Driving at 70mph is the norm. As recently as the 1960s that was only possible in a sports car and only if you were wearing a woollen bobble hat.

At sea, you travel at the speed of a comfortable jog. If you run out of wind you may be parked for a day or two, going nowhere. Distances our modern lifestyle would expect to cover in a few hours may take days or even weeks. As the old saying puts it, yachts have destinations, not ETAs, but cheerfully accepting this requires a step change in mindset; this does not happen to everyone at the same time and to some people it happens not at all, hence the scope for disagreement. If someone is continuously fretting about lack of progress and forever worrying about when you will arrive, they will naturally find it difficult to understand someone else whose attitude is that we arrive when we arrive. If you believe 'mañana' describes an easy going, wait until tomorrow attitude, it is a shock to discover that after a long ocean passage you come to see 'mañana' expressing a sense of unnatural and unnecessary haste. Having flown home to the UK from the West Indies to deal with some family matters, I found the speed and intensity at which people rushed around the streets surprising. I still have the scars from where they trampled over me.

As a rule, if you have survived one passage with your crew then the chances are you will survive the next. The catch comes when you set out on a different type of passage. If you have been coastal sailing happily together, there may be problems when you set out on an offshore passage. Or if you enjoyed offshore cruising together, your first ocean passage may raise difficulties. It is well worth giving this subject some careful thought. Never lose sight of the fact that we sail for fun and more cruises have been ruined by social discord, personnel and personality clashes than have ever been endangered by weather or navigational hazards.

All this applies tenfold if you have a crew of strangers. The days are gone when skippers, as a matter of course, hired and fired professional crew in the same way as they employed valets or ladies' maids. Nowadays, some skippers find volunteers through crewing agencies. In ports that are the start points for ocean passages, boatless hopefuls advertise their availability. Such arrangements can work to everyone's advantage. The skipper finds their crew for free, sometimes the crew even contribute towards the cost of the passage, and the crew have their sail. The downside is that lack of time may make it impossible to properly involve them in the preparation phase and geographic separation may make even a trial sail impossible.

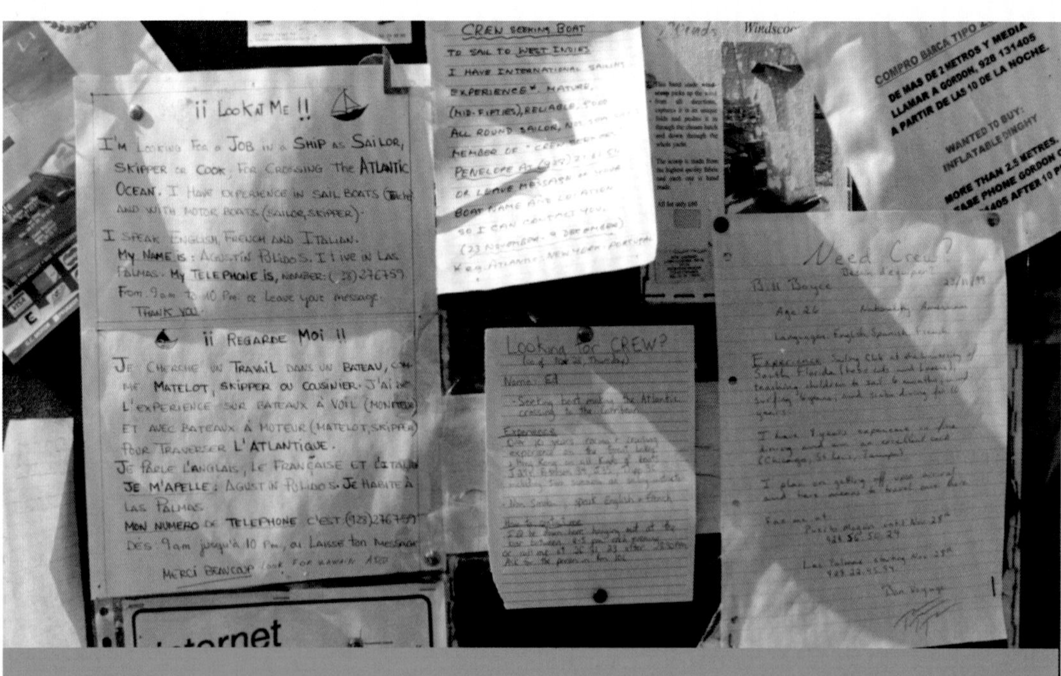

You can find crew through crewing agencies and many seeking a boat leave their details in yacht clubs and marinas in the more popular departure ports for ocean passages

At the start of any passage, everyone believes they are an important and valued member of the same team. Probably the only successful measures to maintain this belief are:

- Making arrangements so that everyone aboard knows each other well enough to accept each other's foibles while appreciating their strengths.
- Giving everyone their own area of responsibility, which contributes to the smooth running of the vessel and enhances their self-esteem. It helps to play to people's strengths, such as mechanics responsible for engines and machinery and radio hams the radios, instrumentation and electrics.

It also helps to have routines that keep people busy, give them a sense of purpose and encourage the feeling that they are contributing to the success of the passage. This may sound condescending or playing people by numbers. It is not. Done properly it is good team management and appreciated by everyone.

PRE-SAIL TRAINING

The purpose of pre-sail training is to ensure that you and your crew know:

- each other
- how you run your boat
- how your boat sails
- the orders you give regarding its handling
- the layout of your boat above and below deck
- where stores and equipment are stowed

Some training can be done onshore or on board when the boat is alongside but much of it involves taking your crew out to sea. You can tell your crew the drills for going alongside or anchoring or how to hoist and set sails until they can parrot them back word perfect, but until they actually try to carry out these tasks neither you nor they know if they can carry them out successfully.

It is worth running through this training even with experienced crews if it is their first time aboard. This ensures that they are familiar with how things are done on your boat. Different ships, different long splices... there is nothing more frustrating than hearing some disaster explained away by the phrase, 'We did it differently on So-and-So's boat.'

- **General:**
  - ✦ Knows the parts of a boat, rigging and sails.
  - ✦ Understands orders concerning the sailing and day-to-day running of the boat.

- **Rope work:**
  - ✦ Can coil, stow, and secure ropes to cleats and bollards.
  - ✦ Can tie and know the correct use of figure-of-eight, clove hitch, bowline, round turn and two half hitches and reef knot.
- **Sail handling:**
  - ✦ Can hank-on, set and reef sails.
  - ✦ Can use sheets, halyards and winches.

- **Anchoring/mooring/berthing:**
  Knows the actions to be taken and the roles played when:
  - ✦ Anchoring and weighing anchor.
  - ✦ Picking up a buoy.
  - ✦ Putting out to sea.
  - ✦ Berthing.
  - ✦ Handling warps and fenders.
  - ✦ Securing cleats to bollards.

- **Watch keeping and helming:**
  - ✦ Is able to keep an efficient lookout at sea.
  - ✦ Can steer a compass course, under sail and power.
  - ✦ Can trim sails on all points of sailing.
  - ✦ Knows how to steer the boat:
    - Under sail and power.
    - By compass.
    - In buoyed channels and by transits.
  - ✦ Knows how to interpret a weather forecast and use the Beaufort Scale.

- **Dinghies:**
  - ✦ Can inflate and launch the dinghy and complies with its loading rules.
  - ✦ Can handle a dinghy under oars.
  - ✦ Knows how to fit and start the outboard motor.

- **Personal safety equipment:**
  Has and knows how to use:
  - ✦ Safety harness.
  - ✦ Safety tether.
  - ✦ Lifejackets.

- **Man overboard:**
  Knows and has practised the man overboard drills.

- **Fire precautions:**
  - ✦ Knows what to do in the event of fire.
  - ✦ Knows how to use fire extinguishers and fire blankets.
  - ✦ Is aware of:
    - Fire hazards.
    - Fire precautions.
    - The locations of fire extinguishers and fire blankets.

- **Emergency equipment :**
  - ✦ Knows how to operate electric and manual bilge and location of all skin fittings.
  - ✦ Knows how to send a Mayday call by VHF.
  - ✦ Knows how to and when to operate the EPIRB.
  - ✦ Understands how to use distress flares and when they should be used.
  - ✦ Knows the abandon ship drills, including:
    - Where the grab bag is stowed.
    - How to launch the liferaft.
    - How to board the liferaft.

PRE-SAIL TRAINING

As planning proceeds it may become apparent that you or your crew could benefit from some additional training to prepare you for the passage you are about to undertake. For example, you may have become aware that it would be wise to:

- take a first aid course
- renew your first aid certificate
- upgrade your existing certificate from an emergency first aid ticket to one covering more ground in more detail

Or you may be considering installing a single sideband (SSB) transceiver. Among other points to consider in making this decision is the requirement, in the UK, to hold a long-range operator's certificate. Should you wish to work the amateur bands as well as the marine band, you would need to acquire a Class A amateur radio certificate and callsign. Amateur callsigns are personal and not linked to your boat in the same way as marine callsigns. Although the equipment used is almost identical, a long-range operator's certificate does not allow you to work the amateur bands and a ham certificate does not allow you to work the marine bands. An amateur radio certificate tests electronics, radio equipment, antennas, radio propagation, RF safety and Morse code. A Class A amateur licence, which is what you need, requires the ability to send and receive Morse code at five words per minute.

There is a wide choice of training courses. You may reckon that it is a good idea for you and your crew to learn the art of jumping into liferafts by taking a sea survival course, which provides some very realistic simulations. If, like me, you are a mechanical illiterate, perhaps a diesel engine maintenance course will help ensure that on an extended cruise you can keep the yacht's engine running.

Unless you think through training requirements before setting out, the need for them may be revealed too late for you to learn the necessary skills. Weatherfaxes are a great way of receiving weather forecasts when beyond the range of Navtex. You need an SSB receiver or transceiver, a laptop and a demodulator, which turns the analogue signal from the radio into a square signal the computer can recognise. In Philipsburg on Saint Martin I had everything to receive weatherfaxes except the demodulator. I had somehow acquired a wiring diagram for a home-made demodulator but my ignorance of electronics was so complete it could have been written in Greek. I sailed that voyage without weatherfaxes but on my return I took an evening class in basic electronics before my next long voyage, and was able to run a small cottage industry making demodulators for other boats while waiting to leave the Canaries for the Caribbean.

Training courses form an important part of your onshore preparations. For each course, you must identify suitable providers and factor their course timings into your schedule. Courses cost money and this makes it difficult to insist that any crew member should attend a particular course unless you are prepared to bear the cost. Bear in mind, pay for one and you pay for all. An exception may be if they are working towards an RYA Certificate of Competence where they could be encouraged to attend, say, the shore-based element of the training.

CIRCUITS AND BUMPS

What I call Circuit and Bumps is the often forgotten, poor relation of pre-sail training – yet ensuring that your crew are familiar with you, each other, your boat and how to sail it is probably one of the most important elements in making sure that when you come to cast off, your passage starts on the right foot.

Circuits and Bumps takes place a day or so before casting off and is going through all the basic drills:

- casting off
- anchoring
- picking up a mooring
- berthing
- setting sails
- trimming sails
- changing sails
- reefing
- tacking
- gybing
- man overboard
- abandon ship

Overlooking this element of training is perhaps forgivable if you sail with the same crew year in year out and you are all familiar with each other and the boat, but a refresher course before you cast off is probably worthwhile. It is *less* forgivable if there is a new member of crew. Whether they are experienced or not, for the first few days of any cruise they will be placed under additional and unnecessary pressure trying to keep up with everyone else who goes about their duties without a second thought. It is unforgivable when the skipper and crew are strangers to each other and your boat. The scope that exists for misunderstandings, mistakes and disaster is simply too great to be acceptable.

I was once part of such a crew. We were a cocktail of experienced and novice sailors to the extent that it was one crew member's first time at sea on any sort of yacht. We had introduced ourselves briefly at a shore-side meeting. Now, a couple of weeks later, we joined the boat in a rush to go to sea. Only the skipper knew the boat but it was some time since he had been aboard. Like the rest of us, he was ignorant of its present state. There was no defects book and the ring-bound inventory prepared months ago was out of date. Nobody was sure how much food was aboard. The original stowage plan was an irrelevance.

Before we sailed we did no drills. We hoisted no sails. We were unsure which halyard was which or what rope went where and we were inept at changing and reefing sails. Even the lead of the headsail sheets was a mystery. We had little idea where anything was stowed or how the plotters and radios worked. Our ignorance and uncertainty about the boat and each other was so complete that, willing as we were, it was hard to work as a team. It was in this state we went to sea to cross an ocean. When we came to anchor at the end of the voyage, it was more slapstick than slick.

We were fortunate that we met no really bad weather. Being aboard a yacht in a gale is rather like taking part in an early bare-knuckle, no holds barred boxing match. There is no referee, no rounds, no time limit and your opponent observes no rules. All that is asked of you is to toe the line and if you fail in that, you lose. In a gale the noise, the constant movement of the boat, the continuous physical effort, and the near complete lack of rest drive you to a point where you would sell your grandmother for a few moments of peace and quiet. There is no time out. The wind and the seas keep coming. It is relentless. There is never a break in the incessant onslaught, which continues with one squall after another smashing into the boat, seeking to destroy what little willpower and reasoning ability you and the crew have left.

This is not the time for untried evolutions on an unfamiliar boat with a mixed ability crew who are strangers to one another. Reefing, changing sails? Lord help us. Man overboard? God forbid.

HEART OF OAK

When skippers resort to making good these sort of deficiencies with a cheery, stout-hearted, can-do, Heart of Oak attitude, it pays to remember that although Heart of Oak is the Royal Navy's official march, it started life in 1759 in a pantomime called Harlequin's Invasion and its claim to fame was that it featured the first ever talking harlequin. Gung-ho works well when the going is easy, and perhaps for a time when the sailing becomes more demanding, but without the back up of skill, effort and teamwork it invariably crumbles in any serious test.

In heavy weather, with an untrained or inexperienced crew there is a real danger that an unfair proportion of the workload, particularly the more time consuming and unpleasant tasks, falls upon one or two willing horses. This does not happen because the remainder of the crew are lazy. It happens because in the beginning the willing horses see what has to be done, know how to do it, and get on with it. This rapidly comes to be seen as the norm, a part of their responsibilities when it is, in truth, a failure of skippering. For the same reason, unnecessary hardship marks an absence of leadership. Being tired, cold and wet is never a challenge. It does not develop character or bring out the best in people. It is downright miserable and dangerous.

If this sort of trouble is to be avoided, there is no substitute for training. Training does not happen by accident. It takes time and effort, first to plan and then to carry out. As skipper, this is your responsibility. It is unrealistic to expect individual crew members to create their own training programmes. Training need not be a chore. If it is, then it is poor training.

For your crew to reach a basic level of competence, the training programme requires three elements:

1. You must design an effective, enjoyable training programme.
2. You and your crew must be prepared to work hard during the training programme. Just because it is fun does not mean that it must be easy or that you will accept anything less than their very best.
3. Your crew must want to learn.

For training to be effective, everyone must clearly understand what it is meant to achieve. Drills of the 'Do this and don't ask questions' nature, as every army recruit knows, are pointless. At their simplest, pre-sail training drills teach your crew how to carry out an evolution when their brains (and yours) resemble three day old porridge, their eyes are closing with fatigue, and their fingers are frozen, useless, unable to loosen a shackle and barely capable of holding the tiller.

Once the crew have mastered a particular skill, remind them that they are expected to be able to do it in fearsome seas on a bucking boat with the wind trying to snatch them off the deck – and have them do it all over again and again.

If you are preparing for a race, all instruction must be complete before crossing the start line. There will be no time for any teaching during the race. If you are cruising, delaying the start of your cruise for a day or so for Circuits and Bumps is of no great matter and, once underway, you can use quiet days in sheltered waters for the crew to practise what they learned. Practice makes for proficiency. It is also worth considering taking individual training to higher levels. If everyone in your crew trains for the next level of competence, their new skills will be reflected in how they carry out their present duties.

Crew members who come along hoping their sea time will help towards them acquiring further sailing qualifications generally appreciate an informal programme of ongoing practical training. Not only are they learning the skills needed for their next qualification but also their sea time becomes a positive means to an end and not just a tally of hours afloat for an examiner to count and doubt sometime in the future.

PERSONAL EQUIPMENT

There is more to preparing the crew than training. It is important to check that their personal equipment is up to scratch. This includes:

- foul weather jacket
- foul weather trousers
- gloves
- seaboots
- boat shoes
- hat
- torch
- personal strobe
- whistle
- knife
- lifejacket
- harness and safety tether

It is important that all this protective equipment is of the right standard and in good condition. Leaking seaboots or foul weather gear promises cold and damp sailors. An overused, well worn safety tether could be the cause of a man overboard. The last chance you have of checking your crew's personal gear and making good any deficiencies is during the Circuits and Bumps. Foul weather and safety gear all look much alike and it could help avoid disputes if you suggest to your crew that, before they come aboard, they mark their personal gear so they can always easily identify it. Other personal gear you may ask your crew to bring along includes sleeping bags (or some suitable substitute) and pillows. For stowing items such as cameras, computers, cellphones and iPods, a small waterproof bag might be useful in keeping them dry.

If you are going foreign they will need their passport, visas (if necessary) and health insurance, along with any personal medication they may be taking. You must insist that you are told if they are undergoing any medical treatment, even if it does not involve taking pills or drugs. Watch them carefully during the Circuits and Bumps to see if their condition has any effect upon their performance.

POWER PLANTS AND PROPELLERS

THE ENGINE

It is rare nowadays for a yacht not to have an auxiliary engine, even if it is only an outboard hanging off the transom.

OUTBOARD ENGINES

An outboard engine is sufficient to take you in and out of harbour and motor-sail in calm seas, but in a seaway the propeller spends at least half its time beating air and progress is somewhere between slow ahead and dead stop.

Most outboards run on petrol. This carries a much greater fire risk than diesel and most harbours and marinas to not have pumps delivering petrol. This means finding a nearby garage. Once, while berthed in Bridlington on England's east coast, I went in search of petrol during a visit by a major politician. I found myself having to explain to a minibus crowded with suspicious, heavily armed policemen why I was towing a couple of cans of fuel on a small trolley. They did not even offer me a lift back to the harbour.

Another drawback is that outboard engines do not produce enough electrical power to charge the ship's battery. This is of little importance when there is regular access to shore power but on long voyages you need good power discipline and either a solar panel or wind generator to keep the battery charged.

DIESEL ENGINES

Diesel powered engines are by far the most common auxiliary on yachts. As a rough rule of thumb, an engine with two horsepower for every 1,000 pounds (450 kilograms) of displacement is enough to push you over a foul tide or to windward in a chop. There is also sufficient power remaining to run a decent sized alternator to keep the batteries fully charged.

ACCESS

It often seems that yachts are not designed with engines in mind. Engines are hidden deep in the bilge and working on them involves hanging upside down groping for unseen nuts and bolts or contorting yourself in positions that leave you aching for weeks afterwards. Since they were originally fitted before the deck went on, builders give little thought as to how the engine comes out, either for overhaul or replacement (besides ignoring how in situ engine maintenance can be carried out). To remove the engine sometimes requires major, hopefully temporary, modifications to either the cockpit or the companionway.

FUEL CONSUMPTION

Diesel engines are more economical on fuel than outboards but it is still worthwhile keeping records so you can always calculate your remaining range under power with whatever fuel you have aboard. An engine hour meter is the easiest way of keeping track of how long you run the engine and either dipping the tank or consulting the fuel gauge will tell how much fuel was used. Keeping this information in the engine logbook will soon build up an accurate picture of your hourly fuel consumption in different types of seaway. Ensuring that you have a range under power of several hundred miles usually requires carrying fuel in cans, either in lockers or lashed down on deck.

SPARES

Another factor that can become important when away from your home port or sailing to distant ports is the availability of spare engine parts. Before casting off, it is a good idea to speak to the manufacturer of your engine, tell them where you are planning to go and ask about the availability of spares. Even if spares will be readily accessible, it is worthwhile carrying a wide range of spares, particularly consumables such as filters and belts. It is also a good idea to have an engine parts manual for your model of engine aboard – while part of your preparations for a foreign cruise may include learning the local language at night school before setting sail, sadly these courses are weak on teaching the names of diesel engine components. With a parts manual you can beat the language barrier by pointing to the item you need.

SHAFT ALIGNMENT

Before setting off on a long passage, it is well worth checking the engine and shaft alignment and the condition of the engine mounts. Engine mounts carry almost all the propeller thrust load and transfer that to the hull. Poor engine mounts allow the engine not only to rock fore and aft but up and down and side to side, jiving to the tune of 'I'm all shook loose'. Unlike cars, boat engines do not stay indefinitely in alignment and if the alignment is out or the engines worn, this can lead to:

- excessive and rapid bearing wear
- increased wear on stuffing boxes, causing leaks
- vibration, which can damage the engine mounts and possibly even the hull
- a bent or damaged shaft
- excessive wear on universal joints
- transmission failure

The larger and longer your boat, the more critical the shaft alignment becomes, for bigger boats generally have longer and bigger diameter shafts. A prop shaft that is 10ft (3m) long can tolerate ten times the misalignment of a 20ft (6.1m) prop shaft.

ENGINE MAINTENANCE

Diesel engines may be more powerful than comparable petrol engines but regular maintenance and more frequent oil changes are essential if you wish your auxiliary diesel engine to keep going. Points to bear in mind on engine maintenance are:

- Engine lubrication is important. Always choose the correct oil for your engine. Make a point of changing the oil filters at the manufacturer's recommended intervals.
- Check and change fuel filters. Diesel fuel injectors work on very small flow passages and tight clearances. Dirty fuel can clog your engine's injection system. Be meticulous about changing the fuel filters as the manufacturer recommends or more often if you question the quality of the fuel.
- It takes several thousand cubic litres of air to burn one litre of diesel. Air filters keep grit out of the cylinders. If grit does enter, and some will, then it increases wear on the pistons, piston rings and liners.
- Diesel engines run at about three times the compression ratio of a petrol engine. This generates more heat than a petrol engine and places extra demands on the engine's cooling system. The cooling system is normally designed to remove about 30 per cent of the heat generated by the fuel combustion. Any less and overheating is likely. If a petrol engine overheats you can often stop, switch it off and wait for it to cool. If a diesel engine overheats it will need major surgery before it can be restarted. The message is always to make a point of checking and maintaining the engine's cooling systems.
- Monitor gaskets and coolant hoses closely. If you should find one leaking gasket, replace all of them, for the rest are about to start leaking.
- Always keep fuel in the tank topped up to prevent condensation building up inside the tank, as this water can end up in the injectors. As it reaches the injectors it turns to steam and blows the heads off the injectors.
  Diesel fuel is more likely to oxidise than petrol. It should never be kept in storage for more than twelve months. In some remote locations the age of the fuel can be questionable.

FUEL TREATMENTS

All fuels contain some water. Dust can introduce spores into your fuel tank. Some of these like growing in the water. The more water, the more microbes. Others – there are over twenty known types of microbes that look on your diesel tank as home – feed on the fuel at the fuel-water interface. If not treated, these fuel bugs will at the very least:

- reduce fuel quality and performance
- reduce the effectiveness of any additives
- produce corrosive acids that damage your engine

At worst, the residue from the bugs turns your fuel into a slimy sludge which blocks fuel lines and filters and eventually stops the engine. There are broad-spectrum biocide additives that prevent this happening. They are not cheap. The only consolation to your wallet is that they are cheaper than cleaning the tank, replacing fuel lines and filters and buying new injectors. Every drop of fuel should be treated with the additive and filtered to remove water before going into your tank. This is especially true in more remote areas, where you have no way of knowing how the fuel you have just bought has been stored or its condition. Yes, it came out of a tank, but how old is the fuel? What was stored in that tank before your fuel went in it? Is the tank full of water? Is the fuel already contaminated with microbes?

Treating and filtering fuel can be a chore, particularly in a seaway. It is difficult to hold a heavy fuel can without slipping over the side, never mind pouring its contents into a funnel with a water filter without the funnel overfilling and spilling fuel everywhere. The easy answer is to forget the funnel and fit a hose over the spout on the can, stick the other end into the fuel tank and pour. But you are gambling that by omitting to filter the fuel you will not pay the price for this moment of ease, with interest, later.

IN THE DOLDRUMS

We spent days motoring out of the doldrums looking for the trades and the skipper ignored suggestions that we should treat and filter the fuel before pouring it into the tank. To be fair, there was no additive aboard and perhaps filtering may not have helped that much. Fortunately we had left the yacht to another crew before the fuel turned to sludge and began a sequence of events that put the boat on the rocks.

When you start your engine, always allow it to run for at least five minutes before applying load. Putting a cold engine under load can cause premature wear or trigger a seizure; before stopping the engine, let it idle for about five minutes.

THE PROPELLER

For day to day sailing, and even for longer summer cruises, it is probably unnecessary to do more than check that the propeller and its prop shaft and couplings are in good condition and that there is no undue play in any of the bearings.

CHECKS

If you are planning an extended cruise, these checks are more important and you may wish to make a note of your propeller's diameter and pitch. This information should be stamped somewhere on your propeller. If the propeller is damaged or lost at sea this information speeds up finding a replacement. You may even go as far as carrying a spare propeller and key.

THE RIGHT PROPELLER?

Propellers convert rotational motion into thrust. The first patent was taken out in the mid-17th century but it was another 150 years before a propeller was first used successfully on a ship and another twenty years before something like the modern propeller appeared. This was by accident. Bits of the prototype under test fell off and the broken propeller worked better. Talk of propellers is complicated by the number of blades, blade size, shape, diameter, pitch and gearbox reduction ratio. If you are serious about confusing your listeners, you can throw in real and apparent slip, wake factor, cavitation, rake and skew.

In the end, all this jargon barely matters. Replacing your existing propeller with one that is more efficient is not as simple as it may first appear and choosing the correct propeller for your boat is still more of an art than a science. No two boats are exactly alike. Even between two boats of the same class there will be features that make them sufficiently different that each should have a different propeller. If you wish to identify the ideal propeller for your boat, you need to know each and every factor to be fed into the formula you are using. Unfortunately the data on most of these factors remains stubbornly elusive.

The usual solution is to find the best possible balance between engine output power and the ability of the propeller to turn that power into thrust. If this is achieved, the engine will provide maximum power at the correct RPM for maximum thrust from the propeller. If the pitch or diameter of the propeller is too great, the engine will be overloaded and never reach the optimum RPM for the ideal power output. If there is not enough pitch, or the propeller diameter is too small, the engine will race and the propeller produce very little thrust. At best, it is unlikely that the propeller's efficiency will ever exceed 60 per cent.

Having gone through all the trauma of choosing the right propeller, there is the satisfaction of knowing that the better the propeller matches your boat, the better your fuel economy and the quieter your engine runs.

DRAG

The other major discussion point on propellers is the drag they create under sail. In the beginning yachts were heavy and slow (comparatively), engines were low powered and the propellers small. Consequently, drag was not a major factor. Then yachts grew lighter and faster, and engines became more powerful. Even in the 1970s it would have been unusual to find an engine of double-digit horsepower in a 25–30 foot yacht. More powerful engines meant propellers had to be bigger to use the extra power efficiently. Drag grew to be a problem. It was discovered that drag increased with the square of boat speed and that the drag of the typical three-bladed propeller cut speed by around 15 per cent. This was less of a problem in strong winds, where the drive from the sails could overcome the drag; but in light winds it slowed performance perhaps to a point where progress could only be maintained by powering up the engine.

A sail drive with a folding propeller to reduce drag when under sail

The cheapest and simplest way of reducing propeller drag is to fit a thin, two-bladed propeller. Unfortunately these are horribly inefficient going ahead and next to useless in reverse. The next answer was the folding propeller. These first came out in the 1920s but it took fifty years before practical folding propellers appeared with geared blades that flew open when the engine was put ahead. Reversing was better than with the thin, two-bladed propeller; but to keep the folding propeller open when in reverse, the weight of the blade, especially close to the tips, had to be increased. This resulted in thick, heavy blades that reduced the propeller's efficiency.

The search for an answer to prop-drag continues. It has seen three- and even four-bladed folding propellers and auto-pitching propellers among others, but so far no one has discovered the drag-free prop.

14 GENERATORS

When considering the best way to generate enough electricity to meet your needs, you must start by estimating your daily power consumption. Once you have some idea of this then, taking into account your type of sailing, you can consider the best way of paying the bill. If, for example, you sail from marina to marina in daily passages and your longest passages are no more than twelve to eighteen hours, plugging into shore power is the most straightforward answer to your power needs. Anything the engine alternator puts in is a bonus. If you weekend sail and wish to ensure that your boat's batteries are kept charged between passages and shore power is not available, a wind generator or solar panel might provide a solution.

Sailing without any means of onboard power generation and relying on shore power to charge the ship's batteries is not impossible. I managed to do this for several years, taking in fairly lengthy summer cruises including sailing round Britain via the Caledonian Canal. For one season I fitted a wind generator and, with it standing proud on the stern, set off on a four day passage across the North Sea. The wind generator whirred away and power was used as if supplies were unlimited. All went well until, on the third day, we sailed into a ring of warships. It took us a couple of hours to clear the circle. The warships mostly ignored us. As we cleared the last warship, every gun in the fleet opened fire and my crew charged out of the cabin, declaring that the Decca navigator (yes, it was that long ago) was dead. For a few minutes we thought the navy was practising electronic warfare and had visions of skippers all over the North Sea demanding to know why they were lost. Then we discovered

ESTIMATED DAILY POWER CONSUMPTION

APPLIANCE	AMPERAGE	DAILY USE (hrs)	AMP HOURS USED EACH DAY
VHF	1	12	12
Plotter	1	12	12
Navigation lights	2	8	16
Domestic lights	4	4	16
Pumps	2	0.5	1
Domestic usage: stereo/laptop/charging cellphone/iPod etc	2	9	18
TOTALS			75

The final column of this table has to be in amps because your battery bank's capacity is measured in amp hours. What you want to know is how much you must put into your battery bank each day to keep it fully charged. This means working in amps.

When manufacturers use watts it is easy to convert watts into amps.

Amps = watts divided by volts

If you have an item of equipment rated at 25 watts and your boat has a 12 volt battery circuit, then:

Amps = 25 divided by 12 = 2.1 amps

This figure means that your 25 watt masthead light uses 2.1 amps every hour it is switched on. On an eight-hour night passage it takes nearly 17 amp/hours out of your battery. For most, this is about a fifth of their total domestic battery capacity.

that the Decca navigator was voltage sensitive and our batteries were flat. Unknown to us, the whirring wind generator had developed a fault and was not generating any power. Another lesson learned the hard way: monitor the state of your batteries and the output of your generators every day.

There are four ways of generating power on yachts:

1 the engine alternator
2 a separate petrol or diesel generator
3 a wind generator
4 solar panels

These are not mutually exclusive. It is possible to mix and match.

THE ENGINE ALTERNATOR

Until the 1960s, cars used direct current dynamos; but as silicon diode rectifiers dropped in price, alternators became more common, and today it would be rare to meet a DC dynamo. Alternators have a number of advantages over dynamos, not least being a longer working life. A rectifier, or diode bridge, is used to convert the alternating current from the alternator into direct current and a voltage regulator is needed to ensure a constant voltage at the battery terminals. At first, voltage regulators were mounted separately from the alternator. From about the 1990s they were incorporated into the alternator and now the alternator's electronic control unit does the job. On many yachts, the alternator is identical to those found in cars or light commercial vehicles with a maximum output of between 50 and 70 amps and a sustained output of about half their maximum. Purpose-designed marine alternators are explosion proof. This is a safeguard against sparking brushes igniting a build up of explosive gases in the engine room.

Most diesel engines have what is called a small case alternator. These are around 15cm (5–6in) in diameter and about the same in length. Most have only a single pulley for one belt but a more powerful alternator may have two pulleys.

If you are planning a long passage, or the addition of air conditioning, refrigerators and freezers has made the output of your existing alternator insufficient, then you may wish to install a high output alternator. This normally has an actual output of 70 to 100 amps or about two to three times the norm. On a long passage, the increased output significantly reduces engine running time when charging the batteries. As a very general guide, your battery capacity in amp hours should be around the same figure you arrive at when multiplying the alternator output by four.

If you opt to fit a new alternator, you must check:

- case size – is there room for the new alternator if it is bigger than its predecessor?
- mounting type – whether it is a dual foot or single foot alternator and if it fits the existing arrangements on your engine
- mounting bolt – this attaches the alternator to the engine at its pivot point. Larger alternators take a 12.5mm or $\frac{1}{2}$ inch bolt; medium sized alternators a 10mm or $\frac{3}{8}$ inch bolt; and small alternators an 8mm or $\frac{5}{16}$ inch bolt. It is important that your new alternator has the same size of bolt, or make the new bolt fit by using bushes
- pulley – the pulley must take the same size of belt as your old alternator. Belt size is measured across the top of the belt, which is its widest part. You must also check that the pulley on the new alternator lines up with the old pulley. If you have a single 10mm ($\frac{1}{8}$ inch) belt, then on a 12-volt alternator you are limited to around 70 amps: a 12.5mm or $\frac{1}{2}$ inch belt allows this to be increased to a maximum of about 110 amps
- regulator – high power alternators tend to come with external regulators, which allow adjustments to fit your particular setup and frequently have digital displays or flashing lights to tell you what is happening

At first sight, fitting a second alternator may appear a simple way of increasing generating power, but it is a serious engineering project normally involving finding a machine shop to manufacture additional brackets, a belt tensioner and even pulleys.

SEPARATE DIESEL OR PETROL GENERATOR

The greatest problem with a separate diesel or petrol generator is deciding where to stow it. For most boats this tends to rule out diesel generators, which usually demand their own, dedicated space, ventilation and plumbed-in cooling systems.

The most popular option is a small petrol powered generator. There are two types. A small two- or four-stroke engine is linked to a mains voltage generator and enclosed in a tubular metal frame. This is heavy and noisy and, although it is fine for battery charging or running hand power tools, its output is, electronically, too rough for laptops and other electronically sensitive equipment. It is also necessary to drain the fuel tank after each use and before it is stowed, as they tend to have open breather caps and not sealable breather caps as found on outboard motors. Since the tubular frame is made of mild steel tubing, it will rust if not very carefully maintained. The alternative is the inverter generator. A small engine drives an alternator and the output voltage from that is stepped up to mains voltage by an inverter. These are much smaller than frame generators, lighter, have sealable breather fuel caps, and since the output is electronically regulated it is smooth enough to run sensitive equipment. They usually come in a plastic case and can be stored in a locker when not in use.

Plugging the normal trickle battery charger into your petrol generator will charge your batteries but only after many hours of running. If you wish to use a petrol generator to charge your batteries, you will need a suitable switch mode battery charger.

WIND GENERATORS

Wind generators are a common sight on yachts but what may appear to be the complete answer has hidden snags. The catch with wind generators is that their output is proportional to the size of their blades: the longer the blade, the greater the output. A small wind generator, with an output of between one and two amps and suitable for trickle charging a battery, will have a blade diameter of around 0.6m (2ft). The spinning blades are a danger and must be mounted somewhere where there is no possibility of them coming into contact with hands, faces or any other body parts. This normally means mounting the generator so that the ends of the blades are a minimum of 1.8m (6ft) above the deck. This usually requires placing the generator on top of a guyed pole, on a mast or some form of framework. Serious wind generators, capable of producing the sort of power required on a long passage, have blade diameters starting around 1.8m (6ft) to over 2m (6½ft).

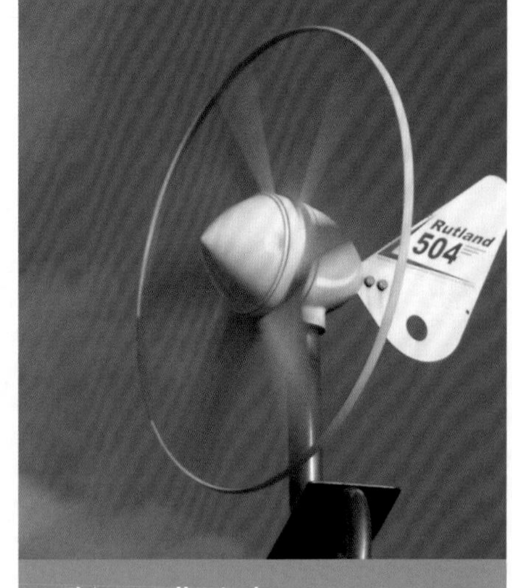

This small wind generator is able to keep the ship's battery charged between weekend cruises but will not produce sufficient power on a long cruise. It is mounted on goalposts on the transom

Few wind generators come with mounting kits and regulators. As a rough rule of thumb, providing these essential items adds between half to two thirds the purchase price of the generator.

Most wind generators are governed to stop producing power in winds around Beaufort force 6/7.

TOWED GENERATORS

Some wind generators come with the option of towing them astern, rather like the old Walker log. Since water is much denser than air, their output when towed is several times that when they are sticking up in the air. This can make them a more attractive proposition than a stand-alone wind generator. There is the question of drag to be considered; and in the same way as a towed log would be recovered when entering busy water, so too must the line of a towed generator. Some towed generators are dual purpose and can be mounted on a pole or hung in the rigging to produce power when in harbour.

SOLAR PANELS

While wind generators do not produce power in gales or calms, solar panels only produce power during the day. To prevent them radiating the power collected during the day into the night, they require a blocking diode or a regulator, which allows power to flow into the battery bank but not out.

A problem with solar panels is their location. They require lots of flat deck space and that is always in short supply. I once mounted a solar panel on the forehatch, which I had sealed down on the grounds that I did not need it, and then lived in fear of visitors using my precious panel as a doormat. Some panels claim to be flexible and yachts tie them round the boom when in harbour, which rather defeats the aim of generating power at sea.

Ideally, solar panels should always point towards the sun and some boats have arrangements that allow the panels to rotate, but in my experience, given how yachts behave in a seaway, this makes little practical difference.

Using a typical summer's day as their yardstick, manufacturers often state the output of their panel in watt hours per day. To see how much this puts back into your battery, take a few hours off to allow for cloudy skies and time of year and, assuming your boat has a 12-volt battery circuit, divide this answer by twelve.

Wind generators are noisy. Solar panels have the advantage of being silent but they work only during daylight hours and require deck space. The answer on this boat is to mount the solar panels on the doghouse roof

15 MEDICAL AND HEALTH

Medical arrangements should be based on the premise that if you leave port with a fit and healthy crew then, unless someone injures themselves, you will arrive with a fit and healthy crew. The greatest demand on the medical equipment you have on board should be to deal with the inevitable minor cuts, bumps and bruises.

For serious injuries or illnesses, the aim is to prevent the condition worsening while you arrange proper medical treatment. This is only possible if there is someone aboard who understands how to use whatever medical equipment you choose to carry. It is better still to have at least two people aboard with this knowledge to cover the eventuality that the lone medical expert is the casualty. Opening a first aid box without the knowledge of how to use it properly is useless and, in some circumstances, possibly dangerous.

FIRST AID CERTIFICATES

The degree of medical knowledge required varies with the distance between you and professional medical assistance. The minimum qualification should be a basic first aid certificate or the MCA Elementary First Aid to STCW standards. This course is part of the basic training of any professional seaman engaged in any capacity aboard ship.

These qualifications are probably adequate for day sailing, coastal and overnight passages but for longer trips it would be prudent to consider the MCA STCW Proficiency in Medical Care On Board Ship. This goes much further than the elementary certificate and includes knowledge of the drugs included in Category A medical kits. It is intended for ships' captains and senior officers (navigational and engineering) on board vessels voyaging worldwide who are designated first aiders, and is a requirement to become an officer of the watch.

One of the objectives of this certificate is that the first aider, besides being able to make a diagnosis and prognosis of a casualty, is able to communicate with a shoreside doctor by radio in a way that each understands what the other is saying. On a long passage, days, perhaps weeks, away from direct professional help, this could be an important skill.

If you consider that formal first aid training is unnecessary, you should ensure that at least two people aboard are familiar with mouth to mouth resuscitation and CPR. After all, it may be you they fish out of the water.

FIRST AID HANDBOOKS

There is a wide range of medical handbooks from which to choose and a copy of the latest edition of the Ship Captain's Medical Guide, the standard work on the subject, can be downloaded for free from www.dft.gov.uk/mca/mcga-seafarer_information/mcga-dgs_st_shs_seafarer_information-medical/mcga-dqs_st_shs_ships_capt_medical_guide.htm.

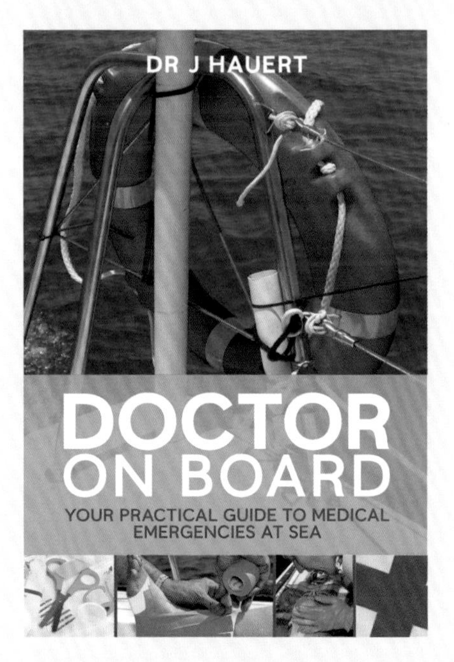

Medical handbooks such as these are extremely useful for when at sea

FIRST AID BOXES

It is unlikely that any two doctors will agree what should be included in your first aid kit. In practice it is often better to have two first aid boxes. One should be a ready-to-use box containing antiseptic creams, sun block, painkillers such as aspirin, seasickness pills, a thermometer, a handful of bandages and sticking plasters. This is stowed where it can be easily reached and is intended to deal with the day-to-day scrapes and grazes. The second, the major incident first aid box, is the one that contains everything needed for a first aider to deal with a more serious illness or injury. When deciding what to include in this, Annex 1 of Merchant Shipping Notice 1768 (M+F) contains much useful information including a list

FIRST AID KIT

There is no ideal or recommended list of contents for a first aid box. This list, like any other, is no more than a suggestion to help you decide what items you may wish to include. If you are planning a long blue water cruise then you will probably wish to include a selection of broad spectrum antibiotics, some frighteningly powerful painkillers and anti-malarial treatments, but speak to your doctor about this before including these items.

The first aid kit should be stowed in a clearly marked, easily identifiable, waterproof, plastic or metal box.

- First Aid manual: to remind you of what you learned on your first aid course
- Adhesive elastic bandages
- Antihistamine cream
- Bandages
- Butterfly strips
- Cotton buds
- Cotton wool pads
- Finger bandage and applicator
- Individually wrapped large sterile unmedicated wound dressings
- Individually wrapped medium sterile unmedicated wound dressings
- Large non-adherent sterile dressings (Melolin)
- Medium non-adherent sterile dressings (Melolin)
- Micropore tapes of various widths
- Non-adhesive elastic bandages
- Oral rehydration salts
- Painkillers
  - Aspirin
  - Codeine
  - Paracetamol
  - Ibuprofen
- Saline for cleaning wounds and washing debris from eyes
- Sterile eye pads
- Sterile gauze pads
- Sterile wipes
- Sticking plasters, various sizes
- Triangular bandages
- Zinc oxide tape of various widths
- Emergency blankets (space blankets)
- Face mask for personal protection when performing artificial respiration or CPR
- Lighter for sterilising equipment
- Safety pins
- Scissors
- Single use disposable gloves
- Small torch
- Thermometer: consider using an ear thermometer (less need to sterilise between use)
- Trauma shears for cutting away clothing
- Tweezers
- Disinfectant spray for cleaning up
- Disinfectant wipes for cleaning up

of the medical supplies needed under the Merchant Shipping and Fishing Vessels (Medical Stores) Regulations 1995. You can either use this information to make up your own first aid boxes or there are a number of suppliers who provide ready-made first aid boxes.

An often overlooked aspect of first aid boxes is that they must be kept up to date. There are two aspects to this: firstly, if any item is taken out and used then it must be replaced as soon as possible. Secondly, many items have a 'use by' date and should be safely disposed of and replaced, ideally just before that date and certainly by that date.

SEASICKNESS

Being seasick is not a sign of weakness or a subject for humour. Most people suffer from it. It just takes some longer than others to show the symptoms. Ask anyone to hang head down in the bilge in a seaway and work on the engine and it is a safe bet they will be seasick.

Seasickness has three stages. Stage one sufferers feel sick but fight it. In stage two they feel like they are about to die but are determined to live. By stage three they wish to kill themselves but lack the energy to throw themselves overboard. Seasickness is a misery and sufferers find no comfort in being told that they will find their sea legs in a couple of days.

Prevention is far better than noble but misplaced suffering. If you are prone to seasickness, take one of the proprietary seasickness remedies before casting off. If any of your crew is also likely to be seasick, encourage them to do the same. There is an argument that some seasickness remedies encourage drowsiness. This may be true, but a drowsy crew member is more useful to you that one suffering from seasickness.

Anyone who is seasick is likely to become dehydrated. Sufferers must replace the fluids they are losing. Drinking water helps but rehydration salts are better – you can buy these in your local chemist. If you have none on board, dissolving six level teaspoonfuls of sugar and half a level teaspoonful of salt in one litre of clean water provides a useful substitute.

SUNBURN

Sunburn can be extremely painful and, like seasickness, prevention is better than cure. The simplest and most effective answer is to cover up as much skin as possible and apply sun block to those areas you cannot cover up. If someone is sunburnt, applying soothing lotions such as calamine and giving them a painkiller like aspirin may bring some relief.

BURNS

On any small craft in a seaway there is always a risk of a kettle or pot flying off the stove and throwing its scalding contents over anyone nearby. The consequences of this can be so awful that when the motion of the boat makes this a possibility it makes sense for the cook to wear oilskins. If the worst does happen, the hot fluids run off and minimise the effects.

If someone is burnt or scalded, it is important to keep the wound sterile. The burn or scald initially sterilises the wound but leaves it very vulnerable to subsequent infection from ministering hands or non-sterile dressings. Treatment begins by cooling down the burn by pouring lots of clean, cold water over it for at least ten minutes or until the pain subsides. While this is happening put on disposable gloves and, if they are not stuck to the skin, remove watches, jewellery and clothing from the affected area. Do not apply any ointment, lotions or cream. Do not cover the wound with sticking plaster or fluffy materials. A clean plastic bag or cling film over the wound are probably best.

Burns greater than 25mm x 25mm (1 inch square) almost certainly require medical treatment. All deep burns must have medical treatment.

SHOCK

There is a good chance that anyone who has been scalded or burnt will go into shock. This can be life threatening. The symptoms of shock are:

- pale face
- clammy, cold skin
- fast shallow breathing
- unnaturally rapid and weak pulse
- yawning
- sighing
- in extreme cases, unconsciousness

The first aid for shock is simple. Lay the casualty down with their feet higher than their head. Loosen tight clothing, keep them warm and seek medical help.

PERSONAL MEDICATION

It is possible that someone among your crew has a temporary or chronic condition for which they are taking medication. Just because someone has a chronic condition does not mean that they cannot sail. Diabetics have made Atlantic crossings but anyone on medication must tell you before you sail and it is then for you to decide whether you accept that they are fit to sail. This sounds harsh but if they should take a turn for the worse at sea, help may be a long time coming.

If you do agree that they can sail, they must bring with them enough of their medication to cover the expected duration of the passage with some extra to allow for delays and diversions. It may also be sensible of them to carry a spare prescription for their medication so they can easily obtain further supplies.

HEALTH INSURANCE

If you are a UK resident and hold a European Health Insurance Card (EHIC) you can receive state provided health care free or at a reduced cost when visiting EU countries and Iceland, Liechtenstein, Norway and Switzerland. You can apply for an EHIC at www.ehic.org.uk. An EHIC may not cover all health costs and never covers repatriation, so it makes sense to have adequate health insurance that provides for repatriation by air ambulance and all medical bills. You may wish to extend this to cover pre-existing conditions. More information can be found at www.nhs.uk/healthcareabroad.

INSTRUMENTATION

When the log was towed astern and a magnetic compass gave you a course to steer, instruments were too simple to go wrong and even easier to repair. Modern electronic instruments are both a blessing and a curse. When they work they are marvellous. They give you your position to an accuracy that human navigators can only achieve in their dreams. Autohelms hold a course better than any human hand and plotters provide information instantly, continuously, to umpteen decimal places. However, when they break they are beyond onboard repair.

We rely upon them, but probably use only a fraction of their capabilities. This is mostly because their instruction manuals appear to be written in a language understood only to those already intimately familiar with that instrument. Consequently, most of us stop reading after the five easy steps on the page headed 'Getting Started'. Worse, in order to keep it simple, each of the buttons that operates the machine has more than one use. The only exception appears to be the power on/off switch and on my plotter even that has two functions. The function of any other button at any moment depends upon which other buttons have already been pushed – which, in their turn, depends upon which buttons were pushed before them. So we learn enough to make the instrument do what we want, and in the right circumstances this ability can appear impressively knowledgeable to the untutored; but if the instrument throws a wobbler we are reduced to holding the manual in one hand and pushing buttons in hope with the other.

I was helping a friend to deliver his new (to him) boat. We picked it up from the yard that had sold it to him and prepared it for the passage. Everything appeared to work, so we set sail. Having cleared the harbour and pointed the bows in the right direction, we attempted to engage the autopilot. Although there was a button that said 'Autopilot', pushing it had no effect beyond telling us that the autopilot was engaged. It lied. We checked the manual. We went over the ship's wiring diagram. We pushed buttons at random. Nothing. Still in cellphone range, we rang the yard, who assured us the autohelm worked but could not tell us how to switch it on. It was a long, tedious trip. Much later, we discovered that if we pressed a button labelled AUX2 on the master control panel, the autohelm came to life.

Mounting instruments on the wheel pedestal is a popular solution to the problems of having the instruments where the helm can see them

Never follow our example and go to sea without first checking all the instruments actually work. The second lesson is knowing how to use the instruments. On a friend's yacht, the instruments are interfaced. This is not uncommon. Then one season the log stopped working and the autohelm came out in sympathy. We are sure there is a cycle of buttons that, when pressed, allow the instruments to operate in a stand-alone mode but so far no one has discovered this magic sequence.

It also helps to have the instruments located where they can be seen by those who use them. The days of the dedicated chart table are passing. Navigation is increasingly being done from the plotter in the cockpit in real time by the watch on deck, rather than by the hourly plot on a paper chart by the navigator. On one boat I sailed, there was a chart table that could take an open, full sized admiralty chart with room to spare. The instruments, including the plotter, were at the back, a long arm's length away, out of sight and out of mind.

The instrumentation you have is determined by your boat, the type of sailing you do, your love of toys, and the depth of your pocket. Curiously, this is one occasion where the further you sail, the less you need. On coastal passages, navigation and boat handling must be precise. The consequences of not knowing exactly where you are and what course you are steering could be serious. Not so in the middle of the ocean. On my first Atlantic crossing I powered up my GPS for a few minutes each day at noon to check my sextant's sun-run-sun fix.

In boats with a wheelhouse or good cockpit protection, the instruments are often mounted either side of the main hatch

LOSS OF INSTRUMENTATION

It is a useful exercise to give some thought to how you would manage if you lost all instrumentation. There are two principal ways this may happen. First, you may have a catastrophic electrical failure. Second, you may lose some or all of your ability to charge the ship's batteries and have to introduce power rationing. This may involve switching off some or all of your instrumentation or severely limiting its use. Wind instruments are nice but not essential. It is always possible to make a fair estimate of the wind speed and a length of yarn tied to a shroud gives the wind direction. The VHF is only switched on when another vessel is in sight and all transmissions are made on low power.

A good magnetic compass mounted where it can be easily seen, a mechanical speed log and, if the main plotter is dead, a battery powered handheld GPS can go a long way to filling the remaining gap – on a long trip, it is a good idea to carry rechargeable AA and AAA batteries with their own solar powered charger to keep handheld instruments going. Loss of instrumentation is also the point when the cry 'Always carry paper charts!' makes good sense; but if they are not aboard there is usually sufficient information in pilots and almanacs to construct a chart that can see you to harbour. If you find you need soundings then a spare line, suitably knotted with a weight on one end, makes a good lead line, although in anything but unreasonably shallow water you will probably have to stop the boat to take an accurate reading.

TIDES AND WEATHER

> *Forecasts are what you expect. Weather is what you get.*
> **Anon**

Information on tides and weather is vital to your route plan. If either of these is unfavourable, it is unwise to sail.

TIDES

What you need to know:

- time and height of high and low water for:
  - your port of departure
  - your destination
  - all alternative ports
- set and drift of tide

If your passage is expected to last several days, you need this information for your alternative ports for each day you expect to be at sea and may need to update it for your destination should you arrive early or late.

SOURCES OF INFORMATION

- Tide tables: The times and heights of the tide may be found in tide tables for local waters handed out by yacht clubs and chandlers, in almanacs, and in Admiralty tide tables. Tide tables are also published by foreign hydrographic offices, the Internet and specialist tidal prediction programmes.
- Tidal atlas: Information on the set of drift of the tide can be found in Admiralty tidal atlases, which cover the UK and most European waters, in almanacs and on specialist tidal software.

The tides determine when you leave port. If you are in a drying harbour, the earliest you can leave is when there is enough water to keep you afloat. When you leave, it is pleasant to have a fair tide under your keel and if the ebb tide is going your way then, whether the harbour dries or not, you would wait until close to high water before setting out. Conversely, if the flood tide were favourable to you, you would leave at the earliest possible moment on the flood.

Favourable tides are also useful and often mandatory for slipping past headlands and through tidal gates and overfalls. It is important to calculate your ETA at these points and, using this information, to check the tide at the headland and adjust your route plan accordingly. It is possible to butt over a foul tide but this should be avoided if at all possible, particularly in places where the tide is doing its worst.

WEATHER

What you need to know:

- wind direction and speed
- sea state
- visibility

FOUL TIDE OFF SELSEY BILL

I had a fair tide and a kind wind slipping through the Looe Channel off Selsey Bill. This is where depths abruptly change from over 10m (33ft) to 6 or 7m (20ft), and for 5 miles or so the seas can be very unkind until the water deepens again. I was having a bouncy passage, but found comfort watching a yacht coming the other way. He was motor sailing and in no danger but their progress was slow and they were being thrown from wave to wave in a most fearful fashion.

One reason for the difference in our comfort levels was that on a reach I was being overtaken by, say, five waves a minute while going upwind. The other boat was meeting, say, ten waves a minute. The difference in apparent wave frequency is one reason why, when beating, there is a tendency to overestimate the roughness of the sea.

It may be that the other boat had no choice but to arrive off Selsey Bill with a foul tide but I could not help thinking that their passage would have been much easier if they had slowed down to arrive as the tide turned or even slipped into Brighton Marina or Shoreham and waited for a favourable tide.

SOURCES OF INFORMATION

- Meteorological Office Inshore and Shipping Forecasts
- weatherfax
- navtex
- yacht club, harbour or marina office
- the Internet
- mark I Eyeball and your boat's instrumentation

WEATHER FORECASTS

When planning a passage, what you are looking for is a weather window that gives fair winds and kind seas for the duration of your passage. This is rare and you must decide what limitations you wish to place on your sailing weather. You should not take the accuracy of any weather forecast for granted. They are predictions, not promises. In the days before your passage, study the weather forecasts and, as best you can, compare them against the actual weather. This allows you to build up a mental picture of the current weather pattern, which continues to grow as you sail. This helps you evaluate the weather forecasts you gather on passage.

Once, national meteorological authorities were almost the only source of marine weather forecasts. They are still very important, but the Internet gives you access to an enormous range of sources. Everyone has their favourites whose reliability they rate above others. Even so, if at all possible it is good sense to compare forecasts from several trusty sources. If every source promises broadly the same weather, you can be confident about the coming weather. If they differ, this is when the time spent watching the weather over the previous few days helps you decide which forecast you think has the best chance of being correct.

GRIB FILES

GRIB files (Gridded Information in Binary weather data) are used by National Weather Services (NWS) throughout the world to store and exchange forecast data with other weather services. Most NWS organisations do not release this data to the general public. Exceptions are the US National Weather Service (a part of NOAA), the US Navy and the Canadian Meteorological Service.

A number of Internet sites offer GRIB files, either stand-alone weather forecasts (most notably Ugrib and zyGrib, which provide free forecasts) or integrated with navigation or routeing programmes, for example, Deckman for Windows, Expedition or MaxSea. Most sources for free GRIB files use the US GFS (General Forecast System) with the US Navy's NOGAPS (Navy Operational Global Atmospheric Prediction System) as a back-up.

GRIB forecasts are good but not perfect. A typical GFS file provides forecasts for seven days ahead. The data is good for the first three or four days but the further out you go in time, the increasingly less accurate the forecast becomes.

Short-term forecasts from any source are pretty accurate. If you are going out for a day or afternoon sail, you can be sure that the weather will be more or less as forecast. The longer you look ahead, the less reliable weather forecasts become. It is the nature of the beast. If you are planning a passage of several days or longer, it is important to have access to the latest forecasts during your cruise.

In coastal waters, forecasts come mostly through VHF broadcasts. Up to around 400 miles offshore, Navtex provides regular forecasts. Further afield you are looking at short-wave voice forecasts, Weatherfax or accessing forecasts through your satellite telephone.

The longer you are at sea, the greater the possibility that the weather will take an unexpected turn, or at least one you did not foresee before you set sail, and it is necessary to modify your passage plan accordingly. This may involve abandoning hopes of reaching your destination and underlines the importance of having properly researched alternative harbours and anchorages.

The forecast may have mentioned the possibility of squalls but by keeping an eye on the weather you can see them coming and prepare to meet them in good time. In this case, there may well be storms as the front passes over and you can sail into the sunshine

SHIPPING BULLETIN TERMS	
TIME	
Imminent	Expected within 6 hours of time of issue
Soon	Expected within 6–12 hours of time of issue
Later	Expected more than 12 hours after time of issue
WIND	
Wind direction	Indicates direction FROM which wind is blowing
Becoming cyclonic	Indicates that there will be a considerable change of wind direction across the path of a depression in the forecast area
Veering	The changing of wind direction clockwise ie SW to W
Backing	The changing of the wind direction anticlockwise ie SW to S
Gale	F8 / 34–40 knots or gusts 43–51 knots
Severe gale	F9 / 41–47 knots or gusts 52–60 knots
Storm	F10 / 48–55 knots or gusts 61–68 knots
Violent storm	F11 / 56–63 knots or gusts over 69 knots
Hurricane force	F12 / over 64 knots
BAROMETER	
Description	**Rate of change in 3 hours**
Steady	Under 0.1mb
Rising/falling slowly	0.1 to 1.5mb
Rising/falling	1.6 to 3.5mb = *depression*
Rising/falling quickly	3.6 to 6.0mb = *Force 6*
Rising/falling very quickly	Over 6.0mb = ***Gale***
DISTANCE APART OF 4mb ISOBARS	
In nautical miles	**Wind force**
360	1
180	2
90	4
60	6
45	8

WEATHER SYSTEMS	
Description	**Characteristic**
Shallow	Central pressure over 1000mb
Deep	Central pressure 960 to 1000mb
Very deep	Central pressure under 960mb
Vigorous	Strong winds expected
Complex	Two or more centres
WEATHER SYSTEMS: RATE OF MOVEMENT	
Slowly	Under 15 knots
Steadily	15–25 knots
Rather quickly	26–35 knots
Rapidly	36–45 knots
Very rapidly	Over 45 knots
VISIBLITY	
Very poor	Less than 1km
Poor	1–4km
Moderate	4–10km
Good	10–20km
Very good	20–40km
Excellent	More than 40km

SHIPPING FORECASTS BBC Radio 4

0048 transmitted on FM and LW. Includes weather reports from coastal stations at 0051, an inshore waters forecast at 0053 and further weather reports at 0055. The broadcast finishes at approximately 0058, and is followed by a short goodnight message and the closedown of the station for the night.

0520 transmitted on FM and LW. Includes weather reports from coastal stations at 0525, and an inshore waters forecast at 0527.

1201 transmitted on long wave only.

1754 transmitted on long wave only on weekdays and on both FM and long wave at weekends.

WIND SPEED AND DIRECTION

The wind speed given in forecasts is the mean wind speed 10m (33ft) above sea level. Closer to the sea, the wind speed is less. The speed shown on a handheld anemometer can be as much as a third lower than the forecast wind speed. This is worth remembering when standing on the pier head wondering if the wind speed is within your range for going to sea. If the only forecast you have is a synoptic chart, a reasonable estimate of the mean wind speed at 10m (33ft) can be found using the distance apart of the isobars.

GEOSTROPHIC WINDS

It may be that the only weather forecast you have is a synoptic chart. The shape of the isobars gives you a good idea of the wind direction. If there is a scale for geostrophic winds on the chart, use that to estimate the wind speed.

If there is no scale on your synoptic chart then for 55°N, using the standard 4hPa between isobars, the following table gives an idea of the wind speed you can expect. For other latitudes, use the graph.

DISTANCE APART OF ISOBARS IN NAUTICAL MILES	BEAUFORT SCALE MEAN WIND SPEED (KTS)	GUSTS (KTS)
48	Bft 8–9 (40)	60
96	Bft 5–6 (21)	32
144	Bft 4–5 (14)	21
192	Bft 3–4 (10)	15
240	Bft 3 (8)	12
288	Bft 2–3 (6)	10

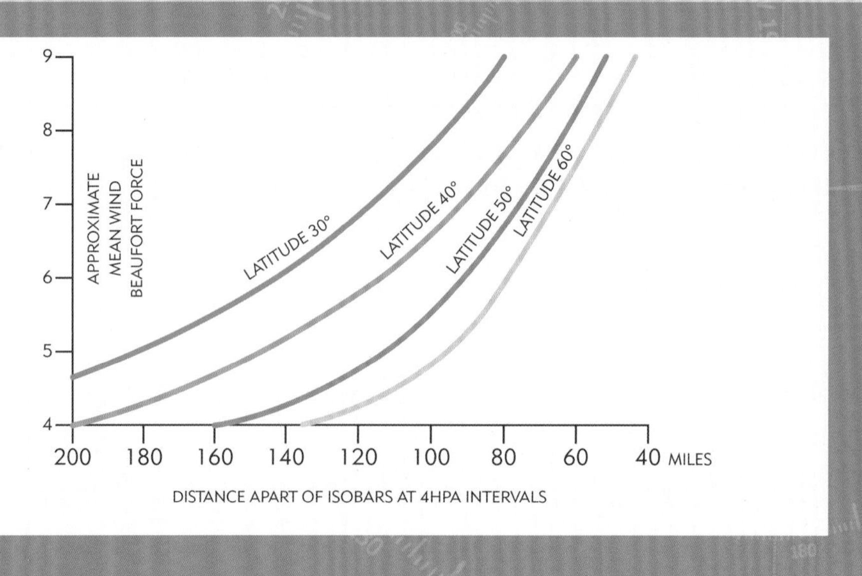

You may decide not to sail if the wind is above a certain speed or comes from a particular direction. The reciprocal of the course you wish to steer is usually classed as an unfavourable wind direction. Your limiting wind speed depends upon your boat, your crew and your inclination. When my son was young I made it a rule not to sail with him aboard if a force 4 was blowing or forecast.

You need to be honest about your boat's upwind performance. Most small yachts pointing their bows upwind in much above a force 5 are probably going sideways as fast as they are sailing forwards. Progress is painfully slow and any increase in the wind speed may mean having to motorsail just to make any headway.

SEA STATE

Even if the wind is favourable the sea state can lock you in, or out of harbour. Years ago there was a wreck of a multihull on the hard by Tweed Dock in Berwick. The story was that, against all local advice, it had sailed out of harbour when conditions were unfavourable. To the surprise of the local sailors, they reached the open sea; but not liking the conditions they turned round to return and capsized on the re-entry. At least one person died.

On a blowy day on the River Tyne some years ago, a yacht out for the day ignored warnings from both the harbour master and the coastguard and sailed out to sea through the piers. They broached as they returned through the piers and two crew members drowned.

Even if we are convinced that at sea the conditions are suitable and all we face is an uncomfortable few moments clearing or entering the harbour, it is wise to listen and heed local advice.

FIVE RULES FOR AVOIDING BIG SEAS

Meeting and beating monstrous seas makes for good bar room tales but sailing in heavy weather and big seas is rarely fun and with some cunning foresight it can often be avoided.

1. Do not sail in shallow water.
2. Do not sail upwind in big seas. If you must sail upwind, the apparent speed of the waves increases, making for a bumpy ride; and when you tack you are sailing across big waves hitting the bows at around 45°. If you are faced with sailing upwind in big seas and strong winds, consider waiting until the wind and seas moderate. If in harbour, then stay in harbour. If at sea and there is sea room, consider heaving-to.
3. Try to sail in the lee of the land where the waves will be smaller and kinder for a given wind force rather than along a lee shore.
4. Pay attention to the weather reports for the days before you sail. You may sail out into a force 3 from the south-west, which is ideal for your planned passage, but if the wind has been blowing force 8 from the north-east for the previous week, significant wave height is likely to be twice what you expected, coming from the wrong direction, and have the beginnings of a cross swell.
5. If you must sail in big seas, then pay attention. Waves do not behave predictably. Staying alert in bad weather is tiring, so keep rotating the helm and never leave anyone on the helm for hours on end.

WAVES

Waves are usually a complex structure of one wave system on top of another. They are formed by the wind and their nature depends, among other factors, upon:

- wind speed
- the length of time the wind has been blowing from that direction
- the fetch of the wind

As a very rough guide, a force 8 with a fetch of 500 miles creates seas around 5m (16ft) high after 24 hours and a force 6 with a 200 mile fetch brings 2.5m (8ft) seas in the same time.

The period of a wave is the time taken between one wave crest (or trough) and the next passing a floating object such as a patch of foam. Once you have found a figure for the wave period, you can play around with the following formulae to learn more about the waves you are meeting.

The speed of the wave (in knots) = wave period multiplied by 3.

The distance between two successive crests is the wavelength and so in the time of one period the wave has travelled a distance of one wavelength and so:

Wavelength = wave speed multiplied by the wave's period.

Wave height (amplitude) is not related to its length, speed or period. The wave height as reported by ships and buoys is the significant wave height, which is the average height of the highest one-third of waves.

Wave steepness is the ratio between wavelength and wave height. When the height of a wave and its period are similar, say 3m (10ft) seas every ten seconds, the wave steepness is considered to be severe and dangerous to small craft, which run the risk of pitch poling or capsizing.

TIME, WIND SPEED AND WAVE HEIGHT

UNLIMITED FETCH				
Time in hours wind has blown	Bft F4 11–16kts	Bft F6 22–27 kts	Bft F7 28–33 kts	Bft F8 34–40 kts
	Significant wave height (m)	Significant wave height (m)	Significant wave height (m)	Significant wave height (m)
1	0.3	0.8	1.2	1.7
2	0.4	1.0	1.5	2.3
4	0.5	1.2	1.8	2.7

6	0.6	1.5	2.3	3.5
12	0.7	1.8	2.7	4.1
24	0.9	2.6	3.5	5.2
72	1.4	3.4	5.2	6.1

The figures are for the wind blowing over an unlimited fetch in the open sea. This is rarely the case and shorter fetches create smaller waves. As the table gives significant wave heights, the highest waves could be 30–40 per cent above these figures. In soundings and shallow water, the pattern of wavelengths and heights will be different.

LIMITED FETCH		
FETCH and TIME	**WIND SPEED**	**WAVE HEIGHT**
Fetch 10nm for 2–3 hrs	F3–4 F4–5 F5–6 F6–7	0.3 0.5 1.0 1.1
Fetch 20nm for 4–5hrs	F3–4 F4–5 F5–6 F6–7	0.4 1.0 1.1 1.4
Fetch 30nm for 5–7 hours	F3–4 F4–5 F5–6 F6–7	0.5 1.0 1.3 1.7
Fetch 40nm for 6–8 hours	F3–4 F4–5 F5–6 F6–7	0.5 1.0 1.4 1.9

OVERFALLS

When the wind blows against the tidal stream, wavelength shortens and the waves steepen. In moderate winds and tidal streams, this can create an uncomfortable chop; but when the tidal runs strongly it causes overfalls, particularly off headlands and through tidal gates. The Portland Race on the south coast is a well-known example of overfalls created by a headland, but they are likely to be found off any promontory.

The Gulf of Corryvreckan between the islands of Jura and Scarba off Scotland's west coast, where the tide can run at over 8 knots, is perhaps the UK's best-known example of overfalls through a tidal gate. Overfalls, even if not considered dangerous to small craft, are best avoided. If that is not possible, they should be taken with a favourable tide.

SHALLOW WATER WAVES

As waves move away from their source, they are classed as swell. Swell waves run on, often for hundreds of miles, keeping their period, speed and wavelength, and only slowly lose height. As waves approach the coast and the water shallows, their character changes: they slow down, change direction, their wavelength shortens and they grow steeper. As the depth of water can vary along a wave, different parts of the wave can travel at different speeds. When the depth of water is about 1.3 times the wave height, the wave breaks.

VISIBLITY

It is a cruel truth that in poor visibility there is no certainty that large craft will see small craft either by Mark I Eyeball or radar. Regardless of the situation under the Rules of the Road, safety for small craft lies in their keeping out of the way of bigger boats. To do so, they must become aware of the presence of other vessels in good time to take avoiding action. Nowadays, many small craft carry radar and this, with the ready availability of cheap receivers for the Automatic Identification System (AIS) for ships, has taken much of the terror out of sailing in poor visibility. Nevertheless, it pays to remember that neither system carries a cast-iron promise of freedom from close encounters.

If visibility clamps down while at sea, you must accept the situation and take whatever measures you can to minimise the risk to you and your crew. Anchoring in water so shallow that if anything hits you it has wheels is a good solution. If you must stay out at sea, radar and AIS can help. Broadcasting your position course and speed every fifteen minutes or so may encourage craft with radar to take a closer look at their radar screen.

If you are in port and visibility is poor or forecast to close down, it is best to stay in harbour. I will not sail if the visibility is less than 2 miles. I once left Cherbourg for Poole with a forecast of 'fog patches'. These fog patches were either larger than anyone could reasonably expect or the forecast was optimistic. I sailed in visibility of less than a mile all the way across. I nearly died of fright crossing the shipping lanes.

Fog is one of the scariest weather conditions for a small yacht. You may know where you are but you probably have no idea what else is out there and what it is doing

ROUTEING: THE ROUTE PLAN

> *You've got to be very careful if you don't know where you are going because you might not get there.*
> **Yogi Berra**

THE ROUTE PLAN

Your route plan is the description of the track you hope to follow from leaving your berth to arriving at your destination. It takes into account factors such as timings, hazards, alternative routes and other destinations.

WHAT YOU NEED TO KNOW

There are seven steps to any route plan:

- clearing your berth
- pilotage to your point of departure
- examination of all possible routes between your point of departure and landfall
- examination of all possible alternative ports

- selection and detailed planning of your preferred route from your point of departure to your landfall
- pilotage from landfall to berth
- berthing at your destination

INFORMATION GATHERING

For each step, you must gather enough information to enable you to complete that phase of your passage in a safe and seamanlike manner. The level of detail that gives you the confidence to do this varies from passage to passage and person to person. Some, like me, delve deep; others take the broadest of broad approaches. Neither is wrong.

Routeing information probably dates faster than most. Even with the best and most up-to-date facts, the reality can challenge your preconceptions. The first time I entered La Coruña, GPS had not been invented and we relied on my astronavigation to cross the Bay of Biscay. The chart showed a lighthouse by the entrance. I should have checked further but I was confident of recognising a lighthouse when I saw one. The tall stone structure that crawled over the horizon looked more like a pele tower than a lighthouse. There was no sign of a lantern (there is one) and a sceptical crew started betting on where I had taken them. Had I done my homework properly I could have impressed everyone by telling them that we were looking at the Torre de Hércules, a lighthouse built by the Romans and still in use today, making it the world's oldest working lighthouse.

Using pilotage notes to draw a simple sketch map is a valuable exercise, especially when entering or leaving an unfamiliar port. It does not matter that the sketch map is not to scale. It brings together information scattered across other sources such as pilot books and charts; it helps you absorb the detail of this information rather than letting your eyes skip across the page, and encourages you to check out any doubts you may have. Ideally this sketch plan should not just be of isolated features, like the Torre de Hércules, however important they may be, but cover the ground from landfall to harbour.

Ports change. Until the 1960s the port of Amble on the north-east coast of England exported coal. Since the loss of the coal trade, the removal of buoyage on the approaches to

Geography means that harbours along any given stretch of coast look similar and it is easy to confuse one with another. On England's north-east coast they are often are tucked away in the northern corners of bays to protect them from the northerly gales that bring the worst weather. This is Robin Hood's Bay, just south of Whitby

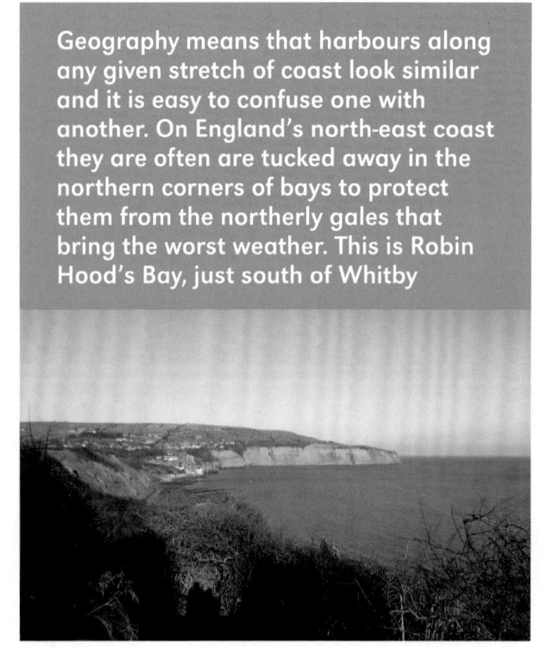

And this is Runswick Bay, just north of Whitby

the entrance and the now variable depths over the bar have made the entrance interesting. On the Yorkshire coast, harbours often cling to the hillside in a corner of a bay, usually but not always at the mouth of a valley where a stream reaches the sea. They could easily be mistaken one for another by a careless navigator. Also, many of the harbours along the north-east coast are not places where boats lie afloat or even dry out, but merely provide shelter for the launching and recovery of the traditional fishing cobles. Many of the fishing ports along the Moray Firth, such as Whitehills and Lossiemouth, have turned fish quays into marinas. In Lowestoft, the yacht club's moorings have become a marina with a new breakwater, and pontoons have appeared in nearby Hamilton Dock.

SOURCES OF INFORMATION

When planning your route, there are many sources of information. Much now comes from specialist sailing programmes or is found on the Internet. If, for example, you wish to know some months ahead what weather you could expect in June, you will learn much by studying the appropriate pilot chart or you could try typing 'weather for June on the north-east coast of England' (or wherever you plan to sail) into Google. Heading the list is the Meteorological Office's report on the climate for that area (www.metoffice.gov.uk/climate/uk/ne/print.html), a splendid starting point for working out the likely weather conditions.

Sources of information include:

- admiralty pilots
- tide tables
- tidal atlases
- yachting pilots
- harbour/marina guides
- accounts in sailing books and magazines
- appropriate charts
- personal local knowledge
- second-hand local knowledge
- the Internet

The more you learn about your route and the ports along the way, the better equipped you are to deal correctly with the unexpected.

STEP ONE – LEAVING YOUR BERTH

In your home port, custom and usage should make leaving your berth straightforward. In a strange harbour, take nothing for granted and remember that time spent in reconnaissance is seldom wasted.

You might, for example, be the inside boat of a raft of boats against a harbour wall. A slick departure requires the good will and cooperation of the other boats in the raft. You must speak to them well in advance so that your leaving does not catch them by surprise. This is especially important if the tides insist on a very early, or late, sailing time. In this case, it is best to invite everyone to a game of musical boats at a time that suits everyone and leaves you the outside boat of the raft, able to leave when you wish without inconveniencing the other boats.

In some harbours it is necessary to raft up with other boats. This requires a degree of give and take from everyone if it is to work, especially when you wish to leave

Never refuse help when leaving a berth. If necessary, seek it out. I was rafted up outside Heinrich's yacht at the end of a long channel in Norderney Harbour in the Frisian Islands. A strong wind was doing its best to keep us both pinned against the walkway. It had been blowing stronger the day before when a large Dutch barge yacht lost control and came down the channel, threatening to crush us. I was happy to stay in harbour but Heinrich, for years a lifeboatman on Borkum and now curator of the DGzRS lifeboat museum in Neuharlingersiel, was adamant that he was leaving. It was time he went home. I explained that, even in the most favourable conditions, when I put the engine in reverse Margo was as likely to swing her stern to port as she was to starboard. I could not even pull forward or aft out of his way. In the present wind I was stuck. Heinrich begged to differ. To prove his point, he produced an enormously long wooden pole, told me to let loose the stern warp, placed his pole against Margo's stern and pushed while his crew held the bow warp tight. At Heinrich's cry of 'Los!' I threw the engine astern, the bow warp was thrown onto the foredeck and Margo raced astern until the wind took charge and swung her round until we were pointing down the channel. I waved to the shorebound onlookers and did my best to give the impression that I had been in control of proceedings.

STEP TWO – PILOTAGE

Pilotage begins once you are clear of your berth. Pilotage is the art of guiding a vessel by day or night by the use of visual features. If you like, pilotage is nautical map reading. The choice of which geographic features to include on a chart is determined partly by the scale of the chart and partly by the hydrographer's opinion of its value to mariners (meaning commercial shipping). Often a land survey chart – such as those produced by the Ordnance Survey, showing features onshore that are not sufficiently important to appear on the chart – is a useful supplement to your nautical chart.

VISUAL REFERENCES

During the pilotage stage, anything you see is a navigational aid. By using a mixture of transits, clearing, cross and back bearings to confirm your position, you are guided safely out of, or into, harbour. Some of the transits and other features you use may appear on the charts as lines with bearings written on them; the rest are those you picked out and used on the spur of the moment.

What features you can see and use depend on whether you are entering (or leaving) in daylight or at night.

In daylight

- Natural geographic features such as cliffs, rocks, beaches, hills, valleys and other landforms including islands, islets and unmarked but charted rocks. For example, if you are sailing along the south coast between Anvil Point and Weymouth looking for Lulworth Cove, the shape of the rock strata around the entrance to the cove is a good signpost.
- Man-made nautical features, including seamarks (such as buoys, beacons and other marks such as withies) and light vessels; and landmarks such as lighthouses and leading marks, piers and jetties. The great value of man-made nautical features is that they have been put there to mark channels, hazards and other features.
- Man-made non-nautical features including conspicuous buildings, high antenna, and roads. To be of use, these have to be on the chart or included in your pilotage sketch map.

At night

- Man-made nautical features such as lighthouses, lit buoyage, leading lights and all other lit seamarks.
- Offshore anchorages outside harbours. Although deck and other working lights on ships may make it difficult to find anchor lights, it is impossible to miss the anchorages like those off the Humber or Tees Bay.
- Man-made lit features such as habitation, lit buildings, high antenna with red aircraft warning lights, working lights and fixed and mobile lights on jetties and wharves. If, for example, you are sailing down the Weser to Bremerhaven at night, the Wilhelm Kaisen container terminal is not just a mass of lights, it is a mass of flashing yellow lights that appear to scurry aimlessly around. When you are closer, they are revealed as the warning beacons on the tractors ferrying the containers from shore to ship.
- The ship's compass to confirm that you are pointing in the correct direction.

It is easy to lose a sense of perspective at night. A bright light, which the chart tells you is several miles away, can look as close as a weak light less than a mile distant. Shadows look like breakwaters where none appear on the chart or make breakwaters look like open water. Looking for one light, it is easy to mistake a distant light of the same characteristic for the much nearer light that you want. Being spatially aware and staying orientated at night is hard work.

Although soundings are not, strictly speaking, a visual feature, depths from an echo sounder, or more rarely nowadays, a lead line, corrected for height of tide, can be an important feature of pilotage.

Provided you are using up to date information, you can prepare your notes on pilotage for entering and leaving harbour before your departure with a high degree of confidence.

USING PLOTTERS FOR PILOTAGE

Plotters, besides encouraging idleness, promote a tendency to treat pilotage as another redundant skill, for plotters see pilotage as no different from any other part of your passage. Just enter the necessary waypoints and follow the flashing dot. This overlooks the difference between pilotage and passage navigation. In pilotage there is no scope for error. At sea, drifting off course by a few degrees usually carries no penalty, apart from adding a few minutes to your passage time. During pilotage, the same error can put you aground before you are aware you are off course.

ENTERING ST ABBS

Entering St Abbs Harbour, just south of the Firth of Forth, you bring the west pier end into line with the apex of the lifeboat house roof and slide between rocks that come too close for the plotter to resolve. Even if it could, by the time you have consulted the plotter and changed course you would be on the rocks.

St Abbs Harbour in Scotland disproves the idea that you can enter any harbour blindfold as long as you have GPS. Always prepare your entry pilotage so you can navigate by Mark I eyeball

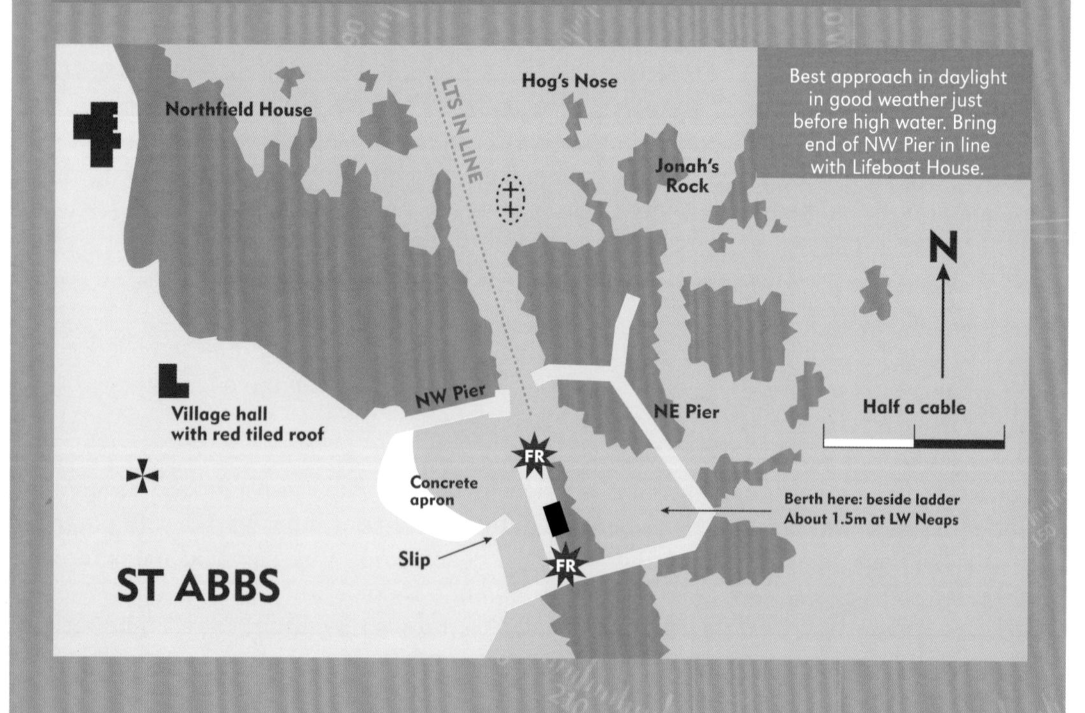

The other great advantage of pilotage notes is that they give an overview and let you know what comes next without the effort of flicking through the pilot book. This is particularly valuable after a long hard passage when you are not at your brightest and the information you need is scattered between the plotter, pilot book and almanac.

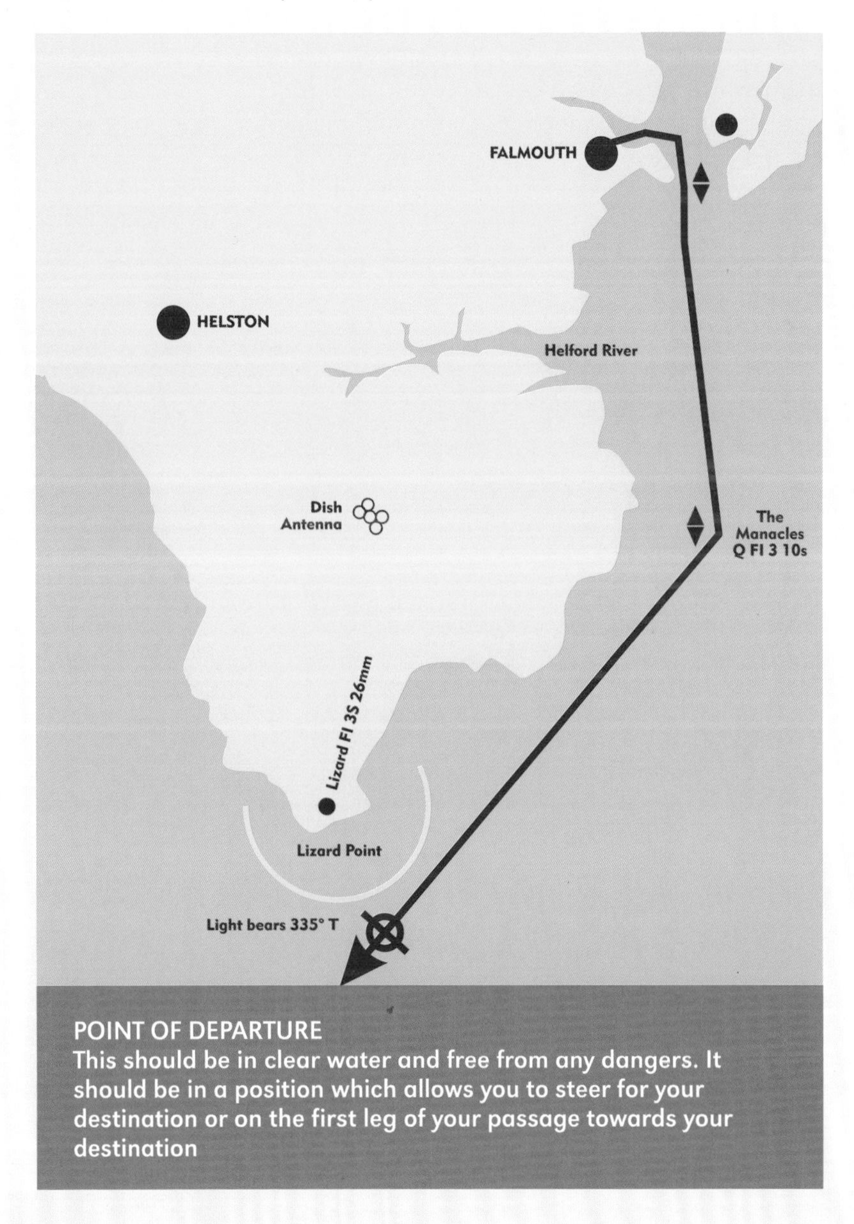

POINT OF DEPARTURE

Pilotage continues until you reach your point of departure. This is a position clear of all the channels and hazards, where you can either lay a course directly towards your destination or begin the first leg of your passage towards your destination. If, for example, you are in Falmouth and making for the Isles of Scilly or La Coruña in north-west Spain, a good point of departure would be somewhere to the south of Lizard Point. If you were making for Guernsey in the Channel Islands, your point of departure would be roughly abeam the Helford River.

STEP THREE – EXAMINATION OF ALL POSSIBLE ROUTES

Passage navigation is where most work is done and most information is required. There is nearly always more than one route to your destination and by dry sailing the various options, you can decide which you believe best suits you.

If you were sailing from Falmouth to La Coruña then, from your point of departure south of the Lizard, it is possible to lay a course directly for La Coruña. Dry sailing this route reveals that it is 410 nautical miles, on a course of south-south-west. Sailing in May, the winds ought to be north-westerly around Beaufort force 4 and there is a south-easterly current of around half a knot. For most yachts, this passage would take around three to four days.

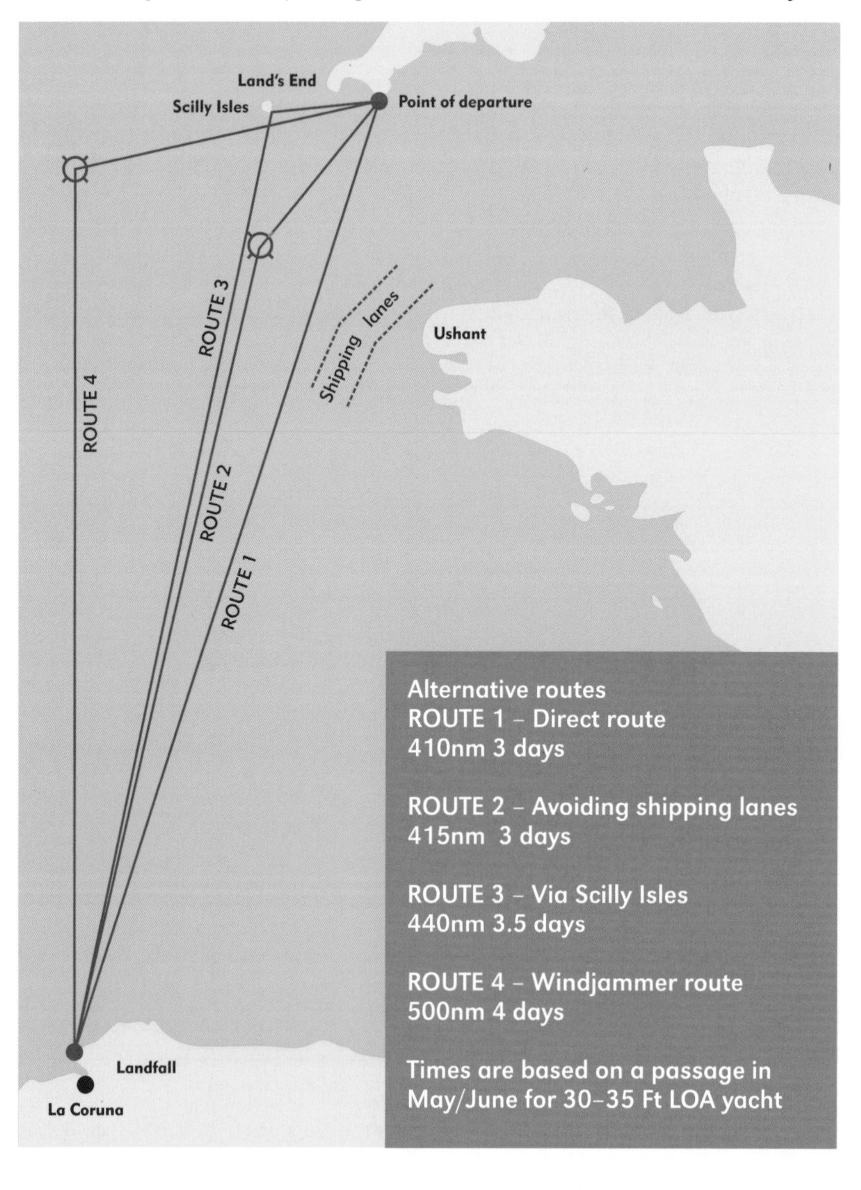

The catch is that this route takes you very close to the shipping lanes off Ushant and if your expected force 4 perked up, you could find yourself in strong winds either on a lee shore off Ushant or being pushed into the Bay of Biscay. Perhaps it would be better, therefore, to give Ushant a wider berth. This can be done in one of three ways. You could sail the 45 miles west to St Mary's in the Isles of Scilly and take your departure from there for a passage to La Coruña. You could insert a waypoint a decent distance off Ushant and steer for that from your point of departure, only altering course for La Coruña when you reach it (this brings you more onto the wind, which is no great problem if it is north-westerly but could be a difficulty if it swings round to the south-west). Lastly, you could follow the advice of the old square riggers who, when they left Falmouth, sailed west until La Coruña bore south and then changed course, which would be no hardship whether the winds were north-west or south-westerly. It removes any chance of sailing too close to Ushant or being pushed into the Bay of Biscay. On the other side of the balance sheet, it adds 80 to 100 miles and at least a day to your passage.

None of these four routes is wrong. All bring you to La Coruña. The option you choose must be the one that gives you the greatest confidence of a good passage.

For every passage you must identify every hazard and limitation along each of your possible routes, including tide races, overfalls, tidal gates, shallows and rocks, and see what effect they have upon your passage along this route. You must also prepare a list of all visual navigational aids along each possible route. This includes buoyage, lights, geographic features and conspicuous landmarks. The information you need to note includes their appearance, characteristics of lights and geographic position.

STEP FOUR – EXAMINATION OF ALL POSSIBLE ALTERNATIVE PORTS

The term 'port of refuge' implies that something untoward has occurred, that you have abandoned hope of reaching your planned destination and are seeking sanctuary in some other harbour or anchorage. I prefer to regard ports of refuge as alternative destinations along your route that you may enter depending on either circumstances or inclination.

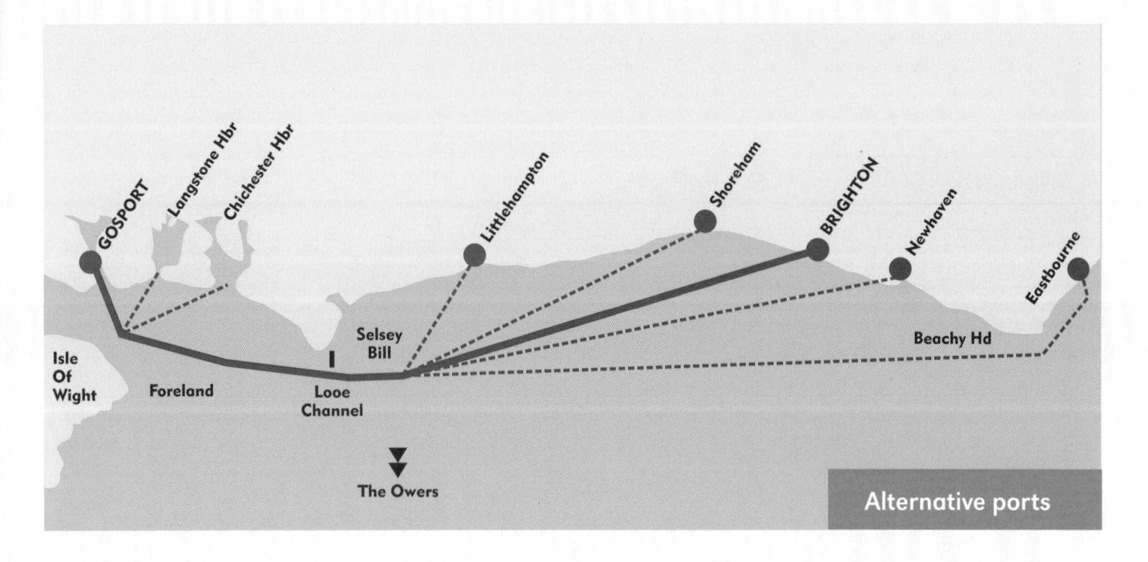

Alternative ports

If you are making a passage between the Solent and Dover and your first day's sail is from Portsmouth to Brighton Marina, there is a long list of ports you could choose to enter. If you are taking the Looe Channel and miss the tide, or if the weather is not as expected, there is a choice of Langstone or Chichester harbours where you could find either a marina or anchorage to wait for a fair tide or better weather. This is an example of choosing to enter an alternative port as a result of something untoward occurring.

Once round Selsey Bill, you pass Littlehampton and Shoreham before reaching Brighton Marina, and if the wind was favourable and progress better than expected then 7 miles beyond Brighton is Newhaven. If all was going very well, you might consider adding another 18 miles, round Beachy Head, and drop into Eastbourne's Sovereign Marina. These are examples of entering alternative ports as a result of events going in your favour.

For each alternative port you must choose a landfall and complete the arrival pilotage and berthing planning to the same detail as your chosen destination. It is not enough to note alternative harbours as possibilities. If conditions are unkind, you do not want to be rushing down a strange channel at night crying 'Hang on a moment' when the helmsman asks for a course to steer.

LANDFALL

Landfalls should be chosen so that you can immediately start using visual features to confirm your electronic navigation. It helps if your landfall is unmistakable. There is a tendency to see what you expect to see and then adjust the rest of the world that happens to be in view to fit. If you are waiting for a tall conspicuous tower to come over the horizon, any feature over 10ft (3m) high becomes a conspicuous tower and you begin constructing a virtual world in which everything is as you expected to see it.

Your entry pilotage starts at your landfall, which should be distinctive and unmissable

Buoys are popular landfalls. Often they are safe water buoys close to the entrance of the channels that lead to harbour. The Needles buoy off the west end of the Isle of Wight is a good example. All along the Dutch and German coasts are landfall buoys marking the start of the safe channel between each pair of islands. Just because a buoy pops up on time, more or less where you expected to see it, does not mean it is the correct buoy. If you can, sail close enough to read its name.

Geographic features are first-rate landfalls. Headlands and high, mountainous islands are good examples. To be sure you have the right island or headland, it helps to have a picture. Pilot books often include photographs or drawings of popular landfalls. Failing that, try Google or Google Earth. If you Google Lizard Point, Start Point, Anvil Head, Flamborough Head, Cape Wrath or even Cape Horn you are offered a choice from hundreds of images that you can download and include in your notes.

If your destination is a low island that is part of a chain or archipelago, give yourself the best possible chance of making a good landfall by aiming for the widest part of the chain or archipelago. When you have found that, head for your landfall on your chosen island.

At night, lights make a good landfall. This means knowing the characteristic of the light you are expecting to see and those of any near by. Timing the characteristic of a light can

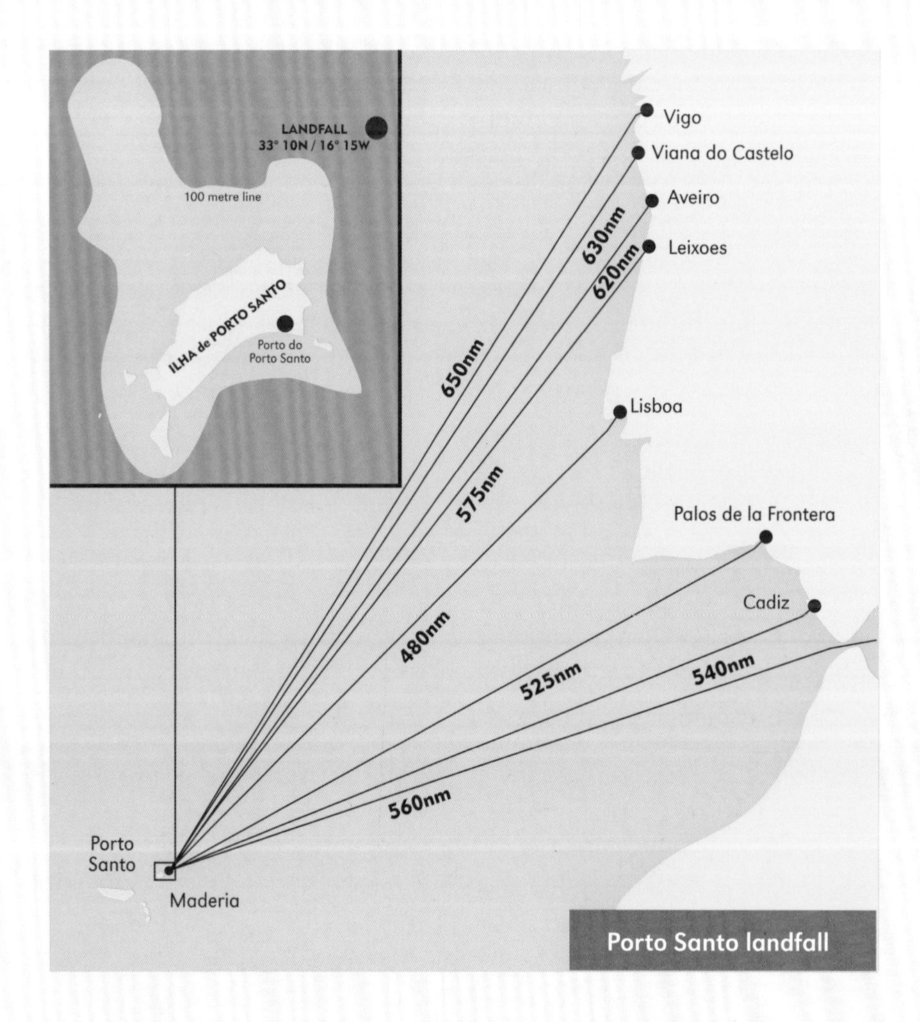

Porto Santo landfall

be difficult if there is a sea running and it may take several minutes before you are satisfied that you have correctly identified a light. Using a stopwatch rather than counting 'One and a two and a three...' can help. In decent visibility, the loom of a lighthouse can be picked up long before the light itself and a landfall buoy is usually seen around 3 or 4 miles away. The loom from the streetlights of towns and ports can be picked up 10 or 15 miles away but beware, a low cloud base can make a small village look like a city. Flashing lights are easier to pick up among shore lights than occulting lights, which disappear into the street lighting. Trying to pick up a light that goes out now and then among a line of similar lights can be a frustrating experience.

At night, aircraft can help confirm your position. Barbados is a low hump easily mistaken at a distance for a swell. I knew I was close. That morning I had listened to Radio Barbados traffic reports; but the sun dropped over the horizon without land coming into sight. A light zoomed across the sky. It had to be a satellite. Tropical skies are so clear that it was unmissable. Then it turned, began retracing its steps, and disappeared. Satellites do not behave this way. Another light appeared, turned back on itself and disappeared. Aliens? Then the penny dropped. I was looking at the landing lights of aircraft heading for Grantley Adams Airport at the south end of Barbados. This was where I was headed. My landfall, Needham's Point, is just south of the airfield. I could not see Needham's Point or its light but I could now confidently point to it and altered course accordingly. Similarly, if you are heading for Howth on Ireland's east coast then, when you are coming abeam the harbour, the landing lights of aircraft heading for Dublin airport form a near unbroken chain overhead. It is almost as good as leading lights.

Good landfalls are popular. This should not be a shock. You chose that particular landfall because you reckoned it gave you the best and easiest lead-in to port. Why be surprised when everyone else makes the same choice? Porto Santo at the west end of the Madeira archipelago is a good example. The island rises sheer out of the sea. Soundings drop from over 1,000m to less than 100m in a matter of yards. After a lonely journey from various points on the Iberian Peninsula, the western corner of Porto Santo resembles Piccadilly Circus as boats from Spain, Portugal, North Africa and the Mediterranean make their landfall before heading for the harbour.

During the summer in popular sailing areas, especially at weekends, fleets of dinghies off harbours and marinas are as good as a signpost pointing towards the harbour entrance.

DISTANCE OFF

When making a landfall it helps to know how far off you can expect to first sight a light, a hill or a headland. This involves doing a couple of simple sums to calculate the distance off. The first sum is the distance from your boat to the horizon and the second is from the feature to its horizon. Adding the two answers together gives the distance off.

The formula used to calculate distance to the horizon depends on whether you are measuring the height of the feature, or the height of your eye, in feet or metres.

Distance to horizon in nautical miles = 1.17 x the square root of height (in feet)
Distance to horizon in nautical miles = 2.12 x the square root of height (in metres)

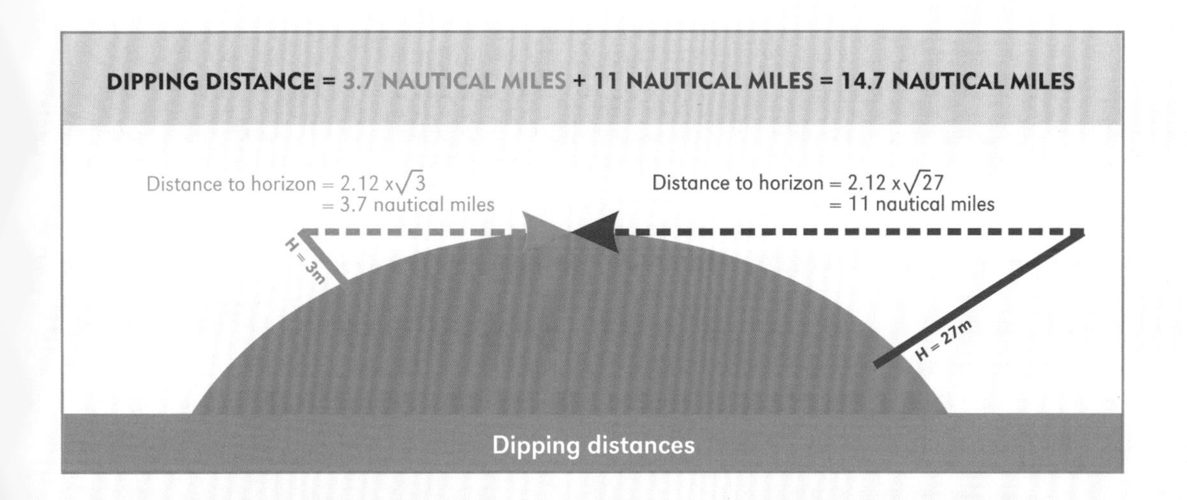

Dipping distances

DISTANCE TO HORIZON

When your brain is mush and there is no calculator to hand then this table gives the distance to the horizon for a range of heights. Even if you have to interpolate the answer is normally good enough to be used with confidence.

Height in feet	Distance to horizon (nautical miles)	Height in metres	Distance to horizon (nautical miles)
1	1.2	1	2.1
2	1.7	2	3.0
3	2.0	3	3.7
4	2.3	4	4.2
5	2.6	5	4.7
6	2.9	6	5.2
7	3.1	7	5.6
8	3.3	8	6.0
9	3.5	9	6.4
10	3.7	10	6.7
15	4.5	15	8.2
20	5.2	20	9.5
30	6.4	30	11.6
40	7.4	40	13.4
50	8.3	50	15.0
60	9.1	60	16.4
70	9.8	70	17.7

80	10.5	80	19.0
90	11.1	90	20.1
100	11.7	100	21.2

ARRIVAL PILOTAGE

Entering an unfamiliar port or anchorage is easiest in daylight. Traditionally, arrivals were arranged so that the coast was approached during the last of the night when lights were easily identified and provided a fix. As the sun rose, the harbour was entered in daylight when you could see where you were going. Even with the assistance of electronic navigation, this remains good practice. Resolving doubts and uncertainties is far easier in daylight than at night.

If you intend to anchor in a drying channel, put out a kedge to make sure you stay in the channel. These boats did not, and very strong winds and exceptionally high tides took them far out of the channel, leaving them with the challenge of getting their boats back into the channel before the tides returned to their normal heights

BERTHING

Wind and tide can make entering your usual berth a challenge and an unfamiliar berth a nightmare. Entering a strange harbour must be done with care, unless you know exactly where you are to berth and how to get there.

Accustomed to sailing singlehanded, I make a practice of entering any harbour with warps and fenders rigged port and starboard, with the warps led back to the cockpit where they are instantly to hand. I know from bitter experience that it is impossible for me to approach a berth, rigged only for portside-to, then to suddenly change my mind without coming close to either farce or disaster. It is also good practice for crewed boats to have warps and fenders ready port and starboard so that, if plans fall apart, they can enter some other berth as though they meant to all the time; but it is surprising how often crewed boats enter harbour working on the principle that weight of numbers compensates for lack of preparation.

It is sensible to prepare for going alongside in clear water rather than leaving putting out fenders and preparing warps as you enter your berth. It is also good practice to enter as slowly as conditions permit. This is not the same as going slowly. In blustery, blowy conditions with fast tides, it may be necessary to enter a berth rather quickly to maintain a decent level of control.

COLLISION AVOIDED

I was lying on a pontoon berth on the island of Kerrera, opposite Oban, when a lovely wooden boat turned to take the berth upwind of mine. Apart from the skipper it had a crew of three or four, all standing on deck. One held a warp, another a fender. They were all chatting. The skipper brought his boat neatly alongside the pontoon. A crew member clambered over the rail, jumped onto the pontoon, ran forward with the bow warp, hooked the rope under a cleat and hauled on it as hard as he could. This pulled the bows into the pontoon, which encouraged the wind to blow the stern onto my boat. Another crew member ran forward and held the fender over the bows.

The skipper reacted smartly. Seeing the danger of collision, he snatched up a boathook, similar if not identical to the pikes Cromwell issued to his Roundheads, drove its point into my rubbing strake and threw his weight on it to hold the boats apart. The fact that the boathook was so readily to hand and the speed of his response suggested that this was not the first time it had been put to this use.

I had a mental image of his weapon splitting the wood of my rubbing strake and then driving through my hull. His crew obviously did not share my concerns. They continued their conversation as though all was well. To be fair, the skipper displayed admirable restraint. He did not panic or, as I would have done, bawled at his crew. He just threw more weight onto his pike. I inserted a couple of fenders between our boats and suggested that it would help if they took a stern warp ashore. The skipper agreed, laid his boathook on deck, opened a cockpit locker and began searching for a line that he could use as a stern warp. I rigged more fenders and kept an eye on the boathook.

If in doubt about which berth to use, go onto the first and easiest berth you see, then find the harbourmaster and sort out a more suitable berth.

LEFT: Pilots and charts often include small chartlets showing the layout of the pontoons in a marina. The reality, particularly in busy harbours, may be quite different

RIGHT: Just because you are entering a marina, do not assume there is no tidal stream or that it will be minimal and can be ignored

19 ROUTINES AND DAILY CHECKS

We sail declaring our independence from the petty restrictions and needless bureaucracy of everyday life, only to learn that the sea is an implacable master with unchanging laws and disciplines that those who enter its domains must follow.

It is trite to say that on long passages your boat is where you live and work twenty-four hours a day, seven days a week. Once at sea, if we do not quickly establish some form of routine to give each day its shape and rhythm then onboard life with everyone doing their own thing, in their own way, as the inclination takes them, becomes first unbearable and then dangerous. Without routines there is a lack of accountability. Too much is left undone and what work is done is to no particular standard.

As skipper, it is your job to introduce routines that fairly share out the work arising from making a safe and seamanlike passage and see this work is carried out in a timely manner and to an acceptable standard. It sounds like a return to shoreside rules but it is not. At sea, rules are not about hammering square pegs into round holes. They are there to make sailing easy. Save for an 'All Hands' call, a good sea routine creates a structure that allows individuals the freedom to do their own thing in their off-watch time. It allows them a personal breathing space that gives them a life of their own outside of the demands of sailing the boat and permits them to make a distinction between work and play.

Additionally, routines keep the boat clean and tidy, and a tidy boat, if not actually creating space, gives the illusion of space. This is important. At sea, four or more people inhabit a space that even the most imaginative, elastic-minded estate agent would be hard pressed to describe as a large dog kennel. Without the discipline of a routine, privacy, always scarce, becomes non-existent. Everyone falls over and falls out with everyone else.

Independence is sometimes confused with anarchy. Both in their own way idealise freedom from direct rule and promote voluntary and cooperative associations between individuals. This may look like teamwork but it is not. It overlooks that the sea is an absolute dictator. If you are to have a safe and happy passage, even the most independent of anarchists must live and work together within the ship's rules and routines. There is nothing voluntary about it.

Singlehanders have only themselves to consider but even they need the discipline of routine to rouse them from their bunk and make sure that every day the day's work is done.

If out for the day, the need for sea routines is limited. You are not living in each other's pocket. Meals are optional, often no more than coffee and sandwiches. In a few hours you are ashore and either sharing a pint in the club bar or going your separate ways. Several days, perhaps a week or more, pass before you go to sea again, and during that time any niggles that may have surfaced at sea have time to shrink into proportion and be forgotten. For day sails there is less need for daily checks on the boat's condition. They become occasional inspections that can be completed in harbour and any maintenance requirements they reveal can be carried out at some convenient time.

On day sails longer than about twelve hours, overnight passages and the passages that make up your summer cruise, the need for sea routines grows. On these longer passages you will probably share the work of sailing the boat by running some sort of watch system. As time at sea increases, the need for regular hot meals moves up scale from being optional to desirable and finally, essential. At the same time, the longer you are away from your home port, the greater the need for frequent checks to satisfy yourself your boat is still sound and seaworthy. On ocean passages the need for good sea routines is absolute.

Carrying out daily checks and insisting that the boat is kept clean and tidy may at first look like small-minded petty bureaucracy in action, but this deck is so cluttered with unnecessary junk that in an emergency at night it could put the crew at risk

The simplest way of making a start is to organise your sea routine around mealtimes. Food is important. It is the fuel that provides the energy to work the boat. Eating breakfast, lunch and dinner together means everyone dines regularly in a social situation. If you are working a watch system, especially a watch and watch system, then consider scheduling meals around the change of watch. The watch off prepares the meal, eats and goes on watch while those who were on watch come below, eat and wash up. If your watch system rotates watches, it is a fair division of labour: one day a watch cooks and the next it washes up. There are other options on scheduling meals but whichever you chose there are two implacable rules: stick to the advertised mealtimes and make sure that meals are served on time.

DAILY CHECKS

On longer passages, some form of daily check of the boat's condition is essential. The sea is a harsh environment. If something can corrode, then it will. Unceasing motion carries the promise of chafe. If you do not watch for it and stop it before it happens, halyards fray and holes appear in the sails.

You must keep a record of fuel and water consumption to make sure you are staying within bounds; grease everything that should be greased; clean the bilges; tighten anything that may have worked loose; replace filters as necessary and service equipment on schedule. Decks must be washed, standing and running rigging checked, and cabins, bunks and lockers cleaned and tidied.

In addition, you must keep the inventories up to date, make sure that navigation lights are working and all emergency equipment is ready to hand, and there are the radio, engine and battery checks to be carried out. Weather forecasts must be checked, logs written and a plot kept up to date. Traditionally, logbooks are written up at the change of a watch.

It is best to carry out these checks during the morning watch. Shared out among the crew, they should not take too much time. It is important that they are carried out every day. Just because a piece of equipment worked yesterday does not mean it will work tomorrow, when it may be desperately needed. You must also make sure that any repairs or maintenance these checks throw up that can be carried out at sea are carried out promptly.

None of this happens by accident. Leaving your crew to carry out what checks they think are necessary as and when they find convenient will not work. However eager or conscientious they may be, some item will be skimped, missed or disappear from the list and remain forgotten until it demands your full attention when least expected. Checks must be a formal part of the ship's routine.

The detail of the daily checks varies from boat to boat. There can be no set pro forma, only guidelines. It is a good idea to write up your own daily checks as part of your onshore planning. Write them so they reflect the areas of responsibility you plan to give to each member of crew. Have printouts of your checks laminated and keep them in a folder. Each crew member then removes the appropriate checklist from the folder and carries out their daily checks, ticking off each point using a chinagraph or greaseproof pencil. When their checks are complete, they transfer any notes to the logbook, inventory or defects book as appropriate. They then wipe the laminated checklist clean and return it to the folder ready for tomorrow's check.

HARBOUR ROUTINE

Life in harbour is different from life on passage. Harbour duties revolve around maintenance, resupply (fuel, water and rations), and keeping the boat clean and tidy. Below deck is often reorganised to provide more living space and in warm climes an awning and table can turn the cockpit into a living-cum-dining room. If you are safely berthed on a pontoon, and provided all commitments to the boat are met, there is no reason why everyone cannot go ashore and explore.

If you are berthed against the harbour wall, your harbour routine depends on the type of harbour. If it is primarily used by leisure craft or you are berthed in an area designated for leisure craft, you need to:

- make sure you are safe from waves, swell and the wash from passing boats
- make sure you are berthed close to a ladder so as to be able to climb ashore
- tend your shore lines as the tide rises and falls
- if the harbour dries, make sure your boat will not fall over
- make sure you do not berth outside a small boat or allow a larger boat to berth outside you

If you are berthed on the wall in a fishing harbour, life can be more problematical. Local fishermen claiming squatters' rights sometimes feel free to move your boat to suit their convenience whether or not you are aboard. Sometimes this does not matter; other times they leave your boat in a vulnerable and dangerous position.

ANCHOR ROUTINE

Dropping the hook for a lunchtime snack in the cockpit is one thing. If the wind perks up or the anchor begins to drag, you can quickly abandon your picnic, recover the anchor and return to the business of sailing. Anchoring overnight or for longer is another matter. Keeping an anchor watch for the occasional overnight stay is no hardship. Everyone takes their turn standing watch for an hour or two in the cockpit, noting the anchor bearings in the log every half hour.

If you are staying in an anchorage for several days or even weeks, standing anchor watches can become something of an imposition, especially if after a couple of days it is obvious the anchor is dug in and without some change in the weather your boat is going nowhere. The reality is that in blue water anchorages it is rare for anchor watches to be kept as a matter of course. The confidence to do this comes from using heavier than recommended anchors and putting out plenty of anchor rode (this does not mean you should not each day periodically check your anchor bearings to reassure yourself all is well so you can sleep soundly that night). This also gives you the confidence to go ashore, leaving your boat alone on its anchor. This can only be done when you are absolutely sure there is no possibility of the anchor dragging and that during your time ashore conditions will not change to put your boat at risk. If there is any possibility of this happening, at least one person who is competent to recover the anchor and handle the boat under power must remain aboard. There must also be a communications link between those left on board and those ashore. This can range from the frantic waving of arms, through cellphones, to keeping a radio watch on an agreed VHF channel. These links are useful not only in an emergency but also to coordinate the dinghy taxi service between the boat and the shore.

As part of your anchor routine, give some thought to dinghy security, both when it is hanging off the stern of your anchored boat and when you take it ashore. A useful rule is to make whoever takes charge of the dinghy for its trips between boat and shore responsible for its security and cleanliness. This means:

- if the dinghy is tied to the boat, it is securely tied with the paddles brought onto the boat
- if the dinghy is ashore, it is securely berthed with the paddles secure
- if the dinghy is carried ashore, it is stowed safe from curious children and passers-by

If you have an outboard engine, consider its security and the safe stowage of its fuel.

20 SAFETY AT SEA

Sailing is one of those activities where however careful your planning and preparation, or whatever steps you take to make your passage as safe as possible, there is always an element of risk outside of your control. Sailing is not a safe activity. You do not rule the waves and there will always be unforeseen and unexpected events coming out of left field that place you and your crew at risk.

Safety at sea is all about risk management or the art of looking deep into the dark side and arranging the risks you find in ascending shades of grey; the darkest, blackest greys with the most serious consequences are at the top and the lightest and least worrisome at the bottom. Conventional risk management wisdom says that your attention and resources should be concentrated on minimising those grave risks that carry the most serious consequences. These are risks that present an immediate risk to life and include sinking, stranding, fire and explosion, and man overboard. Close on their heels follow serious non-fatal risks, including personal injury, medical emergency and gear failure. Given the least encouragement, any in this second class of risk could easily escalate into something more serious very quickly.

Fortunately, great risks are show-offs. They approach drums beating, bugles blowing and flags flying, advertising their presence and drawing attention to themselves. They are not kidding. They are dangerous but their high profile, attention seeking behaviour means that everyone is aware of these risks and deals with them accordingly. It usually takes no more than common sense. Nobody should need to be told not to look for a gas leak with a lighted match.

It is not just for this reason that it is unwise to focus all your attention on the most serious risks. Most great disasters come not from a single catastrophic risk but frequently from small, overlooked events that are the forerunners of an armada of trivial mishaps. Individually, none of these is particularly important and each is easily dealt with in isolation; but en masse their very insignificance makes it impossible to prioritise them and direct resources to where they are most needed. Ultimately, they overwhelm whatever resources you have available. Hindsight inevitably reveals what you ought to have done but has to wait for the enquiry. You must develop the habit of picking up on small mishaps as soon as they appear and crushing them before they can grow into disaster.

MAN OVERBOARD

One of the most important rules regarding safety at sea is that no one should leave the boat before it is safely berthed. Anyone going overboard at sea and being left astern, as they invariably are, is a very poor insurance risk. For this reason, have a rule that says everyone on deck must always wear a harness and always be clipped onto a strong point or jackstay. Having made this rule, enforce it. In rough seas and strong winds, everyone sees its wisdom; but in pleasanter conditions, clipping your harness in and out every time you move around the deck becomes a chore and wearing it an inconvenience. That is, until the moment, one quiet dark night, when someone who should be wearing a harness and clipped in, but is not, stumbles when the boat lurches and dives overboard. The main gybes, the gooseneck breaks, the boom drops and clouts the helmsman on the head. There is confusion in the cockpit, frantic questions from the cabin, the clip holding the lifebuoy in place has seized and will not come undone. The batteries on the lifebuoy's floating light have corroded. The engine will not start. And it had been going so well.

Man overboard drills should begin by walking through them when you are alongside in harbour, then going out to sea in kind conditions and practising them with a fender or lifebuoy representing the man overboard. At first this should be carried out slowly, about the same rate as the harbour walk through drill. As your crew's proficiency improves, the drill can be speeded up with unexpected variations thrown in as their confidence increases.

All drills, whether anchoring, sail changing, reefing, ropework or whatever, should always be taught in three simple steps:

1. demonstrate: you show the crew what has to be done. Repeat this step until everyone understands
2. imitate: have the crew copy what you have demonstrated until they have it right
3. practise: and practise and practise again until it has become second nature and your crew is a slick, well-oiled team

GEAR FAILURE

The risks of gear failure are much reduced by thorough pre-sail checks followed by daily checks at sea and carrying out any remedial work these checks reveal. The most likely areas for gear failure are:

1 MAST AND RIGGING

Once at sea, the daily checks should highlight areas of possible failure and encourage early repairs. If there is a critical failure, such as the mast breaking, try to salvage as much of the gear as possible to help the construction of a jury rig that enables you to sail to safety.

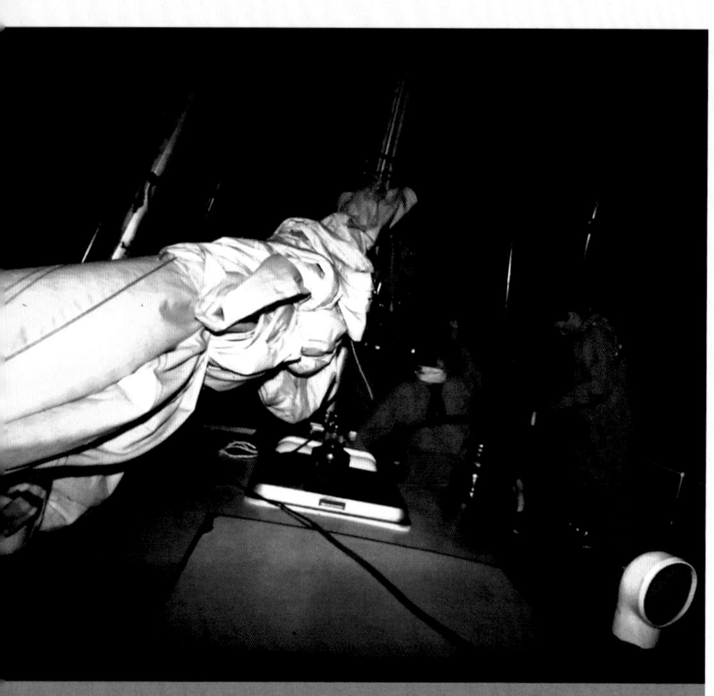

A broken mast in the small hours of the morning is no fun. It took an hour to tame failing rigging and broken halyards and make it possible for the crew to work safely on tidying up and securing the mess. Note that everyone on deck is wearing a harness and is clipped in. With lines in the water, we were powerless to recover anyone who went over the wall

2 SELF-STEERING

On lightly crewed boats on long voyages, the loss of the self-steering can mean long hours on the helm if some alternative cannot be jury rigged.

3 MECHANICAL (probably the engine or a generator)

The loss of the engine or a generator on a yacht should be more of an inconvenience than a problem. It almost certainly means rationing electrical power and switching off many electrical devices so that alternative generators, such as solar or wind generators, can keep a decent charge in the batteries. The question of power becomes more critical if frozen food makes up a significant proportion of your food supplies and your alternative power generators cannot meet the freezer's demands.

4 ELECTRICAL

On a yacht it should be possible to continue on passage even after a complete electrical failure. It does mean a return to navigating by paper and pencil, keeping a good lookout at night with the steamer-scarer handy and being miserly with torchlight below decks; but none of this should present insurmountable difficulties.

ABANDON SHIP

Just as with the man overboard drills, the abandoned ship drills should be practised until they are almost instinctive. Everybody must know how they are to leave the boat and what they are to take with them apart from their personal grab bag. This includes the ship's grab bag and additional food and water.

Until the 1990s, when EPIRBs became commonplace on leisure craft, stepping into the liferaft meant making whatever supplies you had of food and water last until you were picked up. Being picked up was largely a matter of chance and flares were the principal means of attracting the attention of other vessels. On long ocean passages there was a strong argument in favour of having a lifeboat, however small, that allowed you to make your own way to safety rather than drifting about in a liferaft waiting for rescue.

Modern communications have changed everything. A GPS enabled EPIRB will give the rescue authorities your position to within a few metres and in coastal and offshore waters bring rescue within 24 hours. The surest means of attracting the attention of passing vessels and informing them of your situation is not flares but a combination of a handheld GPS and handheld VHF. It is important that your emergency communications are in keeping with the nature of your passage. For coastal and offshore passages a GPS enabled EPIRB and handheld GPS and handheld VHF are probably sufficient. For longer passages, adding a handheld satellite telephone allows real time two-way communication with the rescue authorities.

You should also give some thought to how you keep this electronic equipment fully charged while waiting for rescue. A small solar panel might be the answer.

FIRE

NO SMOKE WITHOUT FIRE

The engine was charging the batteries somewhere between Las Palmas and Barbados when I saw smoke coming out of the engine compartment. Close to panic I stopped the engine, shut off the fuel and, clutching a fire extinguisher, nervously opened up the engine compartment. I could see no flames. Once the smoke cleared I discovered that a fault on the alternator's super clever regulator had caused it to overheat and the fan belt had begun melting. My first reaction on discovering this was a sense of enormous relief.

Fire at sea is always serious. The most likely causes are carelessness, an unnoticed gas leak or an electrical fault. Carelessness is best tackled by making your crew aware of the dangers of fire and insisting those who smoke do so only on deck. The risk of gas leaks is greatly reduced by having a sound gas installation, insisting that when gas is not being used it is turned off at the bottle, and whoever lights the stove is responsible for seeing that it stays alight and is turned off after use. A gas alarm is a sensible safety measure.

As part of your pre-sail drills, make sure that everyone on board knows the locations of every fire extinguisher and fire blanket and how to use them.

PERSONAL PROTECTION

Checking up on personal equipment can demand diplomacy. You know that a long-term crew member has been faithful to one set of oilskins for twenty years, treasures a decaying lifejacket, and does not believe in harnesses. Somehow they must be convinced that an upgrade is necessary.

The aim of personal protection is to keep all aboard:

• WARM AND DRY

This means being dressed appropriately for the conditions on deck. Keeping warm requires sufficient layers of the correct type of clothing and staying dry needs good quality oilskins and sea boots.

• ATTACHED TO THE BOAT

Every crew member must have a harness fitted to them, with a tether fitted with snap hooks at each end. These snap hooks, or karabiners, must have a positive locking device that prevents them from accidentally coming undone. Many lifejackets double as a harness. If a harness is worn separately from a lifejacket, is should be compatible with the crew member's lifejacket.

AFLOAT

Should anyone part company with the boat, it is important that they remain afloat until they are rescued. Do not expect them to swim or to reach any floatation device such as a lifebelt. Every crew member should have a properly fitted lifejacket of at least 150N buoyancy, with a whistle, an automatic SOLAS white light with a working life of over eight hours, retro-reflective material, and a crotch strap or thigh straps. The lifejacket should be marked with either the yacht's or the wearer's name. If it is an inflatable lifejacket using a compressed gas inflation system, this should be periodically checked to confirm that it is in working order and the lifejacket should, from time to time, be manually inflated and checked for air retention. A splashguard/spray hood is also recommended.

DRUNKEN SAILORS

Perhaps if there were regular 'Don't Drink and Sail' campaigns, backed up by random breath tests, we would be more aware of the dangers of mixing alcohol and sailing. In the USA, all forty-eight mainland states have a statutory BAC (blood alcohol concentration) of 0.8 per cent. Blood alcohol concentration or content is a measure of the amount of alcohol present in a certain amount of blood. It is usually described as the amount of alcohol in mg per 100ml of blood. The prescribed legal drink-driving limit in the UK is 80mg/100ml blood or 0.08 per cent.

It is reckoned that around 50–70 per cent of all boating fatalities in the USA involve alcohol and a study by the American Medical Association reported that a drunken passenger is just as likely to die as the skipper or a crew member. Only about 25 per cent of alcohol-related accidents and injuries involve collision between vessels. The remainder happen when people fall off the dock or pontoon into the water, or fall into the water when getting in or out of a dinghy, or fall overboard.

In the UK, drunken sailing is an offence and there is legislation on the books, but not yet brought into law, to introduce a BAC of 0.8 per cent. Statistics on drink and boating are held by the Marine Accident Investigation Branch (MAIB). These are very patchy but indicate a similar pattern to the USA. One significant difference is that in the UK almost 50 per cent of fatalities involve falls off pontoons and getting in and out of dinghies.

ALCOHOL: MYTH vs FACT

MYTH	FACT
Beer is less intoxicating than wine or spirits.	A 330ml can of beer contains as much alcohol as 200ml of wine or 25ml of spirits.
Diluting spirits with non-alcoholic drinks means your body absorbs the alcohol more slowly.	This is true for diluting spirits with water or fruit juice but diluting your gin or whisky with carbonated drinks increases the rate of absorption.

Drinking spirits warms you up.	When you are cold, the small blood vessels close to the skin contract to help maintain a warm core temperature. Drinking alcohol dilates these blood vessels and draws warm blood from the body's core. This can have the effect of creating a momentary feeling of warmth, but the now cold blood returning from these vessels to your body's core can dramatically, even fatally reduce your body's core temperature.
Alcohol is a stimulant and sharpens your senses.	Wrong. Alcohol is absorbed directly from your stomach into your bloodstream. As it circulates through your brain, it weakens body functions and learned restrictions on social behaviour, as well as almost immediately impairing vision, judgement, reaction time and balance. Alcohol is a depressant.
Cold showers, hot coffee and fresh air will sober you up.	Wrong. Only your liver can take the alcohol out of your body, at a rate of about two hours for each drink consumed. Showers, coffee and fresh air only produce a clean, wide-awake drunk.

ALCOHOL AND MAN OVERBOARD

Alcohol makes it much harder to control the involuntary gasping reflex that happens when your face or upper body is suddenly immersed in cold water. This makes it more likely you will inhale water if you suddenly plunge into cold water.

With your blood diluted by alcohol, your body's ability to protect you against cold is lowered. If you have been drinking and fall into the water, the numbing effects of the cold water take effect much quicker than if you had been sober. Within minutes you may be unable to call for help or swim to a lifebuoy, the dockside or the boat.

Some researchers believe that drinking alcohol increases susceptibility to inner ear disorientation, which can cause swimmers to swim down instead of up after they have fallen in.

ALCOHOL AND DECISION MAKING

Alcohol impairs your motor function, skews your judgement and degrades your decision-making ability. This is because alcohol lowers your ability to respond to several signals simultaneously. It takes longer to receive, process, and react to information from your eyes, ears and other senses. Your peripheral vision, focus and depth perception are degraded, making it harder to judge speed and distance, and your night vision is impaired.

There but for the grace of God go any one of us. Banning booze from boats is not practical. Regardless of the legal position and whether you enjoy a drink or are teetotal, as skipper it is your responsibility to know the dangers of mixing alcohol with boats and introduce a common-sense policy of moderation to keep you and your crew safe.

FATIGUE

We appear to have lost our forebears' ability to plod on regardless and endure the cold and wet. It is well recognised that three or four hours' (say one watch keeping period) exposure to wind, sun, glare, vibration and the general motion of the boat slows reaction times to a level where you would be banned from driving a car. A tired sailor is a danger to themselves and others. As skipper you have the task of:

- knowing what conditions cause fatigue
- dealing with the causes of fatigue
- recognising the signs of fatigue and treating it early

CONDITIONS THAT CAN CAUSE FATIGUE

Among the yachting fraternity there is a natural tendency to see fatigue as arising partly from the physical effort of sailing the boat in a variety of unpleasant conditions but primarily from staying on your feet for far too long. This is undeniable; but the wise skipper is also aware that fatigue can be caused by pre-existing medical conditions and other shoreside factors which, when at sea, bring on fatigue that much quicker.

It is estimated that one person in ten suffers from persistent tiredness and that it is more common in women than men. Some of the shoreside causes of fatigue are obvious. If there

SHORESIDE CAUSES OF FATIGUE

Few of us start a cruise fit, rested and raring to go. Last-minute preparations may have meant snatching rest when you could in the days preceding your departure. You may have flown thousands of miles to join the boat and are thoroughly jet lagged and needing several days to become acclimatised to the change from a British winter to tropical heat. You may have home or work worries gnawing away at your peace of mind.

All this, and more, is part of the personal baggage you take to sea. A well-run boat gives you time and space to catch up on your sleep and unwind, and a poorly run boat takes you to the edge and pushes you over. Other causes of onshore fatigue that a wise skipper, discreetly, checks out include:

- **anaemia**
- **bereavement**
- **boredom**
- **cancer**
- **chronic fatigue syndrome**
- **current illness**
- **depression**
- **diabetes**
- **divorce**
- **high metabolism**
- **infections, such as flu**
- **iron deficiency**
- **low metabolism**
- **moving home**
- **poisoning, particularly food poisoning from the local food in that quayside cafe**
- **pregnancy**
- **recent illness**
- **relationship problems**
- **vitamin or mineral deficiency**
- **work problems**

Being aware of such problems allows you to adjust your expectations from that crew member and helps avoid you adding to their woes.

has been a crew change and your new crew has flown several thousands of miles to join you, if you then rush them straight from the airport and out to sea do not be surprised if, for the first couple of days, they complain of being tired. If someone has just recovered from an illness or begins showing signs of illness, they are more susceptible to fatigue.

DEALING WITH THE CAUSES OF FATIGUE

There are three simple steps you as skipper can take if not to prevent fatigue, then at least to reduce the risk.

1. Ensure that all crew members have adequate rest. This sounds obvious, but on passages longer than a few hours it requires a watch system that gives everyone enough time off watch to rest properly and for you to make sure they take full advantage of this opportunity.
2. Crew members who are cold and wet tire quicker than those who keep themselves warm and dry. Macho sailors may like to enhance their reputation by claiming that cold is in the mind. There is no harm in them doing so – but only after you have insisted that they dress appropriately for the prevailing weather conditions.
3. Keep your crew's energy levels high with regular food and hot drinks.

ONBOARD CONDITIONS CAUSING FATIGUE

Any of the conditions listed below cause fatigue. As a rule of thumb, you can be tired or cold or wet and though you may not be at your brightest and best, you remain operational. A combination of any two of these conditions and you are useless. If you are cold, wet and tired then you are finished.

- **High winds and rough sea conditions.**
- **Rain, sleet and snow.**
- **Extreme hot or cold weather.**
- **Holding on and maintaining balance: bracing yourself or hanging on to a grab rail for hours on end is extremely tiring.**
- **Eye strain: staring into wind and spray is more than unpleasant – it is also tiring and saps morale.**
- **Stress and worry: concern over the boat's performance, decisions you have made and whether your performance is up to scratch can eat into your reserves of mental energy.**
- **Exposure to noise: the tiring effect of waves thumping into the boat and the wind whining and moaning through the rigging is well documented.**
- **Lack of personal fitness: this applies to many sailors who look back to their youth through rose-coloured glasses.**
- **Seasickness: an obvious cause.**
- **Lack of sleep: a part of the sailing culture considers it macho to remain awake for hours or even days. The same culture also believes fatigue does not affet their performance. This is rubbish. If you have established sensible sea routines, no one in your crew should be able to truthfully make such claims.**

WATCHING OUT FOR FATIGUE

It is important to catch the first signs of fatigue and treat it early. Everyone on board should know the signs of fatigue. Often the sufferer is the last person to realise that they need a rest. Since that could be you, have everyone watch everyone else for the early signs of fatigue so that it can be nipped in the bud.

HYPOTHERMIA

Fatigue should be treated as soon as it is noticed. If someone is suffering from fatigue, it is not a sign of personal weakness but a warning of worse to come. Ignore it at your peril. It is the first cousin to hypothermia, with which it shares some of its symptoms. Hypothermia begins when the body's core temperature falls below 35°C and comes in three forms.

MILD HYPOTHERMIA

This is when the core temperature is between 32 and 35°C. It is a condition somewhere between full-blown hypothermia and being cold, wet and miserable. It is easy to miss. Symptoms include:

- shivering – the body's attempt to produce heat to keep vital organs warm. It uses a lot of energy
- complaining of fatigue and going about tasks in a slow, rather uncoordinated manner.
- fast breathing
- pale or cold skin. Exposed areas of the face and hands quickly become almost as cold as the surrounding air. This is not necessarily a symptom of hypothermia but it is a sign of losing heat fast

MODERATE HYPOTHERMIA

The core temperature is now between 28 and 32°C. Symptoms include:

- shivering uncontrollably, often violently. Severe shivering is the body's last ditch effort to stay warm. It is a signal that sufferers must receive immediate treatment and must not be ignored. As the core temperature drops, shivering may stop. Do not think that the worst is over. It is a sign that the body has no energy to generate any heat
- sleepiness, lack of coordination, inability to pay attention to their surroundings, cannot follow simple orders and may hallucinate
- slurring their words
- suffering from hypoventilation, which is slow, shallow breathing

Do not be fooled by the term 'moderate hypothermia'. This is a very dangerous condition and sufferers must be given immediate treatment.

SEVERE HYPOTHERMIA

This is where the core temperature is below 28°C. Sufferers:

- are unconscious
- have dilated pupils

- breathe shallowly, if at all
- have a weak, irregular pulse or none at all

They may appear dead, but only a doctor can make this decision. If someone is suffering from advanced hypothermia, only advanced medical intervention can save them.

AVOIDING HYPOTHERMIA

Do not assume that hypothermia is found only in cold and wet conditions. On a side trip up a tributary of the Orinoco, we were trading with the local Indians, who came out from their villages in dugout canoes. They did not understand our poor Spanish and we were bemused by their local dialect, but it was fun. One woman came alongside and held up a very young baby. As far as we could make out, she was telling us her baby needed blankets. We suspected a scam. The daytime temperature was around 30°C and not much different at night. She became frantic. We had no blankets but gave her a selection of large bath towels. Much later we learned that after a tropical rain shower (it was the rainy season), the chilling effect of the rainwater evaporating from a baby's skin can lead to hypothermia and, too often, death.

The surest way of avoiding hypothermia is:

- stay warm by wearing the right protective clothing to avoid losing heat
- eat well and have hot drinks so your body has the energy to generate heat

TREATING HYPOTHERMIA

Probably the best way to treat hypothermia on board is, as quickly as possible, to:

- take the victim below, out of the wind and wet
- remove any wet outer clothing and replace with warm dry clothing
- put them in a sleeping bag or two. If necessary, have someone climb into the sleeping bag with them to share their body heat
- give them warm, sweet drinks and, if they can eat, some glucose-based food. This provides fuels for the body's heat making engine
- if the cabin air is cold, you can warm the air the victim is breathing by LOOSELY wrapping a woollen scarf round his or her mouth and nose

If there is no improvement in twenty minutes, or if there is any deterioration during that time, seek professional medical help.

21 SUPPLIES

Supplies should always be adequate for your intended passage but some definition of 'adequate' is necessary before this statement has meaning. Finding a definition is not as simple as it first appears. Take food supplies, for example: if you are accustomed to silver service, three course meals and vintage wines, your opinion on what is an adequate food supply will differ from someone who is content to live on corned beef, pasta and crispbread.

A useful rule of thumb for any passage is to carry food and water for your estimated time en route plus 50 per cent. This guideline has the virtue of being sufficiently flexible to cover passages of any length and whether or not you see eating as refuelling or a gourmet experience.

The right food is important. It would have to be a very long passage before vitamin deficiency became a problem but it is more pleasant to eat food you enjoy than shovel down a reconstituted sludge because it is good for you. Even on a day trip a poor meal, picnic or otherwise, can throw a shadow over your sailing. On long voyages, meals are a highlight of the day and all the more welcome if it is food you like.

On any voyage, it is a good idea to ask your crew for their culinary likes and dislikes and try to put together a menu from the likes they have in common. On a long passage it is sensible to start your ration plan by putting together a week's worth of different daily menus heavy on what the majority, if not all, your crew enjoy eating. These menus can then be rotated throughout the passage, turning to canned and dried food and vegetables as fresh food runs out. If the job of cook is rotated among the crew, show them the list of menus based on the food they like and ask each member which of these menus they can cook with edible results. Their answers provide the cooks' rota.

If you wish to escape plagues of cockroaches and other nasty beasties of warmer climes, never allow any supplies to come aboard in cardboard boxes or paper bags. These are ideal homes for cockroach eggs. Wash all fruit and vegetables in a mild solution of bleach and water. Cartons of long life milk and wine are a particular problem. Eggs may lurk in the folds of the carton. One solution is to open up the folds and wash down the outside of the carton with your water and bleach solution.

It is always sensible to keep the water tanks full. At sea it is not difficult to use an awning as a rain-catcher and run the water off into the water tank.

It is also a good idea to keep the fuel tank full, if only to discourage the build up of condensation in the tank, which increases the risk of the fuel becoming contaminated. If more fuel is needed than can be carried in the tank, jerry cans of fuel can be stowed on deck. If this is done, make sure they are secure and watertight. Carrying fuel on deck on long passages is becoming increasingly common. Once, apart from entering and leaving harbour, yachts relied on sail power for the passage and accepted dribbling along when the inevitable light airs and calms were met. Now airline timetables and crew changes demand punctuality and the power demanded by electronic instrumentation, fridges and air-conditioning insist that the engine runs for longish periods every day or so to keep the batteries charged.

Liquid Petroleum Gas (also called LPG, GPL, LP Gas or Liquid Propane Gas) is the principal source of cooking fuel on most craft. In the same way as for food, you should very carefully estimate your daily consumption of gas and from that calculate how long you can expect one bottle of gas to last in normal use. Using this information, carry enough gas for the estimated time en route plus 50 per cent. As a very rough guide, a 4.5kg gas bottle lasts for between 15 and 20 hours.

If you are using Calor gas bottles, it is unlikely that you will be able to exchange empty bottles for full ones away from the UK. It may be possible to arrange to have bottles refilled but in some places differences in fittings may make it necessary to buy local bottles and regulators. Campingaz is usually more widely available but outside Europe you may run into the same problems with Campingaz as with Calor gas bottles.

Every item that requires servicing almost certainly needs spares. The list includes engines, fuel systems, heads and winches. The precise range of spares you need is determined by the equipment you have on board. Bearing in mind that finding specialist fittings may be time consuming and expensive, be generous in the quantities of spares you carry and never miss an opportunity to stock up.

Finally, make sure your consumption of supplies is very carefully monitored – firstly to reassure yourself that you are remaining within your estimated limits and secondly to highlight any unexpected excessive consumption early, so that its cause may be tracked down and tackled before it becomes a problem.

B 50

PART 3

EXECUTION AND SAMPLE PASSAGES

EXECUTING YOUR PLAN

You have worked hard and laboured long over your plan. You have carefully considered your goal; revised your ideas to take into account any limitations; discussed your ideas with your crew and finally got yourself a goal. You have decided what you must do to achieve this goal; gathered all the data and information you need; prepared your plan; drawn up a timetable and carried out all your onshore preparations. Now all that remains is to go to sea. There is only one catch. You may have a perfect plan. Sadly, reality is imperfect, imprecise, indistinct and unpredictable – and nothing like your plan foresaw.

A good plan is like a good marriage. You start with the ideal. Making it work means doing your best to make expectations live up to reality. Helmuth von Moltke, Chief of Staff of the Prussian Army for thirty years in the early 19th century, gave this a military twist when he said that 'no plan survives first contact with the enemy'. This is as true of sailing as it is for military operations. If you are not prepared to change your plan, the first wave you meet will overwhelm it and take it to the bottom of the sea. Relying on any plan after it becomes irrelevant to the conditions you actually face is the primrose path to failure. This is not the same as saying that your plan leads to failure. This distinction is important. Failure comes from relying on your plan after it clashes with the real world. Reality never adjusts to fit your plan. Your plan must adapt and evolve to fit in with the real world.

So why plan, why not play it off the cuff? The answer is simple. A good plan means you are properly prepared, trained, and equipped for your proposed passage. You have a very clear idea what you are trying to achieve and what is required to achieve it. More importantly, you have built into its execution the resources and flexibility to handle Donald Rumsfeld's 'unknown unknowns'. Changing your plan does not come as a surprise. It is part of the plan.

CONTINGENCY PLANS

The MCA advises that as you write your plan, you should also prepare a contingency plan. Having a ready-to-use contingency plan sounds prudent but it is a flawed concept. How can a contingency plan be prepared without first knowing the nature of the contingency? Of course you meet contingencies – some big, some small, some good, some bad and some frightful – but until you know their nature it is impossible to prepare a plan to deal with them. If you choose to sail with a ready-to-use contingency plan then somehow it must cover every possible 'what if' situation you think you may encounter.

In addition to accommodating an enormous range of very different contingencies, this plan must also cover the 57 varieties of each contingency. Complicating matters even further, every contingency and every variety of contingency has a number of possible solutions. By the time you have put all this together, the odds on you having a contingency plan tailored for any particular problem you may meet are about the same as winning the lottery. Besides, Murphy's Law says that contingencies you meet are never on your list. It is their nature to be unforeseen and come out of left field, in ways you never imagined. This is not to say that as you prepare your plan various potential hassles and possible answers to them do not occur to you, but that is all they are – possibilities.

PLAN B

There is no Plan B. The notion that you tear up your carefully prepared plan at the first discrepancy between it and reality and then start anew is nonsense. There are always going to be discrepancies. As each appears, do you intend to stop what you are doing, thumb through an alphabet of contingency plans and start all over again? Of course not. You prepared your plan on the best information available, using what you believed were reasonable assumptions of the resources available and the conditions you expected to find when you put your plan into action, but you are not surprised when your bespoke plan comes to resemble a cheap, off-the-peg suit from a cut price chain store. To maintain progress and have any chance of achieving what you set out to do, you must re-cut your plan so that it fits the actual conditions you encounter.

THE EVER EVOLVING PLAN

Your original plan described the tactics you hoped to use to realise your aim. Once the action begins, your aim remains constant but the tactics you employ to achieve it vary as you think best how to deal with the actual conditions encountered. It is a classic example of Darwinian evolution. Planning is strategy. Execution is tactics or, if you prefer, the actions taken in an uncertain environment to deal with the here and now to achieve your goal.

Once the start line is crossed, your plan is in a state of constant development. By selecting and correctly employing the right tactics, it evolves from its initial primeval state to something that, by the end of your passage, can pass for a workmanlike plan. You may even come to believe it was what you planned to do all along.

DISCREPANCIES

You only modify your plan when there are differences between the circumstances you assumed you may meet and those you actually encounter. There are two good reasons why you should not call all these differences contingencies. Firstly, although the term 'contingency'

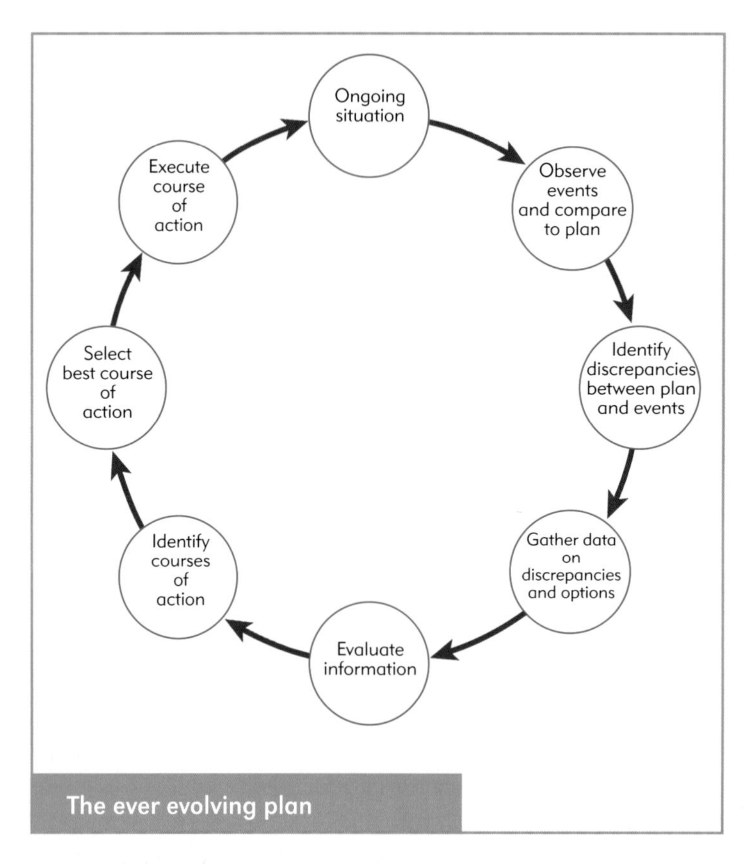

The ever evolving plan

can mean no more than a chance event, it somehow suggests that every chance event brings problems and that any difference between your plan and reality is bad news. This is not true. Some differences are beneficial. Secondly, calling every difference a contingency encourages you to look for problems and perhaps fail to notice those factors that can help you on your way.

As skipper, it is part of your responsibilities to monitor the execution of your passage plan, checking how it is working by continuously comparing the conditions for which you planned with the reality you encounter. When you identify any discrepancy between these two, and regardless of its cause or its advantages or disadvantages, the question is: 'Does the plan remain valid'? If not, then you must make a proportionate, timely and effective response in order to remain on course to achieve your goal.

DISCREPANCIES GOOD AND BAD

Some discrepancies have a positive effect that helps you towards your aim. The wind swings round to the north-east and suddenly, instead of beating, you are sailing on a comfortable reach and romping towards your destination. Other discrepancies are a hindrance. A fierce increase in wind strength means setting the storm jib, which more or less destroys your boat's upwind capability, adding hours to your voyage.

Discrepancies are not necessarily constant in their effect. A positive discrepancy might, in time, become a hindrance. The north-easterly that gave you easy sailing might make entering your chosen harbour dangerous, with the result that you must seek an alternative safe haven.

Flying a spinnaker is a good example of a two-faced discrepancy. It is a sunny afternoon. You are on a broad reach in relatively strong winds and content to run under the genoa or even working jib when, unexpectedly and against the forecast, the wind grows light and progress stops. It is obviously time for the spinnaker or cruising chute. It goes up. Boat speed improves and all is well once more. The wind speed increases but the sailing is good and you carry on. Then you notice the helmsman struggling to hold the course. A squall hits. Your

SOURCES OF INFORMATION TO IDENTIFY DISCREPANCIES

Discrepancies begin appearing the instant you start putting your plan into action. This can be weeks, months or even years before going to sea. Consequently some of the sources that you use to identify discrepancies do not appear particularly nautical.

- Personal observation
- Reports from the crew
- News reports
- Almanacs, pilots and charts, including updates
- Your experience
- Your cultural/social background
- Reports from agencies such as the MCA
- Suppliers
- Contractors
- Boatyard
- Cash flow; mostly involving a shortage of money. No refit ever went to plan or stayed on budget
- Onboard instrumentation including:
  - ✦ Radar, AIS
  - ✦ Wind speed and direction
  - ✦ Speed logs
  - ✦ Barometer
  - ✦ Radio

boat heels and lurches over the ocean. You decide to recover the spinnaker. What would have been an easy task a couple of hours earlier is now a fearsome struggle in the growing dark on a deck that threatens to throw the crew over the side. Happily, only the spinnaker falls in the water.

In this example, you made the correct response to the initial discrepancy but failed to spot that the new situation, resulting from implementing that option, had created new discrepancies that needed your attention. Noticing the wind was increasing would have allowed you to recover the spinnaker when conditions were much easier.

ASSESSING DISCREPANCIES

Deciding the importance of any discrepancy is not easy. Those that flip between being positive and negative can be particularly hard to identify and, when recognised, there is the challenge of deciding which aspect carries the greater importance. It comes down to an informed judgement, which varies from individual to individual. For example, your previous sailing experience can bring wisdom based upon similar past activities. In someone else, the experience gained from their earlier activities can lead to an unthinking, fixed response on the principle that if it worked last time, it will work again.

Again, if you come from a long line of sailors or from a society where sailing is part of everyday life, your assessment of any given situation will be different from someone new to the sea and who is heavily reliant on book knowledge.

EVALUATING DISCREPANCIES

Discrepancies come in all shapes and sizes. Some may contain the seeds of catastrophe; others are so trivial that dealing with them is a waste of time and effort. Simply because you identify a difference between the circumstances you envisaged when writing your plan and reality is not a signal to rush into action. First find the answers to two questions:

1 Has this discrepancy a positive or negative effect upon your goal? In other words, does it help or hinder what you are trying to achieve?
2 What is its significance? How much will it help or hinder? This is the more important question. If it looks like this discrepancy will give you a great boost on your way or threaten disaster, you must take action. If it barely registers on either scale, it can be left alone.

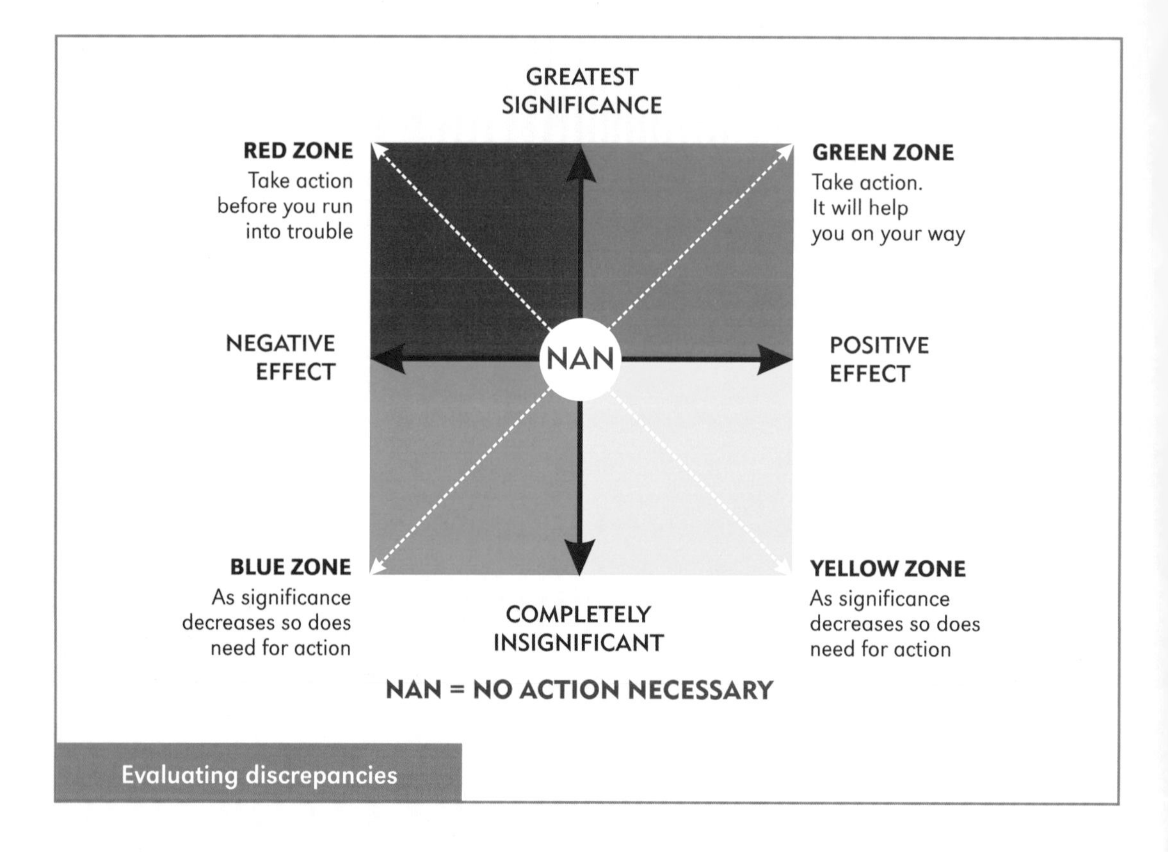

Evaluating discrepancies

With a little modification, the Magic Quadrant can be relabelled to provide a framework to help you evaluate discrepancies. It is especially useful when you are tired and cold and your brain resembles a bowl of cold porridge instead of its usual super-sharp thinking machine. In this version of the Magic Quadrant:

The Green Zone is where discrepancies are always positive in their effect and you should take advantage of them as soon as possible.

The Red Zone is where discrepancies all have a negative effect on your progress. They take priority over discrepancies in any other zone and must be dealt with as soon as possible. If they are not creating problems now, they will in the future and if ignored can bring disaster in their wake.

The Yellow and Blue Quadrants are a curate's mixture. As the significance of a discrepancy declines, so does the need to take action – but do not confuse a decision to do nothing with inaction. You must make a careful appraisal of each discrepancy and if your decision is that no action is necessary then that is an informed decision rather than inaction caused by a failure to assess the situation.

Around the centre of the graph the effects of any discrepancy are small; but as you move further and further away from the centre, the need to take action becomes increasingly urgent.

It is not always necessary to draw the graph on paper – with a little practice, you can visualise it. Sometimes you may even see a discrepancy and the answer to it simultaneously. This is the intuitive response. Again, some discrepancies solve themselves. You see it, start to deal with it, become distracted by some other more pressing matter and when you return to deal with it, it is gone.

RESOLVING DISCREPANCIES

Resolving discrepancies depends more upon individual skill than following some formula or rule of thumb. When preparing your plan you were making strategic decisions. The situation is effectively static. Decisions then are made slowly, with easy access to all relevant information. There is time to clarify doubts, seek additional information to resolve uncertainties, discuss ideas with your crew, seek expert advice and revise your proposals, taking into account the results from dry runs and rehearsals.

When executing your plan at sea, you are making tactical decisions. Time is of the essence. The information available to you is likely to be incomplete and sometimes ambiguous. There is no time for dry runs or rehearsals. The situation is dynamic. Any action you take to resolve one discrepancy immediately generates a new situation. This creates further discrepancies that require assessment and more tactical decisions.

OODA LOOP

The OODA loop is a powerful tool when making tactical decisions. In the 1950s a young USAF fighter pilot, John R Boyd, issued a standing challenge to his fellow pilots: starting from a position of disadvantage, he would have his jet on his opponent's tail inside 40 seconds or pay out $40. Legend says that he never lost. Much later, as a USAF colonel, he developed what he knew instinctively as a young pilot into the concept of the OODA loop.

The term OODA comes from its four steps:

1 OBSERVE

The collection of data from every source available to you at that moment.

2 ORIENT

This is the most important part of the OODA loop. It is the analysis and synthesis of the data relevant to the current situation. In other words, this is when you make sense of the data you have collected and come to understand what it means and how it can best be used. No two people see the world in the same way. We filter the data we receive through our genetic heritage, cultural traditions, previous experience, education, family background and

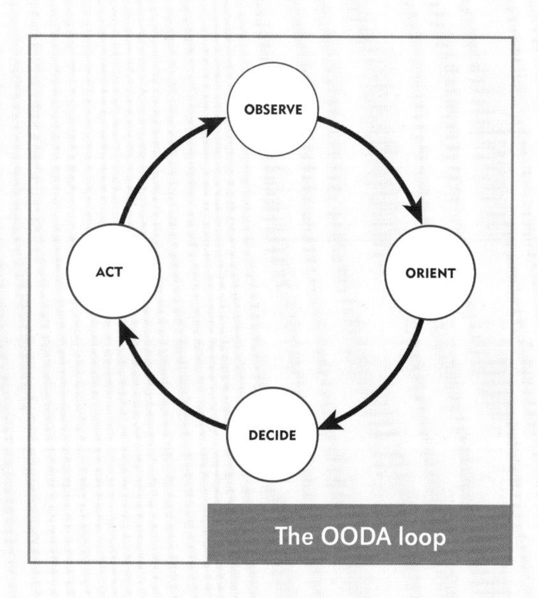

The OODA loop

everything else that makes us different from everyone else. This cocktail of influences gives us our view of the world, and determines how we interpret and use the information we observe. This in turn affects our decisions and how we go about implementing those decisions.

3 DECIDE

Selecting a course of action.

4 ACT

Executing that course of action.

One advantage of the OODA loop is that it is not a closed circle travelling in one direction. You do not take a discrepancy, feed it into its OODA loop, put your decision into operation and that is it, problem over and your OODA loop vanishes. It is a continuous process. The four steps of the OODA loop are not a sequence of discrete steps but interact one with another. The instant you begin to take action to deal with a discrepancy, you create a new situation and a new OODA loop spins off.

The strength of the OODA loop is that you are always aware of what is happening; you understand why events are developing as they are and this allows you to remain in control of the situation. Always remember that each discrepancy you resolve is another step towards your goal, not an end in itself.

Counter-intuitively thinking through a problem, the Orient step of the OODA loop buys you time, and with time in hand you can:

- recover from mistakes
- learn from experience: in other words, be less likely to make the same mistake twice
- control and shape the situation
- try more than one solution to your problem

OODA LOOP MADE SIMPLE

There are options to and variations of the OODA loop but whatever system you adopt it is important to develop the habit of observing the world around you. Skippers admire the view after they have observed what is happening.

If you adopt the OODA loop then at first you may find it easier and quicker to work through a recurring and non-stop ten step cycle.

STEP	ACTION
1 OBSERVATION	Stay alert from the instant that you begin to implement your plan and continuously monitor the relevance of your prepared plan against what is actually happening

2 IS THERE A DIFFERENCE BETWEEN YOUR PREPARED PLAN AND ACTUAL EVENTS?	YES: Is the difference significant? Is it positive or negative? What is its priority? NO: then carry on implementing plan. Go back to Step 1
3 EVALUATE DISCREPANCY	Gather all the relevant data and information necessary to resolve this discrepancy
4 WHAT OPTIONS DO YOU HAVE?	Use the data and information you have collected to identify the various options that you have to resolve this discrepancy.
5 EVALUATE THE OPTIONS YOU HAVE IDENTIFIED	Place options into order of preference
6 CHOOSE OPTION YOU WILL IMPLEMENT	Select the option you believe is most likely to be successful taking into account the skills and resources that you have onboard. This may not be your preferred option but it is an option you believe can be made to work
7 CHECK OUT YOUR CHOSEN OPTION	Seek the crew's views and ideas on your choice of option and then identify the available resources
8 MAKE A PLAN	Plan how you will implement your chosen option using the resources available to you. Remember, the situation is changing as you plan
9 BRIEF CREW	Brief the crew. Allocate tasks and resources. Confirm timings
10 GO FOR IT	Put plan into action and return to Step 1

THE OODA HEIRARCHY

The OODA loop is not something to keep to yourself. Boyd believed that, within any organisation, OODA loops work at each level within that enterprise, giving a faster, stronger and more positive approach to developing events than one relying on a rigid chain of command.

If you sail with a crew, most of us allow the mate, watch officers and others to act, within limits, on their own initiative. Nowadays we call this a decentralised chain of command controlled through directives, but it is just another way of describing what Von Moltke called mission orders. He believed that subordinates, if correctly trained and having the right ethos, would achieve better results if allowed to carry out the task as they saw fit. The concept of mission orders and a hierarchy of OODA loops uses the talents of crews to better effect than the skipper shouting orders and reprising the role of Captain Bligh.

How far you go with this approach reflects how you choose to organise your crew and how much authority you are prepared to give to your mate and watch officers. If you adopt it, then to make it work you must also ensure that they are trained for their role and that they understand the concepts of the OODA and how to use them.

TAKING ACTION

When you come to act on a discrepancy, then go for it. In his book *Maxims of War*, Napoleon noted 115 maxims that guided his actions. Over 2,000 years earlier, Sun Tzu, in his book *The Art of War*, listed thirteen principles of war; but the American Civil War general Nathan Bedford Forrest had only one: "Get there firstest with the mostest.'

When you decide to act, overkill is good. A hesitant, half-hearted, under-resourced response comes with the absolute promise of failure. Any action you take must be prompt, generously proportionate, confident and enthusiastic. You will be identifying, assessing, making tactical decisions and acting on discrepancies from the minute you cast off until you are securely berthed. Do not assume it is over when you enter harbour. I once entered a marina on the south coast of England. I was told over the VHF to take berth 19 on Pontoon B. 'You'll see it ahead of you as you enter,' said the radio. What could be simpler? Easy peasy. Once I had found pontoon B, the berth numbers would give me a clue on the whereabouts of berth 19. I could then use that information to position my boat for the turn into the berth, taking into account that, once I began the turn, the wind would be pushing sideways. Simple.

Pontoon B was prominently marked but its berths were not. There was not a berth number in sight. With a strongish wind astern and aboard a yacht that, in those conditions, measured its turning circle in nautical miles, I was reluctant to sail too far into a dead end with the chance of hitting another yacht or two as I struggled to turn round. It did not help that a much larger yacht, its businesslike crew holding warps and fenders, was hanging on to my transom. Feeling hemmed in, I swung into the first empty berth, jumped ashore and discovered that the berth numbers were on the walkway and invisible from the water. Having found the location of berth 19, I made my way there – after apologising to the skipper of the yacht whose berth I had temporarily occupied and who, while waiting for me to vacate his berth, had with great difficulty turned round before hitting the end of the pontoon. The marina manager later explained that he put the berth numbers on the walkway because if he put them where they could be seen from the sea, the yachts broke them off. His response to a problem serves to reinforce the fact that no two people see the same situation in the same way.

In the beginning, you move through each stage of systems such as the OODA loop in great clunking steps, consciously moving from one to another. Soon it becomes second nature. You suck in information wherever you find it in the same natural way that you breathe; you process it instinctively and tweak your plan automatically. It is almost effortless and, unless something really significant has happened, most of the adjustments you make to your plan are small because you are catching problems early and dealing with every discrepancy as soon as they appear. It would be embarrassing to call your responses contingency plans. After all, reality is nothing more than one continuous contingency.

SAMPLE PASSAGES

Using a more or less random selection, let's look at how you could plan and prepare for different types of passage. There is no claim that these passages are typical of each type – there is no such animal as a typical passage. Some may be better known than others; the Solent to Cherbourg, for example, is probably the UK's most popular offshore passage – but does that make it typical? If you use the number of boats making a particular passage as your measure, then going through the Crinan Canal is probably Britain's most typical passage. Nor does it help that there is no clear boundary between the different types of passage. When does a short coastal passage become a long coastal passage? How far must you go offshore before it counts as an offshore passage? If you go out on a day sail and return a couple of hours after the sun has gone down, is that a night passage?

Hopefully, although you may never sail these passages, their preparation and planning may be helpful to the passages of your choice. To help you plan, there is a checklist of sorts, complete with caveats (see page 217).

There is no discussion on how you might execute these passages. There are three reasons for this decision. Firstly, the planning and preparation done before casting off is the key to a happy, successful passage. Secondly, although you may have made similar passages in the past, it might be the first time you have considered making this particular type of passage. Of course the planning, preparation and execution of those earlier passages gives you a useful stock of knowledge and experience to draw upon when planning and preparing for this passage, but not necessarily on its execution. Thirdly, speculating on the execution of your plan involves creating imaginary situations followed by unreal solutions and entering a make-believe world of pretend passages. I've lost count of the times I've sailed up and down England's east coast and no two passages have ever been alike. I have had idyllic cruises, passages from hell, and everything in between – but I cannot recall meeting a 'what-if' situation that I had included in my preparations. Sometimes I got close but I never won a cigar.

Done well, planning and preparation takes time. Simply collecting the information necessary for an offshore passage can easily take a couple of days' hard work. Only when you have this information can you begin writing your plan. Try not to confine your information to waypoints, tides and weather. It helps to know more than that about the waters you sail through. What is its history? What tales does it have to tell? How did the land and seascape come to look like this? Not only does it make your cruise come alive, it is surprising how often this information proves helpful. For example, many of the smaller harbours along the Frisian coast dry, but they dry to 'schlick', the sort of mud in which seagulls swim. Keel boats sink in and sit upright. On the other hand, local boats often have a centreboard to help them navigate the drying channels. Just because you see a 50 foot boat approaching, do not assume there must be enough water for your 30 foot boat.

Planning forces you to work through your passage step by step, to ask what you need in terms of skills, equipment and experience to make it a success. Only when you have ticked all these boxes and satisfied yourself that you are up to scratch can you cast off. Once at sea, you are on your own. Then the key to making your planning and preparation work is a mix of an awareness of what is happening around you and flexibility. This is when training and past experience along with proper planning and preparation keeps you, if not your plan, on track. Do not mistake training for drills such as 'man overboard' or 'abandon ship'. Good training teaches you to think before you act and to make the best response, not necessarily the same response, to a given situation.

Although the passages in this section follow a line from day sailing to ocean crossings, it must be stressed that this sequence is not a measure of difficulty – just time and distance. There is no hierarchy of passage making. Regardless of the length or type of your passage, the sea demands the fullest respect all of the time, whether you are in harbour or the middle of an ocean. There is also a strong case that coastal and inshore navigation with its tides, shoals and rocks demands a higher degree of precision than offshore or ocean sailing. Inshore, you must know exactly where you are to within a few metres all of the time or you may get a fix the hard way. When you meet problems inshore, there may not be much time to grovel before Neptune. If you lose your mast, a sail or your engine, you may have only moments to resolve your difficulties before you are on the rocks. Offshore, there is generally time to carefully think through any such difficulties. That alone is a huge safety factor. I once spent two days debating whether or not to tack and then put off a decision to the weekend.

TYPES OF PASSAGE

Sailing is a broad church; an agreed classification of passages is as rare as a typical passage. You may not agree with the seven different types of passages used in this section, particularly if you sail on North America's Great Lakes, which take inland waters to a new level, or cruise in the Baltic or Mediterranean, where tides are not significant but I hope there are elements in each useful to all.

24 ROUND THE BAY

Round the bay sailing is leaving port, sailing around for a few hours and then returning to the same port. This is not as restricting as it first appears. Harbours are usually in sheltered locations with several miles of protected coastline where it is often possible to sail in conditions that would deter you from going further afield. It may even be possible to raise the wind force a notch or two above your normal stay in harbour limit.

There are many good reasons for a sail round the bay. The British coastline has thousands of bays, creeks, estuaries, inlets and lochs crying out to be explored. The local bay is where many yacht clubs hold their evening and weekend races. You could be a trailer sailor eager to explore new waters. You might be making sea trials after the winter refit, testing some new item of equipment, training the crew, going fishing, spending a warm summer's day afloat or simply sailing round in circles, washing the cares of the day out of your system.

It is a lucky sailor who lives within easy driving distance of their boat so they can leap aboard and head out to sea whenever they wish and the weather suits. Having a boat you can handle alone makes this even simpler. There is no need to round up family and friends as crew. If they wish to come aboard, they are welcome – but your fun is not dependent on others having both the leisure and inclination to spend time afloat with you.

Best of all, day sailing planning and preparation is quick and simple, especially if you have acquired the habit of sailing at every opportunity. Pre-sail checks are essential but they are short and sweet. Not only do you know the condition of your boat but also constant use picks up and puts right defects as they appear. It is amazing how quickly a boat rots when left unloved on the pontoon.

If you are sailing from your home port, navigation is straightforward. You already have the charts and know the waters. Of course the chart is always at hand but navigation is often by Mark I Eyeball. The only variables are tides and weather and not only are short term forecasts reliable but you can also look out of the yacht club window and tailor your plans to the actual weather.

If you are trailer sailing and the port is new to you, planning means finding harbour plans and passage charts on a decent scale covering a radius of about 20 miles either side of the port, and checking out berthing, pilotage and launching information. It is possible that the launching ramp is only available at certain states of the tide or has restricted opening times. It is also a good idea to check out car parking arrangements. In addition, it is necessary to prepare a passage plan, however simple, and note hazards, clearing bearings, tides and tidal streams and, if there is any possibility of sailing after dark, all lights.

If the port dries, or has limited lock or bridge opening times, your departure and return is controlled by these restrictions. Years ago I spent a couple of seasons sailing out of Watchet on the Bristol Channel. The harbour dries completely and my boat was afloat an hour either side of high water. Day sails lasted either an hour and a half or all day.

Your destination is often open-ended and rarely more than 10 or 15 miles from the port. Often it is no more than a decision to head for your favourite fishing ground, find a lunchtime anchorage, or sail upwind and up tide on the outward passage and romp back when the time comes to return to the yacht club bar.

SCARBOROUGH TO FILEY BAY

This passage is typical of thousands around any coastline: a pleasant sail leads to a sheltered anchorage for lunch onboard or ashore, followed by a gentle sail home.

WHY GO THERE?

Filey was a small, isolated fishing village until 19th-century holidaymakers sought peace and quiet from busy Scarborough. In 1835 John Wilkes-Unett, described variously as a Birmingham solicitor, property developer or West Riding gentleman, bought some land from Admiral Mitford of Hunmanby Hall and built The Crescent, with the Crescent Hotel (now flats) as its centrepiece. For the next hundred years, The Crescent in Filey was among England's more fashionable holiday addresses.

It was a different world a hundred years later, in 1939, when Billy Butlin began building his third holiday camp at Filey, complete with its own railway station. This served as an RAF station during the war. It closed in 1984 and is now a 600 holiday home complex and Filey a busy holiday town.

Just south of Filey Brigg is the Spittals. This appears on some charts as the Spittles. It is made of rounded boulders and is some 600m (1,970ft) long, some 8m (26ft) high and somewhat resembles a railway embankment. On big spring tides, over 200m (650ft) of it can dry at low water. It was first recorded in the 1500s and is variously reckoned to be:

- the remains of a Roman breakwater linked to the remains of a nearby Roman signal station. This is my favourite. It is easy to imagine being berthed alongside the breakwater and wagons carrying their cargoes to York
- a glacial moraine

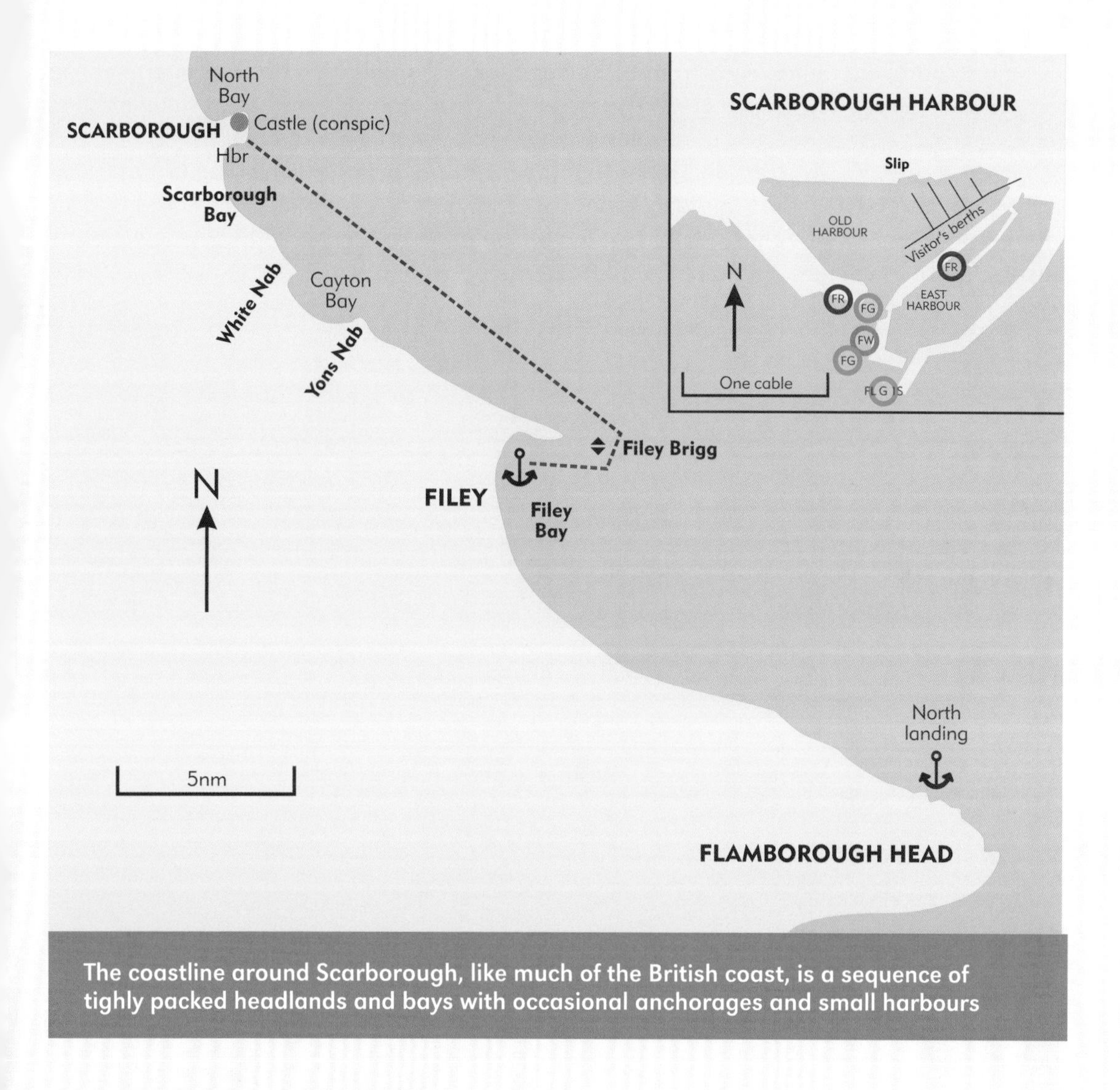

The coastline around Scarborough, like much of the British coast, is a sequence of tighly packed headlands and bays with occasional anchorages and small harbours

- an accumulation of tidal boulders
- the original shoreline before the erosion of the glacial till

PRE-SAIL CHECKS

The big pre-sail check to your boat will have been carried out at the start of the season. All that is needed is to confirm that all defects have been made good, that there is sufficient food and fuel aboard, the radio and electrics work, and your boat is ready to go to sea. If you have strangers onboard, it is necessary to familiarise them with your boat and go through the safety procedures and drills before casting off.

PILOTAGE

Filey Bay faces east. Filey Brigg runs out 6 cables or so into the North Sea, which gives some protection from winds and seas just east of north through to the west. Flamborough Head provides reasonable protection from the south. It is completely open from the south-east through to north-east and winds from these directions bring heavy surf. Do not attempt to enter or anchor in Filey in onshore winds or swell, which can run long after the wind has gone.

Anchor in around 3m (10ft) above chart datum or to suit draft. The holding is good.

Dinghies can launch from the coble landing at all states of the tide and larger trailer sailers about two hours either side of high water. Be prepared to wade the last few metres when you take the dinghy ashore. Filey offers all the amenities you expect in a small seaside resort.

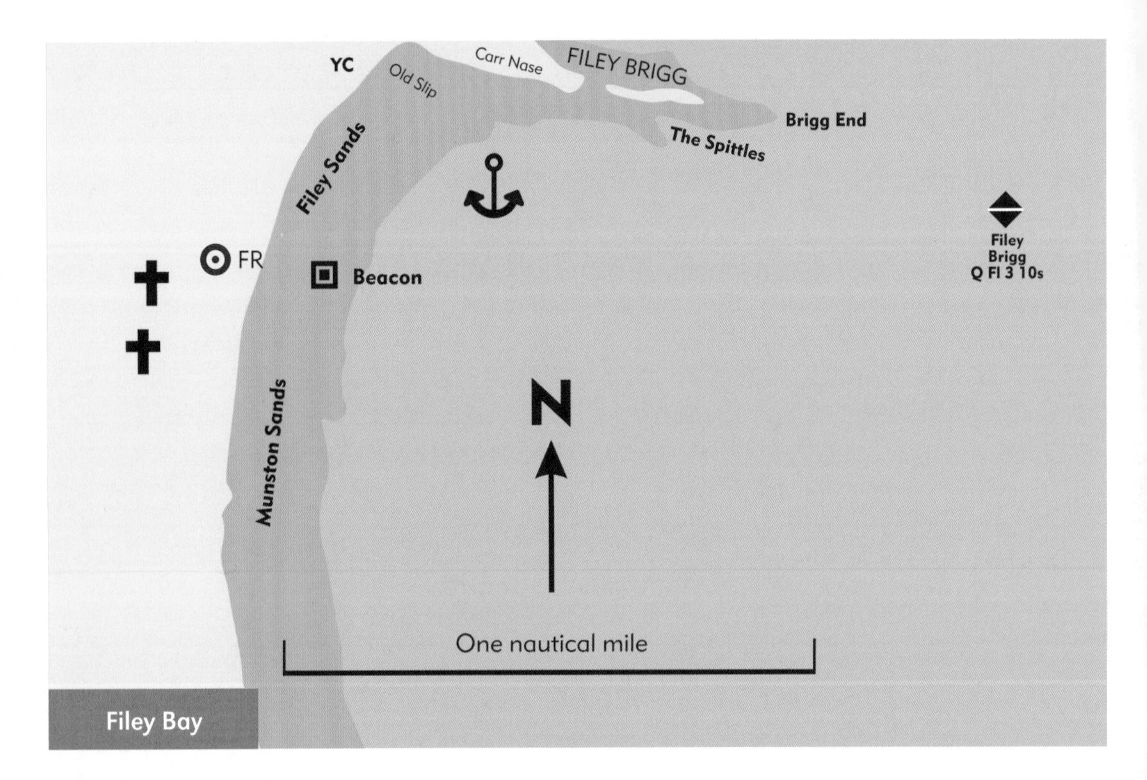

TIMINGS

Leave Scarborough as soon as convenient after low water to have the maximum lift from the south-going flood tide. For the return passage, leave Filey Bay anchorage aiming to arrive at Scarborough a couple of hours before low water.

ALTERNATIVE ANCHORAGES

An alternative lunchtime stop is a little further on at North Landing on Flamborough head, where the history of fishing can be traced back to the 13th century. Today it is home to the North Landing Café and the adjoining Caravel Bar. It was a lifeboat station until 1992.

North Landing is a narrow inlet and the beach is steep-to. The anchorage offers protection from winds from the south-west to the south-east. The holding, mostly rock and weed, is generally good. Just round the corner, to the east of North Landing, is Thornwick Bay, which does have something approaching a small sandy beach but no café or bar.

25

SHORT COASTAL PASSAGES

CRINAN TO OBAN

No passage can be taken for granted, coastal passages least of all. Their variety is endless. With ever changing seascapes and landscapes, there is always something new to see and much to learn. If you are tired of coastal sailing then take up golf.

The passage between Crinan and Oban is taken by the annual exodus from the Clyde to the west coast of Scotland or is part of your route if you are sailing round Britain via the Caledonian Canal.

From Crinan, or sailing northwards out of the Sound of Jura towards Oban, your aim is to break through a ring of tide rips and enter the Firth of Lorne. The first tidal gate is Dorus Mor, otherwise known as the Big (tidal) Gate. Dorus Mor is the channel between Craignish Point and the island of Garbh Reisa. It is an easy introduction for what lies ahead. In Dorus Mor the SE-going ebb starts about two hours before Oban high water and the NW-going flood begins three and half hours after high water at Oban. At springs, the tide rushes through and even on calm days the sea is covered in eddies and swirls.

Once through Dorus Mor, off to port is the Gulf of Corryvreckan. This sometimes appears as Coirebhreacain and translates as the Speckled Cauldron. Corryvreckan separates Jura and Scarba. On the chart it is apparently a hazard free channel. It might appear an easier way into the Firth of Lorne than sailing north and taking the Sound of Luing with its shallows and submarine peaks. It is not. A mile long and six cables wide at its narrowest, Corryvreckan

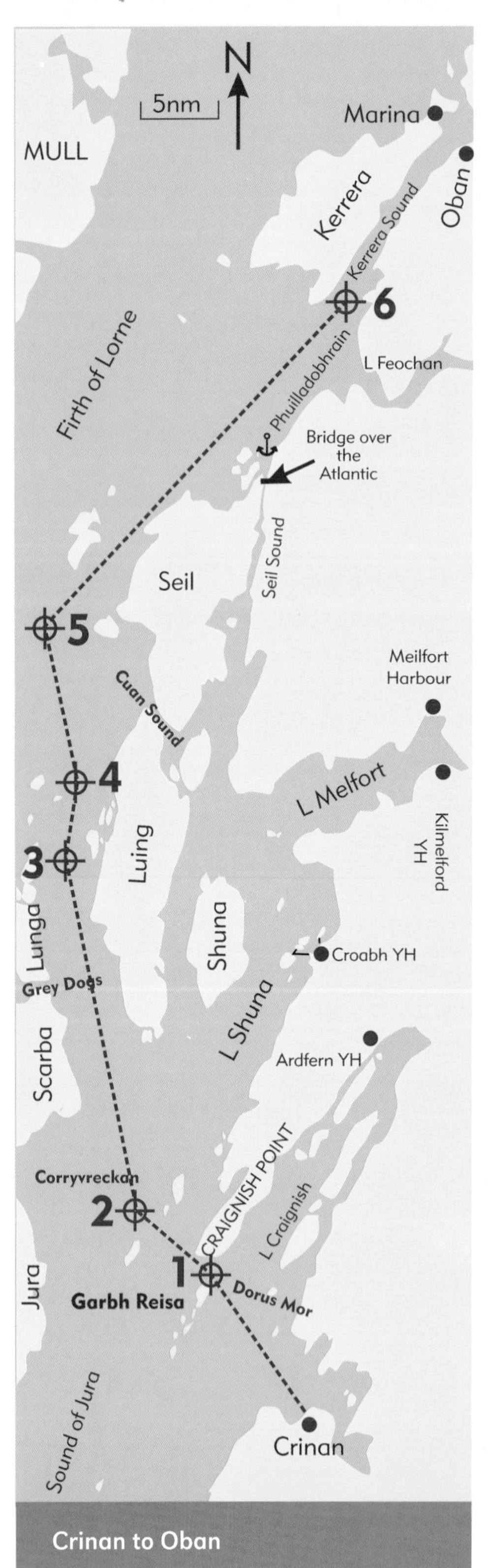

Crinan to Oban

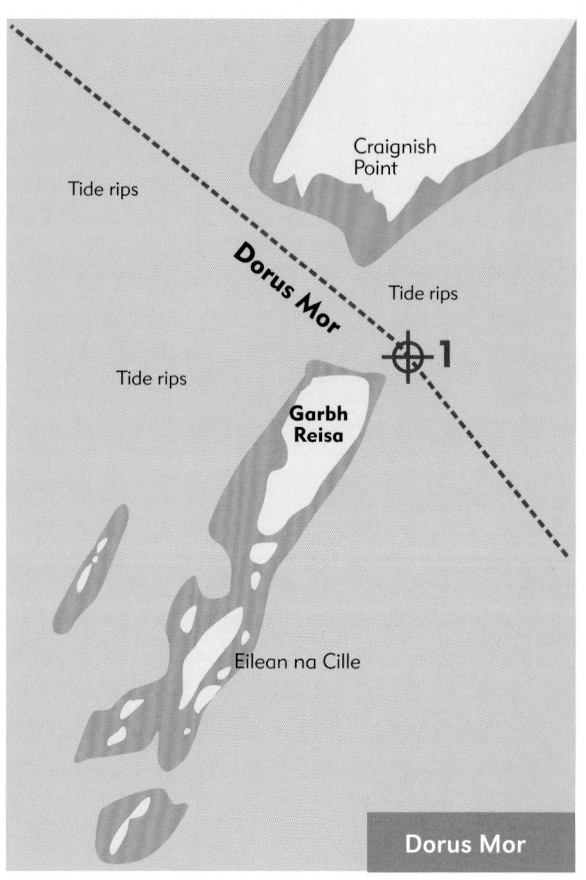

Dorus Mor

is famous for its tide race. The west-going stream begins around four hours after high water at Oban and the east-going stream about two hours before high water at Oban. At springs, the tidal range at the west end of the channel is 3.4m but only 1.5m at the east end. It is this difference in sea levels that explains spring rates of over 8 knots. It is perhaps the most fearsome tidal gate on the coast. It even has its own maelstrom, called the Hag. It should not be attempted without local knowledge, and never with wind over tide. If you insist on taking it then choose calm weather, slack water and a neap tide.

Leaving Corryvreckan to port you pass Bealach a' Choin Ghlais, also known as the Grey Dog or Little Corryvrekan. This is the narrow sound between the islands of Scarba and Lunga and doubled for the real Corryvrekan in Powell and Pressburger's 1945 film *I Know Where I'm Going!*.

You may know where you are going, but do not go through here without local knowledge. Like its bigger cousin it, too, leads to the Firth of Lorne and has tidal streams running at over 8 knots at springs. During the west-going stream there is a bad eddy close to the western end of Lunga, which then runs along the north side of the channel, and in strong westerly winds this can extend almost a mile out from the western entrance.

Next comes the Sound of Luing, the passage of choice into the Firth of Lorne. It is a narrow, shallow underwater ridge joining the island of Lunga with the isle of Luing. In the sound there are no soundings over 10m (33ft) and its bottom is blighted with pinnacles and pimples of rock coming to within a couple of metres or less of the surface. As the tide forces the water up and over the narrows, it picks up speed and even on good days the uneven bottom creates a chaos of eddies and miniature whirlpools.

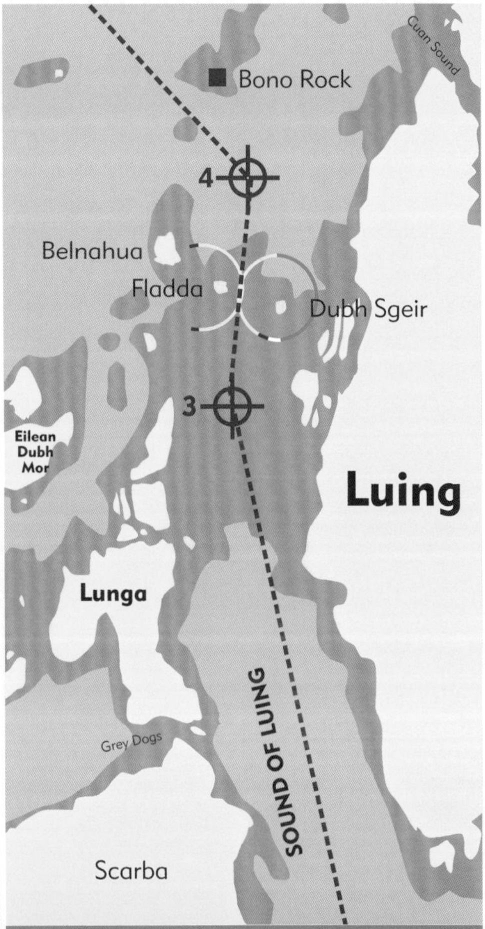

Sound of Luing

Once clear of the narrows, it is plain sailing to Oban. For those sailing south from Oban the Cuan Sound, a narrow 200m (650ft) wide gap between the islands of Luing and Seil, offers an interesting shortcut to Craobh Haven and Loch Melfort. The sound has curious tidal streams going from slack to its maximum rate in the first hour. At springs, the rate can reach 7 knots. On the ebb it is relatively calm but on the flood, especially with a north-westerly wind, it can be rough.

At the north end of Seil is the Clachan Sound. Between 1792 and 1793 Robert Mylne, a local engineer, built the 22 metre (72 foot) long Clachan Bridge, designed by Thomas Telford, over the narrows. Nowadays it is better known as the Bridge over the Atlantic. It is still in use as part of the B844 road. In 2011 the Scottish government decided that, after 218 years of continuous use, this bridge meant the Isle of Seil was no longer an island but could now be considered part of the mainland.

Among the houses next to the bridge is an 18th-century inn called the Tigh an Truish or House of Trousers. The failed Jacobite uprising of 1745 was followed by the Disarming Act of 1746, which stretched beyond weapons to include the bagpipes (regarded as an instrument of war) and the wearing of tartan or kilts. Legend has it that the inn was where the Seil islanders changed from their tartan kilts to plain trousers when they went to the mainland. True or not, the inn is a popular watering hole for yachts moored in Phuilladobhrain (Pool of the Otters) on the west side of Seil. This was Scotland's most popular anchorage in 2011 and a fifteen-minute walk from the pub.

PRE-SAIL CHECKS

This passage is almost certainly part of an ongoing cruise. The big pre-sail check will have been completed before you began the cruise, as will the crew familiarisation, drills and safety briefings. All that should need to be done before casting off is to check that there is nothing outstanding in the defects book, and a walk round the boat to confirm that all is fit for sea.

This passage should take no more than four or five hours. An informal watch system is probably adequate, as are snacks and hot drinks for sustenance. It has been known for boats to carry a fair tide as far as Tobermory. If you go for this option, your passage time doubles and it would be prudent to have proper watches and make provision for decent meals.

ROUTEING

This passage is a good example of the detailed and precise navigation that coastal passages demand. The route goes through rock littered shallows where a moment's inattentiveness or a few degrees off track puts you aground. You must be constantly alert. Even when you think it is all over and it is easy going pilotage up Kerrera Sound to Oban, there is a sting in the tail. About half a mile south of Heather Island, there is a green buoy on the west side of the sound and a red buoy on the east side of the sound. The careless navigator may think that the channel lies between these two buoys. It does not. Going north, leave the green buoy to starboard or the red buoy to port, otherwise you go aground on the rocks in the middle of the sound.

CRINAN TO OBAN – WAYPOINTS			
Waypoint Number	**Name**	**Latitude**	**Longitude**
1	Dorus Mor	56° 07.5N	05° 36.3W
2	Reisa Mhic	56° 14.4N	05° 38.4W
3	Sound of Luing 1	56° 14.5N	05° 40.6W
4	Sound of Luing 2	56° 15.5N	05° 40.4W
5	Bono Rock	56° 16.6N	05° 42.3W
6	Kerrera Entrance	56° 22.8N	05° 32.1W

From Kerrera Entrance navigation is by pilotage.

TIMINGS

On short coastal passages you expect to carry a fair tide from start to finish. The catch comes when a favourable tide is the ebb and arriving at your destination close to low water you must anchor until the harbour fills once more. Timings are ruled by the tides. This passage is not the exception. There is no way a yacht can force its way through the tidal gates against the tidal stream.

Some coastal passages require catching two tides. A good example is from Borkum, close to the mouth of the River Ems, to Norderney in the East Frisian Islands. This passage is often made by yachts heading for the Baltic. You need the ebb tide to take you down the Ems and then the flood to carry you up the coast to the Dove Tief and into Norderney. Do not

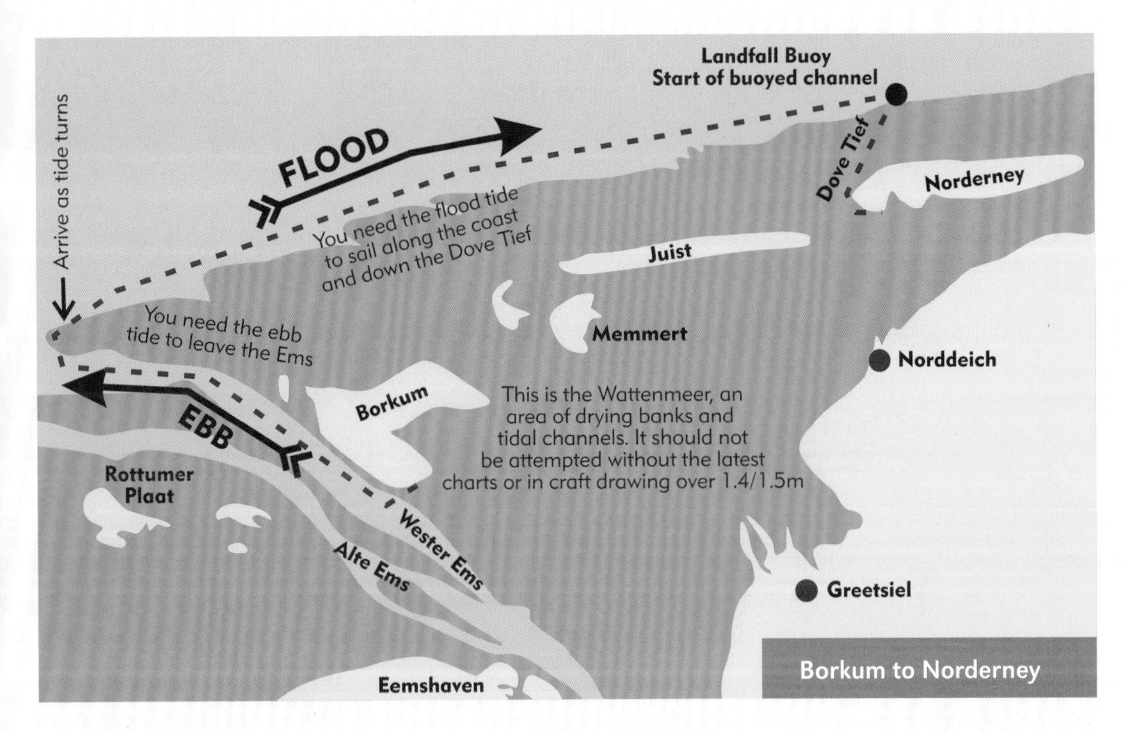

Borkum to Norderney

be fooled by the word 'Dove'. It has nothing to do with birds of peace. It is Platt Deutsch for 'crazy'. The Dove Tief should not be attempted in onshore winds much above force 4. It is possible to cut the corner at the east end of Juist, but only with local knowledge.

THE DECISION TO SAIL

The weather, especially the wind, on the day decides whether or not you sail. It is prudent to have a wind speed above which you will not sail. This limit will vary depending on whether you are running, reaching or beating. It will also vary with the tide. Any wind over tide kicks up a sea. Strong winds over tide turn tidal gates into cauldrons. There are accounts of boats bashing over the tide and crashing through overfalls. You may wish to consider having a modest limit to the wind force, above which you do not sail when the wind is against the tide.

ALTERNATIVE PORTS/ANCHORAGES

As always on this coast you are spoilt for a choice of anchorages, which you may be tempted to explore, and a good selection of well appointed, usually busy, marinas such as Melfort Harbour, Kilmelford YH, Craobh YH and Ardfern YC.

LONG COASTAL PASSAGES

SOLENT TO DOVER

Long coastal passages are rarely an end in themselves. The usual reason for making a long coastal passage is to visit distant cruising grounds, often so far away that reaching them is broken into a chain of lengthy legs. If you are based in the Solent and wish to explore the Baltic, the first day's sail could take you to Brighton, the next to Dover or Folkestone and the third across the Channel, heading either for the Dutch canals or up the Dutch coast as weather, time and inclination dictate.

ONSHORE PLANNING

As you intend to be away for some time, onshore planning is more detailed and time consuming than for a day sail or short coastal passage. As gear failure during the cruise could ruin it for everyone, your boat and its fittings and equipment need to be thoroughly checked out and all defects and deficiencies made good.

If your crew includes anyone not familiar with your boat, you may wish to arrange a couple of day sails prior to leaving on your cruise so that everyone knows each other and learns to work as a crew. As you are making passages longer than twelve hours, there must be some sort of watch system. In turn, that means appointing a mate and introducing some sort of command structure so that someone you trust is in charge of the boat while you are asleep. This leads to considering allocating areas of responsibility to crew members, writing standing orders and night orders, and laying down logbook discipline. After four hours off watch you do not wish to discover a blank logbook. Of course, the plotter tells you where you are and where you have been – but what has happened during the time you were off watch?

It is also necessary to source all the pilot books and charts you require, including port and pilotage information and local weather forecasts. For example, in German waters DP07 Seefunk (www.dp07.de) broadcasts weather forecasts for the German North Sea and Baltic waters. It is in German but at dictation speed and easily understood. Alternatively, there is the Deutscher Wetterdienst (www.dwd.de), which has an English language version of its forecasts.

When all this is completed, you can begin your pre-sail checks, which also need to be more than usually thorough if you are to avoid the embarrassment of discovering that the cruising chute sheets are at home, hanging up in the garage.

ROUTEING

If you are making for the Baltic from the Solent, the first day to Brighton can be treated as a shakedown cruise, changing sails, reefing sails and carrying various manoeuvres to confirm all is working as planned. Brighton is close enough to home for equipment that was overlooked, or if it needs repair it can be quickly made good using your usual contacts. It is also a chance to tweak stowage and berthing arrangements. Building in a short shakedown cruise is a valuable exercise. It means that when you leave Brighton for Dover, you are as certain as you can be that you are in all respects ready for sea.

The longer the passage, the easier the navigation – a short coastal sail may have you forever changing course to wriggle through twisting channels but any long sail tends to be made up of two or three lengthy legs, topped and tailed by some pilotage.

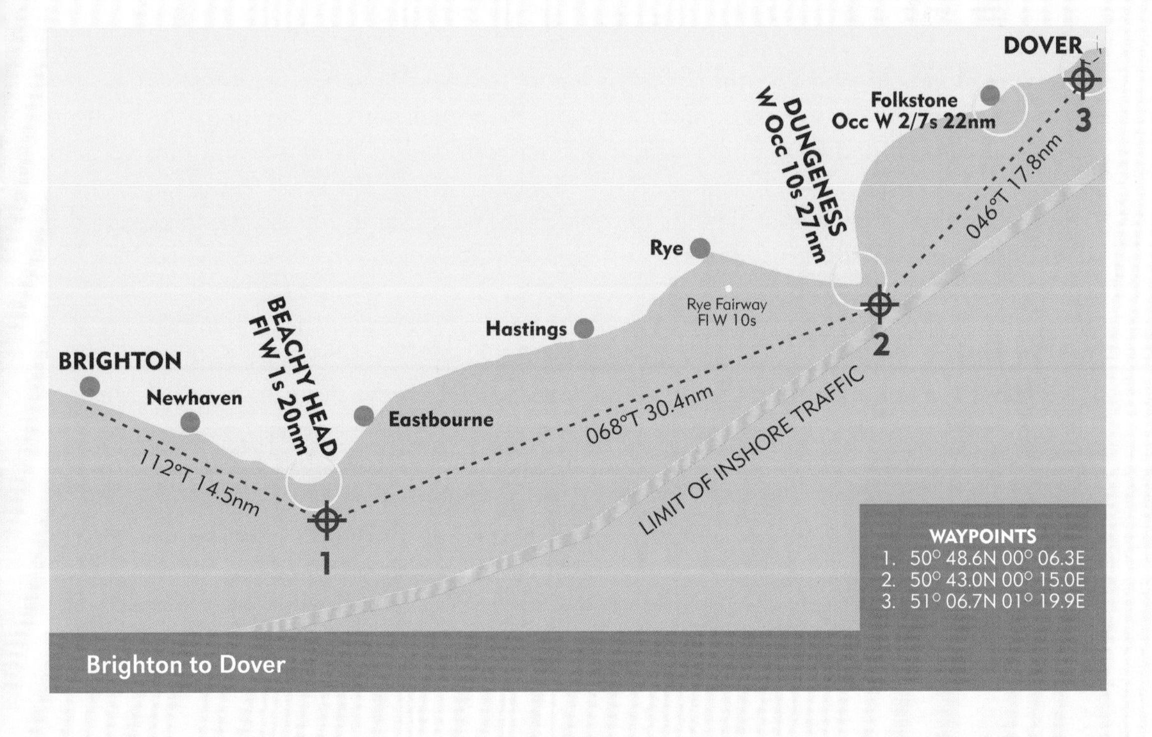

Brighton to Dover

LIGHTS

The timing of the tides means that long coastal passages involve starting out in the dark, arriving in the dark or sailing overnight. This passage is no exception and it is necessary to prepare a list of the lights along your route. You may find it useful to classify lights as:

- passage lights such as Beachy Head. Besides listing their characteristic, it helps to make a note of the range at which you would normally expect to pick up these lights
- landfall lights such as the Rye Fairway buoy, which normally have a range of 3 or 4 miles and take you to the channel leading the harbour
- channel lights in buoyed channels, with a range of 1 or 2 miles. In the days of paper charts it was common practice to note the course and distance between buoys and to tick them off as you passed each buoy. This is difficult to do on a plotter. It may help to prepare a simple sketch plan
- leading lights such as transits or sector lights
- harbour lights, which mark or control entry into and out of harbours, marinas and locks
- isolated lights marking, for example, sewer outfalls, or restricted areas set aside for activities such as waterskiing and cardinal lights

ALTERNATIVE PORTS

Newhaven is rather too close to Brighton to be a serious choice. Sovereign Marina at Eastbourne is a possibility if the weather suddenly turned or some problem meant seeking shelter. Hastings is one of the medieval Cinque Ports but nowadays it is a breakwater offering very limited protection and the largest fleet of beach launched fishing boats in the UK. Rye and Folkestone both dry. The Downs were the anchorage for the square riggers but have less appeal for yachts.

TIDES

The only certainty of long coastal passages is that, as tides flow back and forth along the coast, at some point you will encounter a foul tide. The trick, if you can manage it, is choosing where you meet it, and by cunning sleight of hand you do this by identifying those places where you really do not wish to sail against a foul tide. Having identified these points along your intended route, plan your timings to avoid them or, if that is impossible, to escape the worst of them. These spots include:

- Headlands. Just because the chart does not show overfalls does not mean they are not there. None are shown off Flamborough Head. Believe that, and be surprised.
- Narrows. The tide squeezing through a narrow channel always picks up speed. A familiar example is the Alderney Race between Alderney and Cap de la Hague.
- Channels. Channels are lengthy narrows. Sailing north from Lowestoft you are, effectively, in one long channel until close to Cromer and you probably will not relax for another 10 miles and Cromer is astern. If there is sufficient space, it is sometimes feasible to escape the worse of the tide by sailing in shallower water outside the channel.
- Rivers. As a rule, in rivers the flood tide helps counteract the river flowing to the sea. For small craft, movement in rivers is nearly always controlled by the tide. I once, foolishly, thought I could leave Lisbon and dodge over the last of the flood in the Tagus by sticking

close to shore. I was so close inshore that I was almost on the coastal highway and my progress was embarrassingly slow. Worst of all, it was noticed and later commented upon.

On this passage the two places where you wish either a fair or weak tide are Beachy Head and Dungeness. It is under 20 miles from Brighton to Beachy Head. If you leave Brighton an hour after low water, you carry a fair tide round the headland and around six hours later arrive off Dungeness around the start of the flood that takes you from there to Dover.

PILOTAGE

On this passage there is almost no pilotage or need for points of departure or landfalls. Once clear of the marina breakwater at Brighton you can lay course for Beachy Head, round that and point the bows at Dungeness, and when that is astern head for Dover West Entrance. When 2 miles out, give Dover Port Control, VHF Channel 74, 12 and 16, a call. They usually tell you to give them a call when you are a couple of cables off the entrance, when you will be told to either wait or go in. The western entrance is straightforward but at night the sheer number of lights can be a little confusing and it may help if you have prepared a simple sketch showing the way into the marina.

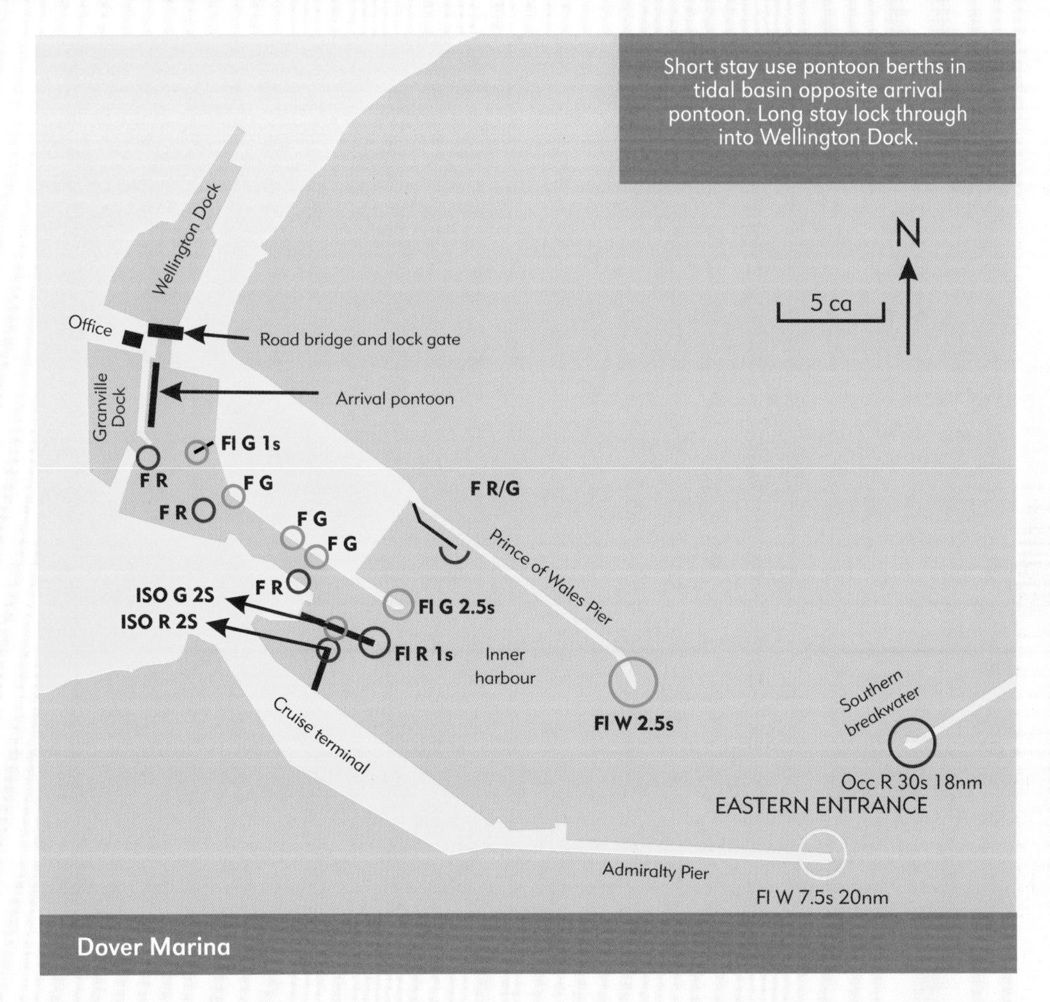

Dover Marina

SHORT OFFSHORE PASSAGES

DOVER TO DUNKERQUE

Going foreign for the first time is a landmark passage and for most British boats this involves heading across the Channel for France. The Channel's funnel shape means that the further west you are, the longer the crossing. The Solent to Cherbourg is probably the most popular and one of the least complicated routes. Steer 180–185°T for 60 miles from the Needles Buoy and you arrive at Cherbourg.

It is not much further to the Channel Islands but as they lie almost due south-west of the Solent there is a higher chance of meeting unfavourable winds and there are strong tidal streams waiting for you towards the end of your passage. It is a more daunting prospect. If you wish to visit the Channel Islands, it may be preferable to sail first to Cherbourg then play the tides and creep westwards along the Cotentin Peninsula. Or perhaps sail west to Weymouth or Dartmouth and trade a longer cross-channel passage against better odds on a fair wind.

There is no standard or typical channel crossing. Yet deciding where to cross is a decision that can make or break a summer cruise. If you are heading eastwards from the Solent towards the Baltic do you cross early, say to Fécamp, and then cruise along the French coast? Or do you hurry the length of the south coast to Dover and the short crossing to Calais? This route is often underrated because you are barely, if at all, out of sight of land, and swimmers consider crossing in a boat as the soft option. This overlooks a traffic separation scheme that almost fills the Dover Strait and unbroken streams of rush hour shipping. It is not just the nose to tail traffic in the lanes. Ferries, like small boys running across a motorway, duck and dive their way between England and France. Include the shallows and sandbanks lying in wait close to the French coast for the careless sailor and you have some challenging navigation.

For those heading east to Holland or the Baltic there is much in favour of a Channel crossing from Dover and arriving off the French coast with the flood tide carrying you eastwards as far as possible, certainly as far as Dunkerque, possibly Oostende, perhaps Zeebrugge. From any of these ports you can choose to charge up the North Sea along the Dutch and German coasts for the Elbe, Brunsbüttel and the Nord-ostsee Kanal or take the more leisurely fixed mast route through Holland.

PRE-SAIL PREPARATIONS

In addition to all the now familiar pre-sail planning and checking, when you go foreign you also have to:

- Confirm with your insurance company that your cover extends beyond British Inland and Coastal Waters.
- Make sure your vessel's Certificate of British Registry is in order.
- Check you hold a valid Certificate of Competence. The basic level is the ICC.
- Check all customs procedures are completed.
- Check everyone on board has a valid passport.
- If your crew are British Nationals, check that they have an NHS European Health Insurance Card (EHIC) backed up with adequate personal medical and travel insurance. British nationals who are also British residents and who do not have an EHIC can ring the NHS on 0845 606 2030 to obtain one.

THE ICC

Going foreign can involve finding a safe channel through a minefield of bureaucratic acronyms. These start with the letters ICC – the International Certificate for Operators of Pleasure Craft, usually shortened to the International Certificate of Competence or ICC.

BACKGOUND TO ICC

The Inland Transport Committee (ITC) is the highest transport policy-making body of the United Nations Economic Commission for Europe (UNECE). In 1979, an ITC working party introduced Resolution 14 to standardise certificates of competence on European inland waters and encourage 'waterborne tourism'.

Resolution 14 was replaced in 1998 by Resolution 40, which introduced a minimum age of sixteen for skippering boats on inland waters and broadened the definition of inland waters to include coastal waters and bareboat charter. From 2011, either Resolution 14 or 40 is accepted and signed in whole, in part or with caveats, by twenty-one countries of the fifty-six UNECE member states. It may also be accepted, but is not actually required, by countries such as Spain and Portugal, which have not signed up.

The twenty-one countries that have signed up are Austria, Belarus, Belgium, Bulgaria, Croatia, Czech Republic, France, Germany, Hungary, Ireland, Lithuania, Luxemburg, the Netherlands, Poland, Romania, Serbia, Slovakia, Switzerland and the United Kingdom.

GETTING HOLD OF AN ICC

An ICC is awarded after a test of boat handling and seamanship at an approved centre and is valid for five years.

UK CUSTOMS PROCEDURES

CLEARING OUT

Since 1993 there has been no need to advise Customs of your departure if you are bound for a port in the EU. If leaving for a destination outside of the EU, it an offence not to tell Customs. You do this on their Form C1331.You can sail as soon as you have completed and posted Part 1 of the form to Customs. Keep Part 2 safe. Customs ask to see it on your return.

The Channel Islands are not part of the EU and if sailing directly to the Channel Islands from the UK you must complete Form C1331. British citizens do not require a passport when visiting the Channel Islands but the passport numbers of all crew members are needed to complete Form C1331.

CLEARING IN

Vessels returning home from an EU port need not advise customs unless:

- you are carrying non-EU persons
- you have duty-free goods onboard
- you have tax owing on the boat
- you are carrying prohibited goods or animals

Vessels returning from outside the EU, including the Channel Islands, should fly a 'Q' flag when entering UK waters (they start 12 miles offshore) and clear in with customs. They should have C1331 Part 2 to hand. Customs can be contacted through the National Yachtline on 0845 723 1110.

If you go to the HMRC website (www.hmrc.gov.uk) and enter *Notice 8 Sailing your pleasure craft to and from the United Kingdom April 2011* you can download a copy of the latest rules.

TIMINGS

As ever, timings are determined by tide times and tidal streams. For this passage you wish to arrive off the French coast with an east-going tide. On a passage of at least 40 miles it is likely that you will either leave or arrive in the dark. It is a surprise to discover that it can be reassuring crossing shipping lanes in the dark. If you must cross ahead on an approaching vessel then at night, in the west-going lane, you first see their green sidelight and steaming lights. Then, as you cross their bows, you have the red-white-green triangle of death as they point their bows straight at you and finally their green sidelight disappears and you heave a sigh of relief. You know you are clear. It is difficult to have this level of certainty during the day.

ROUTEING

Navigation is straightforward. An important consideration is laying a course to cross the shipping lanes at right angles. Of greater importance is avoiding the traffic in the lanes.

LEFT: To cross in front of a commercial vessel, you must be absolutely certain that you can do so safely. AIS, which gives the time to CPA and the distance off, is a great help but not a promise. It is far safer to go round their stern rather than insist that power gives way to sail
RIGHT: At night, the other vessel's navigation lights give you certainty that is impossible during the day. Out of the arc of the port hand light, and with the steaming lights opening up, the yacht crossing ahead of this ferry is clear and there is no risk of collision

They will not, often cannot, change their course or speed. Nor should you rely on them being aware of your existence. They may be, but some ships have so many blind spots that they should fly a white stick from the masthead. To be sure of being safe you must avoid them.

It is surprising how little time there is between a big ship coming over the horizon and crossing your bows. Taking bearings to determine if there is a risk of collision may help, but after allowing for the time between bearings there may be precious little left to take avoiding action. The Automatic Identification System (AIS), either stand-alone or incorporated into your plotter, tells you immediately not only if there is a risk of collision but also gives the time to closest point of approach (CPA) and the distance off at the CPA.

Even if you are sure there is no risk of collision, it is not good practice to cut under the bows of commercial traffic. All it takes is a lull in the wind and your faith in your arithmetic and electronics has sunk you. If there is any risk of collision or even a close encounter, sail round the stern of larger vessels so that if they wish to hit you they must reverse. This results in losing ground to the east in the west-going lane and making it back up in the east-going lane.

Your objective is to arrive around Waypoint 2 with the maximum amount of flood tide left to carry you as far as possible along the coast before you must enter the harbour of your choice, for which you have prepared the necessary pilotage.

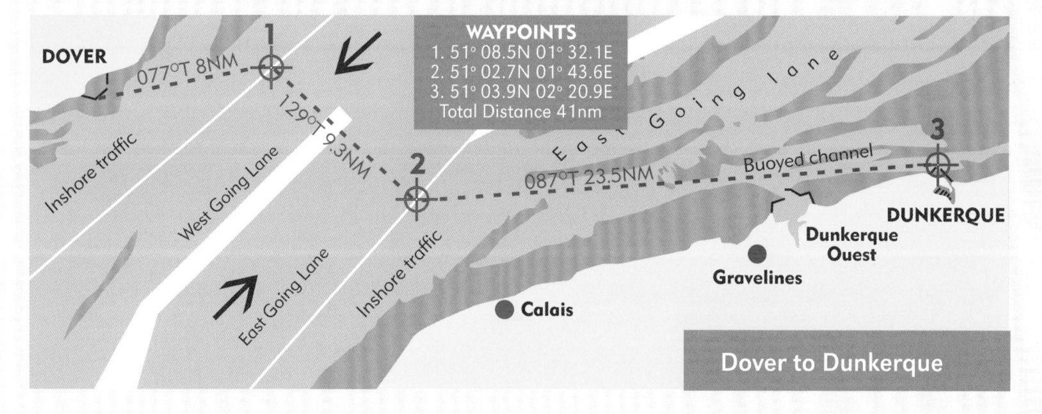

Dover to Dunkerque

LONG OFFSHORE PASSAGES

EAST LOCH TARBERT TO VILLAGE BAY, HIRTA, ST KILDA

This offshore passage is very different from a Channel crossing and illustrates how some passages demand an acceptance by the skipper and crew that circumstances, mostly weather related, may mock your well-laid plans. You may not be able to sail at all or find circumstances insist on your remaining at sea longer than planned and perhaps never reaching your intended destination. All this must be reflected in your planning and preparation.

Other examples of such passages include North Sea crossings from Britain when heavy weather can close many ports along the Dutch, German and Danish coasts. My copy of the German pilot covering the Elbe bluntly warns that 'in stormy weather small SHIPS attempting to enter will be stranded'.

WHY GO THERE?

Lying in the Atlantic 36nm off the west coast of North Harris, the archipelago of St Kilda claims to be the remotest part of the British Isles. It is made up of five islands, which in descending order of size are Hirta, Soay, Boreray, Dun and Levenish. Close to Boreray are two sea stacks, Stac an Armin and Stac Lee. The islands and stacks are all remnants of a tertiary ring volcano, which glaciers, winds and storms have weathered into a dramatic, precipitous landscape. The stacks off Boreray are the highest in Britain. The cliffs are riddled with caves, arches and blowholes.

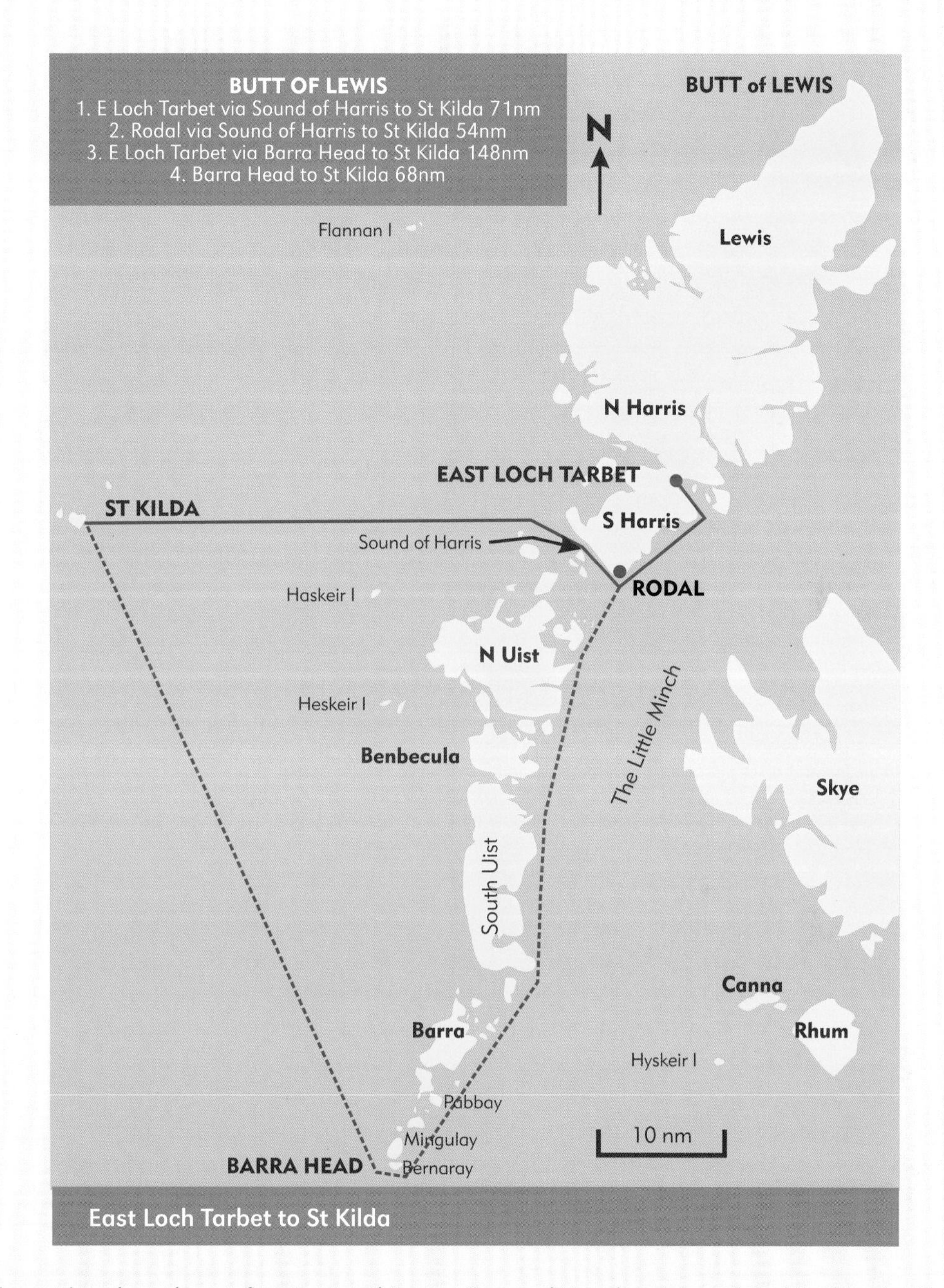

East Loch Tarbet to St Kilda

The archipelago has a fascinating history. Some claim that it was inhabited in the Bronze Age (around 2000 BC) and recent finds of the remains of bronze boats from Dover and Hull suggest that Bronze Age sailors had boats capable of the passage from the mainland in the right weather.

Whether or not the islands were continuously inhabited is debatable. The Vikings swallowed them up and until 1930, when Hirta was evacuated, they were home to a hundred or so hardy souls. The first written account of their life was by Martin Martin who visited the islands in 1697 and published an account of his visit, A Late Voyage to St Kilda, the following year (see page 42). The book was a great success and its effect was to give the islands, the islanders and their way of life a rosy romantic glow that has never faded. After his tour of the Hebrides in 1773 with Dr Johnson, Boswell expressed a wish to buy them. 'Pray do,' said the good doctor, introducing a needed note of sanity, 'and we shall go and pass a winter amid the blasts there.'

In 1957, the ownership of the islands passed to the National Trust for Scotland (NTS). In the same year, with Operation Hardrock, the Army established a guided weapons base on Hirta. It is still there, although it is now run by civilian contractors. Since 2003 the NTS have managed the islands for Scottish National Heritage.

The deeper you dig, the greater the urge to be one of the two thousand or so people who visit the islands each year.

ROUTEING

For 130 miles, from the Butt of Lewis in the north to Barra Head in the south, the Hebrides form a near continuous rampart protecting the Scottish mainland from the Atlantic storms. St Kilda is a rare outlier. It lies 35 miles west of the North Uist coast, which is an academic figure. It is at least 50 miles from any harbour.

The straits between the islands of the Hebrides tend to be shallow and rock strewn and require fair weather and good local knowledge. The one worthwhile exception is the Sound of Harris, between South Harris and North Uist, which boasts two channels. The more northerly, the Stanton Channel, is not just the safest but also the shortest route for a vessel starting out from East Loch Tarbert. This 8-mile channel is the key to the entire passage. Heavy weather prevents boats from leaving or entering the channel. If you are shut in the Minch by bad weather, it may be possible to sail south down the east coast of the islands to Berneray, round Barra Head and sail north-west for 70 miles.

DESTINATION PORT

St Kilda has no port, only anchorages. The best of these is Village Bay on the main island of Hirta. There is another on Loch a' Ghlinne on the north-west side of Hirta, about which little is known, and Martin Martin reported riding out a storm while anchored under the cliffs of Boreray. There is no all-weather anchorage. Village Bay always has some swell and is untenable in winds from the south through to the north-east. When these winds blow, anchored vessels must clear out immediately. They once pinned an LCT on the beach for three days. If winds turn to this sector while you are en route to Hirta, you have had a wasted passage in the sense that you add your name to the long list of boats that have tried and failed to visit; but it may still be possible to cruise round the islands.

Alternative ports/anchorages

The east coast of South Harris is broken every few miles by deep sea lochs, any one of which could provide shelter if required. Rodal is favourite if it is necessary to wait a couple days for the weather to transit the Sound of Harris. Situated on the south-west tip of the island, Rodal is ideally placed for a dash through the sound.

If it does prove necessary to continue south to Barra Head, this becomes a cruise in its own right and choosing from a huge selection of harbours and anchorages is determined by inclination and weather.

On the west coast of the Hebrides there are no alternative ports. There are occasional

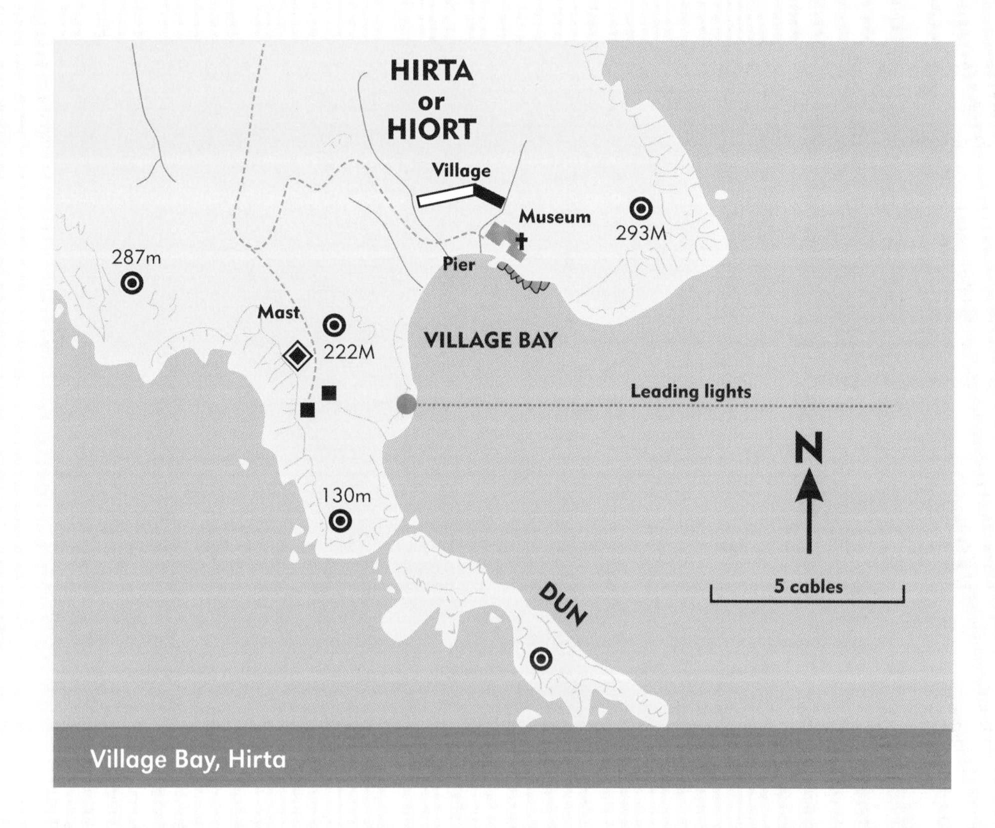

Village Bay, Hirta

anchorages but entering them safely in heavy weather, even if they offer protection in the prevailing conditions, would require great care and local knowledge. In a southerly gale Martin Martin headed for shelter in the Haskeir Islands (rocks might be a better description), but failed to reach them – although from the chart it is difficult to see where they could have found any shelter. There are also reported to be anchorages in the Monarch Islands, which are, confusingly, sometimes also called the Heskeir Islands. To complete the confusion over names, there are the Hyskeir Islands near to Rhum.

WEATHER

The weather patterns, and in particular the winds, determine what time of year you should plan to sail. The weather on the day determines whether to sail or wait for better conditions.

Weather patterns

St Kilda lies along the track taken by the Atlantic depressions. The prevailing winds are south-westerly, but during spring a build up of high pressure over Scandinavia can bring a prevalence of north-easterly winds.

Weather data specific to St Kilda is scarce. By putting together weather data from nearby locations, May or June look like good months to sail.

Weather on the day

Weather patterns are all about averages, which are rarely found in real life. From the routeing information it takes a day to sail to Hirta, allow a day ashore and another to sail back, add

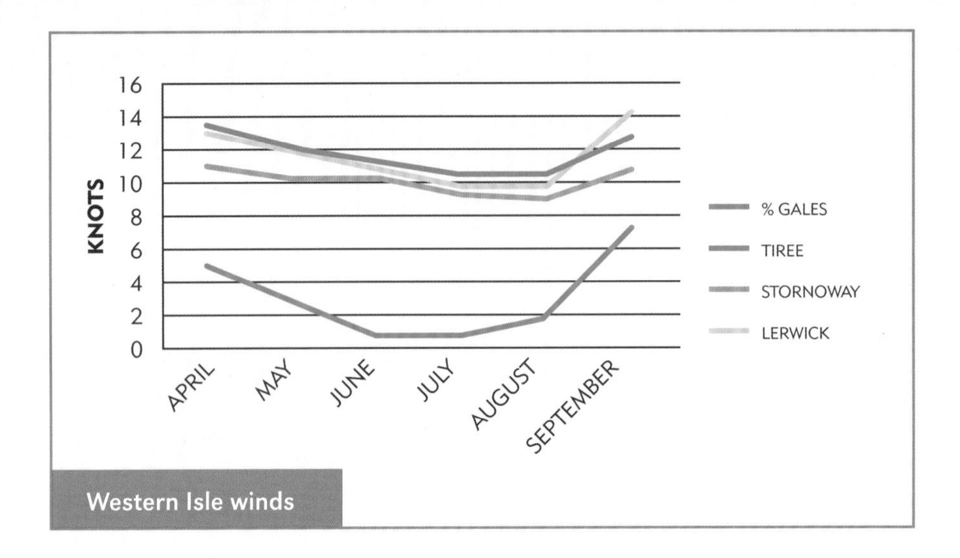

Western Isle winds

a day in hand, and a four-day weather window is required when the winds are from north through to south-west with an upper limit of Beaufort force 5/6.

GRIB files (from GRIB.US or zyGrib) are reasonably accurate up to four days ahead. The best plan is to track the weather forecasts in the days before sailing. If necessary, some of this time can be used to position the boat in East Loch Tarbert or Rodal and then, when a four-day weather window appears, go for it.

TIDES

An ebb tide is necessary to clear the Sound of Harris. Around St Kilda, the average tidal range is 2.9m. For most of the year the Atlantic swell creates 2m high waves. For the rest of the time, 5m swells make the anchorage in Village Bay untenable.

SUPPLIES

On Scotland's west coast, once away from the principal sailing centres, yachting supplies and facilities are thin on the ground. Yachts cruising these waters tend to carry a good selection of spares as a matter of course.

After leaving East Loch Tarbert there is little possibility of topping up on rations, fuel and oil. Although only a four-day cruise is planned, the possibility of having to stay longer at sea makes it prudent to carry supplies for a week or even ten days.

PRE-SAIL CHECKS

This might be the first long cruise following the winter refit. This should have brought everything above and below decks up to scratch. Even so, after comprehensive sea trials a full pre-sail check should be carried out. This should be done at least a month before the planned departure date to allow time for any defects the check reveals to be made good.

OCEAN PASSAGES

The greatest difference between coastal and offshore cruising and blue water sailing is time. It is usual to regard an ocean passage as a stand-alone, three- or four-week voyage, about the same length of time as the average summer cruise but without stopping off in port. This is far from the complete picture.

Normally, any ocean voyage is preceded by a series of day, coastal and offshore passages over several months, which carry you from your home port to the start point of your ocean passage, and when you have made your ocean voyage you are faced shortly afterwards with a second ocean passage, together with another series of coastal and offshore passages, to take you back home.

An Atlantic circuit sailing from Europe to the Caribbean and back includes two ocean passages of three to four weeks each and involves spending fifteen months at sea, covering a distance equivalent to at least five seasons' normal cruising. This is what your planning and preparations must take into account, not a single three- or four-week ocean passage.

Spending over a year continuously at sea opens a new set of problems. Top of the list is how best to equip and rig your boat. Domestic facilities that are fine for a summer cruise, with easy access to shoreside facilities and never spending more than a single night at sea, almost certainly need upgrading to provide a decent quality of life aboard. This may involve more work than you first thought. On many boats, the accommodation below decks is multi-purpose and rejigged each night to turn settees into bunks or tables into beds. This is fine in a marina but not for weeks at sea. There are also your books, DVDs, music, computers and other possessions to be accommodated. Most important is your private space, where you can shut out the world and wash away niggles.

If you are sailing as a family with children, you may wish to arrange a distance learning programme for the children so that their schoolwork does not suffer. Just because you are sailing does not mean that the rest of everyday life stops. You might also wish to look at simplifying sail handling, install self-steering and – since much of your time is spent at anchor – look to your anchor(s), bow rollers and anchor rodes. Since you cannot plug into shore power, you must have some means of keeping the batteries charged at sea and at anchor or return to oil lamps.

Do not overlook crew compatibility. It is never a problem until you cast off and probably the best solution is to sail with friends where the scar tissue of shared experiences, good and bad, is so thick it is impossible to find fault or take offence at each other's behaviour, language or mood ... at least, not for long. Failing that, everyone on board must accept that living in peace and harmony depends on an unbroken supply of mutual toleration. Like good intentions, this never lasts for long.

It is impossible to say how long the planning and preparation phase should last. Some people start from scratch, buying plans and building a boat in the backyard. Others strip out and completely refit and re-rig an existing boat. It will probably be several years before they cast off. Some buy what they believe to be a suitable boat, new or second-hand, and add whatever extra equipment they consider necessary for an ocean passage. This would normally take about a year. A lucky few give their existing boat a more thorough than usual winter refit and set sail the following spring.

AN ATLANTIC CROSSING

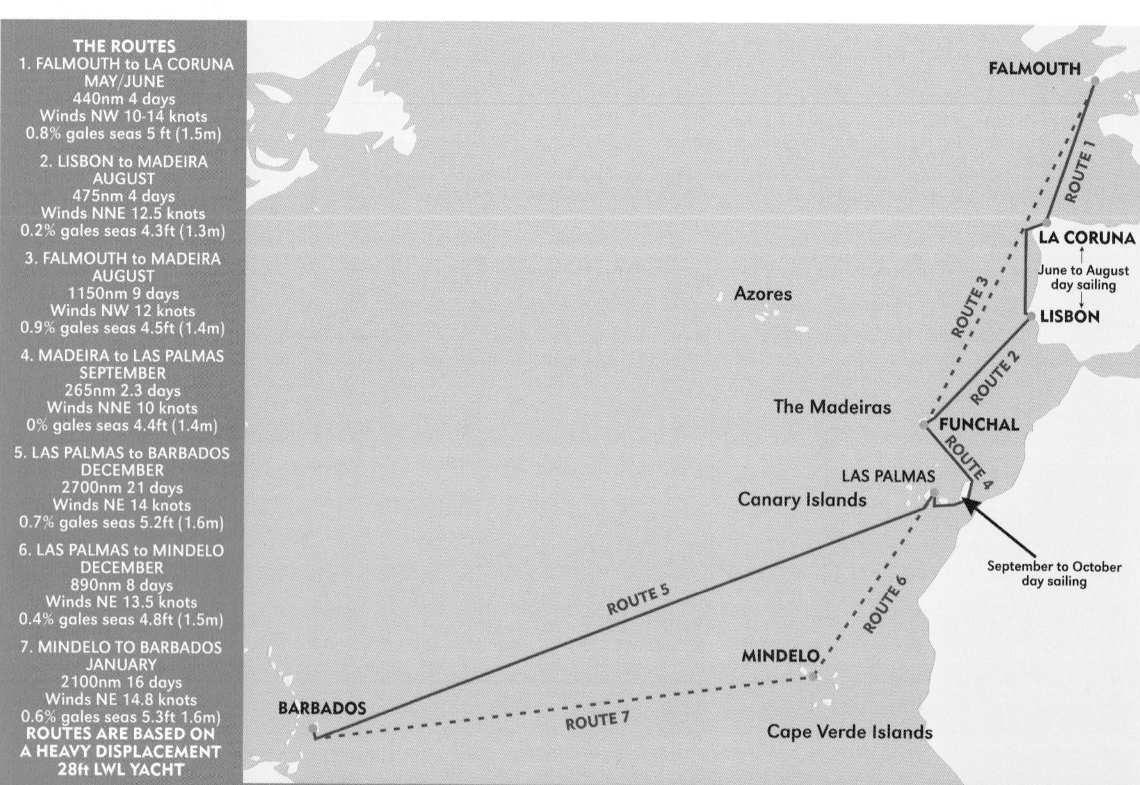

The cruising boat's Atlantic crossing: The trade wind route

ROUTEING

As always, there is a choice of routes. Take sailing from Europe to the Caribbean. Starting out from Falmouth, there are four possible routes.

1 You can sail non-stop. Nicolette Milnes-Walker, the first woman to make a singlehanded transatlantic passage, did so in 1971. Unless you are prepared to brave Biscay in November, the weather window for this passage is from May to early July, after which there is a real possibility of meeting an early hurricane. Once in the Caribbean, it would be necessary to find a good hurricane hole or head south of 10°N to escape the hurricane zone. Milnes-Walker left in early June and arrived in Newport RI in late July. She was probably lucky not to have met really bad weather on her crossing. On the return journey she avoided the risk of meeting bad weather by travelling on the *Queen Elizabeth*. In 1996 two boats left Saint Martin in May, ten days apart, for the Azores. The first arrived after a pleasant sail; the second encountered an extra-tropical storm. This is a hurricane that has left the tropics, lost some of its power, and is heading for Europe. The second boat had a very uncomfortable few days.

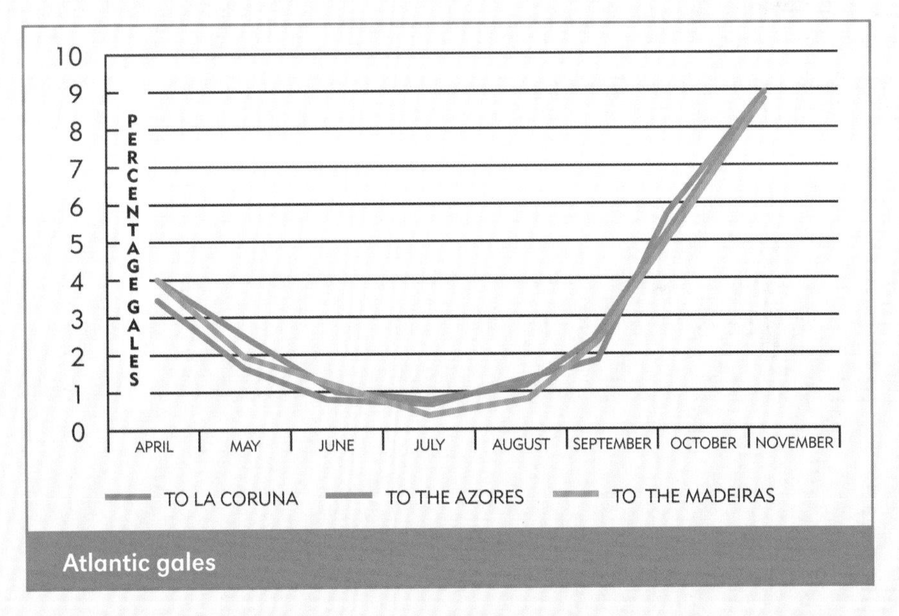

Atlantic gales

2 You could sail via the Azores but if you continue directly towards the Caribbean the same weather restrictions apply. However, you could leave Falmouth in July or August, possibly as late as September, and from the Azores sail to the Canaries and explore them until the hurricane season is over.

3 Sailing for the Azores from the Channel takes you head to head with the prevailing south-westerlies and it may be wiser to pay off a little and head for the Madeira archipelago. The distance is about the same and the option of exploring the Canaries remains open. This could be your best choice if you leave Falmouth late in the season.

4 You could sail from Falmouth to La Coruña in the north-west corner of Spain, then sail southwards down the Iberian Atlantic coast to Lisbon or even Cadiz before heading for the Madeiras and the Canaries. This is the trade wind option and probably the most popular

choice. When you leave the Canaries in late November or early December, you can then either sail direct to the Caribbean or break the journey in the Cape Verde Islands.

WEATHER AND WEATHER ROUTEING

Weather forecasts are treated differently on an ocean passage. You begin by looking for a weather window of three or four days that takes you far enough offshore to give you the sea room to deal with bad weather should it arrive. After that, you must deal with the weather as it comes.

You have four main sources of weather information:

1. If you have satellite communications, you can make arrangements to download GRIB files for your part of the world.
2. There is a wide range of forecasts, amateur and professional, that you can listen to with an SSB receiver.
3. You can download weatherfaxes with an SSB receiver and a computer.
4. Finally, there is what the books call 'single observer forecasting', where you keep track of the weather where you are.

Weather routeing to avoid bad weather for small craft is problematical. The systems travel so fast and small boats so slowly that the weather is upon you before you can escape. You need to keep a careful watch on weather trends – try to look three or four days ahead and plan accordingly.

The USCG broadcasts its High Seas forecast, which reaches across the Atlantic almost to the Azores. It gives the present position of weather systems and their expected position 24 hours later, and the information on each system ends with something like 'Winds 25–30 knots, seas 15–20ft 600 miles south of centre'.

JOIN THE DOTS

Heading for the Azores from the Caribbean, I daily plotted each system on a laminated chart, came south 600 miles (or whatever the figure was) plus a few more miles for luck, and put a dot. Joining the dots produced a line wriggling across the Atlantic, which I regarded as a barrier that I would not cross. It was very primitive weather routeing but it worked. Two boats headed beyond it, looking for the westerlies to carry them swiftly to the Azores, and both sailed back south to escape the gales.

TIMINGS

Timings for small boats crossing the Atlantic are determined by avoiding the hurricane season. This runs from July to November, with the number of hurricanes peaking in September and October.

Every three to seven years, much warmer than average conditions are experienced off the coasts of Ecuador and Peru. This event is called El Niño. Much colder than average conditions off the coasts of Ecuador and Peru is called La Niña. Both El Niño and La Niña are extreme phases of a naturally occurring cycle called the El Niño/Southern Oscillation and

READING A WIND ROSE

Pilot charts describe the average ocean winds and currents. Yachts are most interested in the winds. Every ocean has a pilot chart for each month of the year and the information on these charts is built into programmes like Visual Passage Planner.

Pilot charts, both paper and electronic, are divided into 5-degree squares and each square has its own wind rose based on averages from historic data. At the centre of each wind rose is a circle and the number inside that circle is the percentage of calms that can be expected for that month.

The winds on each wind rose are shown blowing from eight directions. These correspond to the cardinal and ordinal winds of the traditional compass rose. The length of the arrow indicates how long the wind blows from each direction. The longer the wind has blown from a particular direction, the longer the arrow. If one direction has dominated and its arrow would be too long, a figure appears on the arrow. This figure is the percentage of winds from that direction. Giving the percentage wind direction as a figure starts around 30 per cent.

The average wind strength from each direction is shown by ticks on the arrow. One tick is Beaufort 1, three ticks represents Beaufort 3 and so on.

The wind direction is the direction the arrow travels.

Do remember that the figures on the wind roses are averages and fine for planning purposes – but do not be surprised if the weather you actually experience is rather different.

both seriously affect the weather worldwide. Blue water sailors are particularly interested in the research showing that, during a La Niña phase, there is substantially increased hurricane activity in the Atlantic. This makes it all the more important that you should not creep out into the bosom of the sea until the end of November or early December.

NAVIGATION

GPS has made fixing your position in the middle of the ocean no different from and just as accurate as wriggling up the coast. Routeing is more likely to be affected by a desire to place your boat in the Trade winds and a favourable current. Where the Trades are found varies not only from year to year but also with the time of year. Once in the Trades, and with the current under your stern, all that remains is to point your bows towards your destination and wait for it to appear over the horizon.

SAFETY

Difficulties that you cannot handle and for which you require outside assistance are, by definition, major problems. The rest are minor hassles dealt with using onboard resources.

A major problem may be a crew member falling seriously ill. This could involve seeking medical advice by SSB radio or satellite telephone and rendezvousing with a vessel carrying a doctor.

Gear failure that prevents you continuing your passage means either being taken off by another vessel or taking to the liferaft before your boat sinks. Both mean activating the EPIRB and then waiting to be picked up. Rescue on an ocean passage does not include salvaging the boat, even if it is still afloat.

The common factor in coping with all major problems is a GPS enabled EPIRB and good long- and short-range voice communications.

THE CROSSING PLAN

A good crossing plan would be to leave Falmouth for La Coruña around the end of May, spend the summer enjoying the fiestas on the Spanish and Portuguese coasts, head out for the Madeiras some time in August, and arrive at the eastern end of the Canaries in September or October. Autumn is spent wandering west through the Canaries before arriving somewhere like Las Palmas on Gran Canaria to make your final preparations for the crossing.

When you leave Las Palmas you are looking for the north-east Trades and the North Equatorial Current. The easiest way of finding them is to sail to Mindelo in the Cape Verde Islands and spend Christmas there. When you leave early in the New Year you are in both the Trade winds and the current and can expect to arrive in the Caribbean in about three weeks.

Should your departure from Falmouth be delayed for any reason, then up to around mid-August it would be possible to sail directly to the Madeiras and pick up the rest of the route from there. Much later than mid-August the chances of meeting a gale on the way to the Madeiras becomes unacceptably high.

A PACIFIC CROSSING: PUERTO AYORA, GALÁPAGOS ISLANDS TO NUKU HIVA, MARQUESAS ISLANDS

The early explorers discovered the hard way that most of the Pacific Ocean was empty water. It is no surprise that one of the world's longest non-stop passages for small boats is from the Galápagos to the Marquesas Islands. On paper it is not that much further than an Atlantic Crossing, only two or three hundred miles more than the crossing from Las Palmas, but there are no alternative harbours and once you have left the delights of Puerto Ayora and Academy Bay astern, there is only water for the next 3,000 miles.

The Galápagos Islands are more remote than the Canaries, the Marquesas Islands even more so. It is no surprise that fewer yachts make this passage than cross the Atlantic. The need for self-reliance is much greater and this should be reflected in the preparations, which should have been complete long before they arrive in the Galápagos.

PREPARATIONS AND SUPPLIES

Unlike Las Palmas, the Galápagos have no support service for visiting yachts. Facilities of any kind are limited. There are no alongside berths, not even a fuel jetty. You take fuel out to your boat in cans. There are a couple of small supermarkets but their stock, both in range and quantity, is limited. Two or three hungry boats could strip their shelves of goodies. Far better to prepare and victual your boat in Panama, the departure port for most

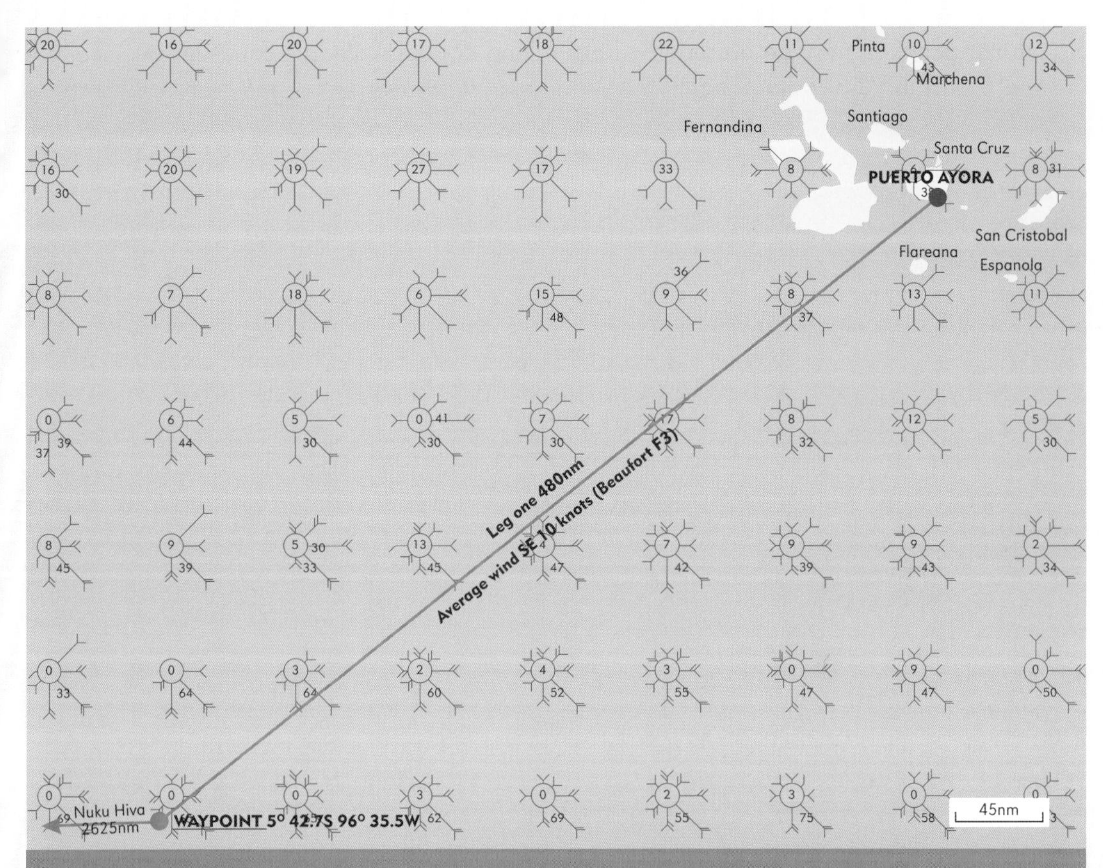

Leg 1: Puerto Ayora, Galapagos Islands to Nuku Hive, Marquesas Islands

The anchorage at Nuka Hiva in the Marquesas Islands

The anchorage at Puerto Ayora in the Galápagos Islands can be quite uncomfortable and yachts must put out a kedge anchor to haul their bows round so that boats point their bows into the swell

boats heading for the Galápagos. Treat anything you find in Puerto Ayora as a bonus. Wise skippers look even further ahead. Facilities in Nuku Hiva are not much better than in Puerto Ayora.

ROUTEING

Perhaps the greatest problem for a sailing yacht is that the Galápagos straddle the Equator and lie in the calms and light winds of the Doldrums. There are two ways of tackling this challenge. The first is to wriggle your way south through the calms until you find the Trade winds. The second is to load the decks with diesel and motor south, rather like those boats returning from the Caribbean to Europe who choose to motor through the Azores High rather than sail around it.

The best time is around spring and the purist dry sailing the pilot chart learns that creeping south-west under sail for around 450 miles to just below 5°S is not impossible and should take between four and five days. After that the winds are more or less steady for the remainder of the passage.

WHALES

Watch out for whales. Around 1790, Captain James Colnett RN discovered that whales calved in their thousands around the Galápagos Islands. Whalers received this information gratefully and rushed to slaughter them. Thirty years later, and a thousand miles west, a new whaling ground was discovered and in November 1820 Captain George Pollard, of the whaler Essex, and his crew found themselves sitting in their three dories after a whale rammed and sunk their boat. Fearful of the cannibals he believed were waiting for lunch in the Marquesas, Captain Pollard led his tiny flotilla against the winds and currents towards South America. Eighty-nine days later two dories and five men were rescued. Ironically, they had survived by turning cannibal. Their experience inspired Melville to write *Moby-Dick*. In the 1970s, two yachts – the *Lucette* and the *Auralyn* – were sunk by whales and although both incidents occurred no more than 300 miles from the Galápagos, their crews spent weeks adrift before being rescued. It seems whales are unforgiving and have long folk memories.

INLAND WATERWAYS

Inland waterways require a different approach to other forms of passage making. The size of Britain's lakes, lochs and reservoirs make passages day sailing without tides. On canals there is the option of pulling in to a canal-side café for lunch and, on the continent, the choice of berthing overnight in the middle of nowhere or in the more picturesque parts of city centres.

Some canal locks and bridges keep shop hours: open at nine o'clock, close for lunch and shut by five in the evening. On continental canals, major road and rail bridges open briefly every few hours at set times throughout the day and night. If you arrive two minutes late then accept with a good grace being stuck on the wrong side until the next opening. On canals such as the Caledonian Canal, arriving at a staircase of locks just as some boats have started travelling the other way leaves no alternative to waiting. Lock capacities are limited and, if the canal is busy, you may have not so much to wait for your turn in the lock as to fight for it.

You can plan each day's programme with the knowledge that it is possible to sail in weather conditions that would otherwise stop you going to sea, although on shallow lakes such as the IJsselmeer a force 4/5 that would normally give no cause for concern when sailing along the coast creates horrible, steep, short seas that make upwind progress for small craft all but impossible. The traditional Dutch boats glide past with their crews playing billiards on the foredeck and the skipper giving you a cheery wave.

A high standard of confident, close order manoeuvring skills are needed. In locks and marinas you squeeze into spaces that appear too small to take your boat, or manoeuvre so close to other boats that a coat of paint counts as sea room.

TIDES AND CURRENTS

It can come as a surprise to discover that some inland waterways are tidal – for example, after entering the sea lock below Tönning, the Eider Canal is tidal until the Nordfeld lock over 20 miles away. When canals are tide free, do not assume that there is no current. Canals are usually part of a drainage system with quite fierce streams and significant changes in level as water is moved from one section of the system to another. Be careful if you creep into a touch-and-go berth for a night's sleep. You may find yourself aground in the morning with no certainty when the water level will rise again.

PAPERWORK

On European inland waters you need to check that your ICC has a CEVNI endorsement and that your VHF is, or can be made, ATIS compliant.

CEVNI RULES

These are the rules and regulations governing navigation on European inland waterways. It is their version of the COLREGS. You can download them from www.unece.org/fileadmin/DAM/trans/doc/finaldocs/sc3/ECE-TRANS-SC3-115r3e.pdf.

If you intend to enter any European inland waterway, your ICC must have a CEVNI endorsement to prove that you know the CEVNI code. The endorsement is made after passing a short multiple-choice written examination conducted at an approved centre. This test is usually taken at the same time as you are tested for your ICC. If you pass, the appropriate section of your ICC will be signed. There is no separate CEVNI certificate. In other words, you cannot hold a CENVI certificate without first holding an ICC.

ATIS

Another acronym to catch out the unwary. ATIS means Automatic Transmission Identification System.

ATIS is not used in the UK but on continental waterways it automatically identifies the sender of any VHF transmission. It was introduced in 2000 under the Basel Arrangement by the RAINWAT (Regional Arrangement concerning the Radiotelephone service on Inland Waterways) Committee under Article S6 of the Radio Regulations of the ITU (International Telecommunication Union) to harmonise RT services. You can read the document setting it all up at www.unece.org/fileadmin/DAM/trans/doc/finaldocs/sc3/ECE-TRANS-SC3-115r3e.pdf.

When you use an ATIS enabled VHF, it transmits a unique number identifying the sender in much the same way as a DSC VHF transmits your MMSI number. This data burst of your ATIS number allows officials to check the ATIS database for details of your vessel.

Sadly, DSC and ATIS are not compatible and if you wish to use ATIS then your first step is to ask OFCOM for an ATIS number. This means requesting OFCOM to vary your ship's radio licence and issue an ATIS number for your boat. For UK vessels this is their MMSI number preceded by the number nine. The OFCOM website tells you how to go about obtaining an ATIS number. Next you need an ATIS compatible VHF. Some VHF sets can switch back and forth between ATIS and DSC in much the same as they switch from international channels to USA channels.

If your radio does not have ATIS but has multiple channel plans that allow it to switch between International, USA and Canadian channels, some manufacturers will, for a fee, modify your radio so that either the USA or Canadian channels can be switched to ATIS. You lose one of these channel plans but it is cheaper than buying a new radio. Otherwise probably the best solution is buying an ATIS enabled handheld VHF. If neither of these options appeal, all that is left is to keep a listening watch and maintain radio silence.

ATIS does not allow scanning, dual watch or DSC operation and only low power transmissions on channels 6, 8, 10, 11, 12,13,14,15, 17, 71, 72, 74, 75, 76 and 77.

On all inland waters, boats should have a holding tank for the heads. Maps showing pump locations are normally freely available locally.

On many canal systems it is necessary to buy a licence that allows you to sail their waters. These can often be purchased beforehand or bought on entering the system.

UK CANALS

The UK has three main canals that yachts visit as part of a summer cruise.

1. Caledonian Canal. This is usually taken as part of a Round Britain sail or as a means for east coast based yachts to visit the west coast of Scotland. It is some 60 miles long and normally takes about three days to sail from end to end. Masts stay up.
2. Crinan Canal. This was built to provide a link to the Clyde Estuary and the west coast of Scotland that avoided the Mull of Kintyre. It is 9 miles long and can be traversed in half a day or less but it is better to allow a full day. Masts stay up.
3. Forth and Clyde Canal. Opened in 1790, closed for the building of a motorway in 1963 and reopened in 2002. It links the Clyde and Forth Estuaries between Bowling and Grangemouth with thirty-nine locks in 35 miles of waterway. For suitable boats it provides an alternative to the Caledonian Canal. Masts come down and low bridges mean that there is a height restriction, with a maximum air draft of 9ft (2.75m).

Staircase locks: this is the staircase at Fort Augustus on the Caledonian Canal. Life is much easier if you can switch the engine off and put a couple of crew ashore. They tend the lines and walk the boat from lock to lock. At the last lock they step aboard and tend the lines from the boat

CONTINENTAL CANALS

The continental canal system is vast. The two systems probably of greatest interest to UK sailors are the French and Dutch canals.

FRENCH CANALS

The appeal of the French canals is that they provide a means of avoiding crossing the Bay of Biscay on the way to the Mediterranean, although they are only for boats whose dimensions do not exceed:

Draft	1.8m (6 ft)
Beam	5.0m (16 ft 5 in)
Air draft	3.5m (11 ft 6 in)

The classic route (there are several to choose from) starts at Calais or Le Havre, where the mast comes down. It then takes you through Paris, Chalon, to Lyon and Rhône and then via Arles and Avignon to Port St Louis and the Mediterranean.

For information on how to obtain a licence to use the canal system and for details of closures, repairs and maintenance to the canal, visit Voies Navigables de France (www.vnf.fr) who since 1991 have been responsible for Europe's largest canal system.

DUTCH CANALS

Holland has almost 2,500 nautical miles (4,400km) of canals and over six hundred marinas, which make it as easy to travel by water as by road. A full list of marinas can be found, in Dutch, at www.allejachthavens.nl. For British yachts, the great attraction of the Dutch canals is the fixed mast route, which allows you to sail the length of Holland without having to drop the mast. For that reason Holland is popular both as a cruising area in its own right and as a sheltered route for boats heading for the Baltic.

Dutch canals are heavily used by commercial traffic, which has priority over leisure craft, and with boat ownership in Holland estimated at 1.64 per head, simple arithmetic tells you that the Dutch canals are very busy, with over 10 million boats or about 4,000 for every mile of waterway. And that is before any visitors arrive.

There are no speed limits on the larger rivers but on the canals it varies between 5 and 9 knots. On canals, boats mostly keep to starboard and if under sail must have the engine ready for use. If motorsailing you must display a black cone, point downwards.

PAPERWORK

You must have a CEVNI endorsed ICC.

Yachts must carry a copy of the Inland Waters Police Regulations. ANWB, a Dutch motoring organisation roughly equivalent to the AA or RAC, publish annually the Almanak voor Watertoerisme. Part 1 contains, in Dutch, a copy of the Police rules. Part 2, also in Dutch, has information on tides, bridge and lock opening times, general sailing directions and port/marina information. The ANWB also publish a range of charts covering all inland waters. If you intend to visit the Waddenzee, make sure you have the latest marine charts onboard. These are updated and republished annually to reflect changes in the drying channels.

Travel on the Dutch canals is generally free but some towns ask boats going through to pay bruggeld. This is usually no more than a few euros but paying it can be fun and the bridge or lock keeper lowers a clog to collect your money as you sail through.

Since 2009 it has been illegal to discharge toilet waste from pleasure boats on all inland waters and within 12 miles of the Dutch coast.

THE USA INTRACOASTAL WATERWAY

For boats returning to Europe from the Caribbean, the Intracoastal Waterway along the US eastern seaboard is an attractive way of gaining northing without going to sea.

From early in the 19th century, the seas off Cape Hatteras were famous as a graveyard for ships and it was reckoned their remains explain the magnetic anomalies shown on today's charts. Various ideas were mooted on how small ships could avoid the hazards of the eastern seaboard. The answer was a 3,000-mile long waterway called the Intracoastal Waterway, which runs along America's Gulf and Atlantic coasts. It is part natural inlets, rivers, bays and sounds and part artificial canal.

It is a popular boating area in its own right, particularly with the Snowbirds, US boats that head south for the sun in the winter and north to escape the heat in the summer. One observer has described it as 3,000 miles of Solent. Travel on the canal is free. Details of facilities can be found at www.icwfacilitiesguide.com. If your computer can handle them, raster charts for the ICW can be downloaded from www.charts.noaa.gov/OnLineViewer/AtlanticCoastViewerTable.shtml.

Boats heading for Europe are most interested in the section that begins at Key West, Florida and ends at Norfolk, Virginia. This is known as the Eastern ICW. It is possible to continue further northwards to the unofficial terminus at Manasquan River, New Jersey.

The ICW has a nominal depth of 12ft (4m) but in places this can fall to 7ft (2.1m). The mast stays up. Bridges either open or have a clearance of 69ft (21m).

PAPERWORK

Sailors from Europe need to obtain a visa before entering US waters and clear in with customs and immigration at their first port of call.

TEN CANAL TIPS

A few simple preparations can take much of the drama out of cruising inland waterways.

1. Sail with mooring lines rigged fore and aft and fenders ready port and starboard so as to be able to berth instantly.
2. It is usual in locks to lead the bow and stern lines round shore bollards and take them back to the boat. The crew stay on board, adjusting the length of the line as necessary, and when the time comes to leave they simply haul the lines inboard. In some canals, particularly those where crew members go ashore to operate the locks this may be impossible. If so consider leading the bow through a block on the samson post back to the cockpit so both lines can be tended by one person.
3. If the lock is busy then raft up to a vessel already lying alongside the wall. This is cheating. They tend their lines and you sit in your cockpit.

4. If you expect to berth alongside the bank carry a handful of large metal spikes and a hammer to drive them in. Remember the underwater profile of a canal is normally saucer shaped and often there is not enough water for yachts to lie alongside the bank. When they try to approach the bank parallel to the shore they run aground and come to a stop several feet from the bank. Take lines ashore by putting the bows into the bank. A volunteer leaps ashore carrying the lines. Later you can square off and lie parallel to the bank. Carrying a plank to bridge the gap between your boat and the bank is a good idea if you wish to go ashore or retrieve your volunteer.
5. On Dutch canals there are overnight berthing places at regular intervals. These come with mooring bollards and sometimes there are rubbish bins and a chemical toilet. It is usually possible to berth against the bank in these spots.
6. If you must take the mast down build a framework to support it at the bow and stern and consider removing the masthead light, antennas and wind instruments to avoid damage. Put buckets over the head and heel of the mast.
7. If you do take the mast down then make alternative arrangements for navigation lights in case you find yourself sailing in the dark.
8. In a rising lock try to keep as far back as you can to avoid the worst of the eddies when the sluices open.
9. Keep a knife handy in the cockpit in case a mooring rope snags while you are in a lock. In a rising lock there is time to sort it out but in a falling lock there are only seconds before you are hung up.
10. Be aware that in places weed can be a serious problem and can be so thick that it wraps around the propeller and stalls the engine. Crews on other boats leaning over the stern and stabbing the water with a boat hook is a warning that you are approaching weed infested waters.

Urquhart Castle: all inland waterways are different. Few are end-to-end man-made waterways. This is the best view of Urquhart Castle on the shores of Loch Ness. Coachloads of tourists walk round it but never see it as the castle was meant to be seen

ENVOI

> *Managers do things right, leaders do the right thing.*
>
> **Richard Pascale, *Managing on the Edge* (Penguin, 1990)**

Every successful passage depends largely upon careful and thorough planning and preparation followed by imaginative and flexible execution, but it requires one further component to make it a perfect passage – leadership. This is the secret ingredient that, more than any other, determines how well your planning and preparation are put into practice. Two boats of the same class making the same passage on the same day, carrying out the same preparations, using the same routeing plan, can have wildly differing outcomes. One boat can arrive happy and cheerful having had a great time; the other arrives with the crew inflating the dinghy, having taken a vote to cast the skipper adrift. The difference is down to the skippers and the style of leadership they displayed.

Do not confuse leadership with decisiveness or the ability to make 'hard decisions'. Hard decisions usually go easy on those making them. In that sense they are both simple and painless to make.

In June 1816, the French frigate Méduse, under the command of Viscount Hugues Duroy de Chaumareys, left Rochefort with a cargo of settlers for Saint-Louis in Senegal. De

Chaumareys had spent most of his life in post-revolution France as a postmaster. He had almost no seagoing experience, none for over twenty years and none in command. Through a mixture of masterly incompetence and near complete ignorance, on 2 July he ran his ship aground on the Arguin Bank off the East African coast. There were insufficient boats to take all those on board and at least 146 men and one woman were put aboard a raft made of spars. This had so little buoyancy they were up to their waists in water. De Chaumareys' intention was to tow this contraption to the shore, after which one boat would go to Saint-Louis to arrange the rescue of those left on shore.

Displaying decisive leadership, de Chaumareys assured the people on the raft that he was in control. He told them they were not to worry. He was with them. He then leapt into the best equipped, most seaworthy ship's boat and left for Saint-Louis. The other boats towed the raft for a couple of miles before cutting it adrift and following de Chaumareys' example. After thirteen days, the fifteen survivors on the raft were picked up by HMS *Argus*; Théodore Géricault's painting of the moment Argus spotted the raft can be seen in the Musée de Louvre in Paris. There is no evidence that, once he left for Saint-Louis, de Chaumareys gave the survivors on the raft another thought. He made no arrangements to search for them when he arrived in Saint-Louis.

Leadership is not a component or sub-skill of management. Managers fit into hierarchies, establish systems and follow procedures. Often, their credo is that doing nothing can never be wrong. Leadership demands rather greater imagination and flexibility. This is not to say that a manager cannot be a leader – but there are many managers with delusions of leadership. For much of the time, when the demands for leadership are low, they may even pass muster; but when the going gets tough they are inevitably among the first to get going, travelling rapidly towards the horizon and safety. The kindest interpretation of de Chaumareys' behaviour is that he fell into this category of manager.

Leadership has been defined as acting with grace under pressure. I am unsure whether or not it is a skill that can be taught, an innate talent, or is acquired through the bruises of hard won experience. Perhaps it is a mix of all three. I do accept that the elements of leadership, like parroting the times tables, can be learned, but putting them together and making them work when it really matters is something else.

There is more to leadership than simply acting with grace when matters go awry. A friend who knows much more on this subject than I do points out that when I am sailing singlehanded, I may well act with grace under pressure – but having no one to lead, I am not displaying leadership. I cannot argue – my actions in circumstances where leadership may be required are mostly motivated by self-preservation.

True leadership is not just acting with grace under pressure, but persuading others to do the same – and then having them follow your lead. How this is done varies from situation to situation and moment to moment as circumstances change. It is only when you stir the right leadership style for you and your crew into the mix of planning and preparation that the perfect passage will emerge.

If you command wisely, you will be obeyed cheerfully.

Thomas Fuller (17th-century churchman, doctor and writer)

APPENDIX: PRE-SAIL CHECKLIST

This is not a checklist, at least not in the sense that you tick the boxes and then go to sea. It is intended as an aide-memoire to help you prepare your own checklist for any passages that you are planning. This checklist is neither prescriptive nor exhaustive.

Highlighting which elements should be included in different types of passage (day, coastal, offshore etc) initially appealed on the grounds that there should be a logical progression, with the length of the checklist keeping more or less in proportion to the length of the passage.

In practice this proved extremely difficult to do and picking better brains than mine led to widespread and heated arguments. There is, it seems, no agreement as to what items are appropriate to particular types of passage.

I suspect this is partly because there is no accepted definition of the different types of passage. One person's day sail is another's coastal passage. The obvious solution was to play politician, sit on the fence and advise that your checklist must include those items you believe are appropriate to your passage.

PLANNING AND PREPARATIONS
Decide on goal
Identify limitations to goal: • time • equipment • skills • weather
Identify what elements must be included in your plan to achieve your goal
Gather the information required to achieve your plan
From the courses of action open to you, select what you consider to be the best for you
Identify the resources required to carry out your chosen options
Calculate the onshore workload necessary to carry out your chosen options
Cost workload and adjust to suit budget
Prepare timetable to carry out workload
If timetable over last possible sailing date, then revise timetable and/or workload
Start implementing your timetable
Monitor progress and adjust workload or timetable as necessary

SHIP'S PAPERS
Logbook
Standing orders
Night order book
Certificate of Registry
Proof VAT paid
Insurance certificate
PERSONAL PAPERS
Passports and visas
Medical/travel insurance
Vaccination and medical certificates
Personal equipment insurance
DAILY CHECKS
Checklists prepared and duties allocated
DEFECTS BOOK
To hand; all crew aware of importance of recording all defects, however small
INVENTORIES
Inventories prepared and tasks of keeping them up to date allocated: • fuel inventory • water inventory • food inventory • spares inventory

CREW

Crew selection

Familiarisation with boat

DRILLS

- MOB drills
- Abandon ship drills
- Sail handling drills
- Boat handling drills:
  - leaving berth
  - at sea under power
  - at sea under sail
  - acting as lookout and making reports
  - heaving-to
  - anchoring
  - weighing anchor
  - berthing
  - engine start/stop procedures
  - fire precautions, location and use of fire extinguishers
  - using the heads
  - location and use of bilge pumps
  - location and rules on seacocks

COMMAND STRUCTURE

All crew aware of the onboard command structure

WATCH KEEPING

Watch keeping system agreed

All crew aware of the watch keeping arrangements and handover lead times and procedures

All crew aware which watch they are in

CREW DUTIES ALLOCATED

Mate

Watch officers

Navigator

Engineer

Electrician

Purser

CREW TRAINING

All appropriate training courses identified and crew enrolled as appropriate

ABOVE DECKS

ANCHORING/MOORING/BERTHING

Tape/seal anchor rode hawsepipe

Tie down anchor or stow securely above or below deck as convenient

All fenders and berthing lines have secure, readily accessible stowage

All warps have secure, readily accessible stowage

PULPIT/PUSHPIT/STANCHIONS

Pulpit/pushpit feet secure

Stanchion feet secure

Stanchion straight and in alignment to guardrails

RIGGING/MAST

Clean and lubricate sail tracks

Inspect all fittings including:

- rigging screws
- sail reefing hardware
- fittings between spreaders and mast and rigging

Inspect all shrouds and stays

All winches checked and in good order

SAILS

Condition of:

- main sail
- headsail(s)
- staysail
- cruising chute
- spinnaker
- storm sails

Sails for sea hanked on

Halyards and topping lifts in good condition, coiled and secured

Sheets, running free, blocks correctly set

Reefing systems checked

HELM

Check helm swings freely and easily from hard a'port to hard a'starboard

Check pintles, bearings, cables etc are in good condition

Emergency steering checked and in good working order

All heavy items on deck securely tied down or fastened to deck

DINGHY

If an inflatable:
- deflated and securely tied down on deck
- paddles
- repair kit
- anchor and lines
- marked with vessel's name

If a rigid dinghy:
- securely tied down on deck
- paddles and crutches
- anchor and lines
- fenders
- marked with vessel's name

OUTBOARD ENGINE

Engine stop procedures followed before stowing for sea

Securely stowed

Protected from seas and weather

Fuel for outboard engine securely stowed

HATCHES AND LOCKERS

All deck hatches open outwards and are closed at sea; hatches opened only with skipper or mate's permission

Washboards for main to hand

Cockpit lockers closed but unlocked

COCKPIT DRAINS

Of adequate size, clear of obstructions and working properly

GUARDRAILS

Also called lifelines, enclose the working deck

Lifelines are of 5mm stainless steel wire, not plastic coated

Upper guardrail at least 600mm above the deck

Lower guardrail at least 300mm above the deck

Lashings attaching guardrails to pulpit/pushpit not longer than 100mm (4in)

TOE RAIL

If fitted, at least 25mm above the deck

Has adequate scuppers allowing easy drainage of water from deck

GAS LOCKER

Gas bottles securely stowed

Regulator(s), pipework and cut-offs in good condition

Outboard drain clear and open

BELOW DECKS

ACCOMMODATION

Accommodation is adequate for the numbers onboard and the nature and length of voyage

Bunk spaces allocated to all crew members

Sea berths made up, lee cloths fitted

Personal locker space allocated

All personal kit stowed

Adequate handholds to allow safe movement below decks in heavy weather

Wet locker for oilskins convenient to the main hatch

STOWAGE

Sufficient stowage to adequately take all supplies, equipment and personal belongings

All loose items securely stowed

All lockers closed

Check that the heel of a keel-stepped mast is securely fastened to the mast step or adjoining structure

Check that adequate handholds are provided below decks

All lockers closed

GALLEY

Check that the stove is securely fastened with a safe accessible fuel shut-off control and that it is capable of being safely operated in a seaway

Stove gimbals unlocked

Gas alarm checked

Smoke alarm checked

Check stove works

Gas supply turned off at stove

Pots, pans, crockery securely stowed

Safety strap for cook in good condition

Check all cold water taps work

Check all hot water taps work

Fire blanket close to stove

HEADS

Check heads work

Check showers work

SEACOCKS

Check open/shut as required

Check a wooden plug is taped to hose close to every seacock

SAFETY

All crew know how to make a CH 16 Mayday call

LIFERAFT

Securely stowed on deck and ready to launch

MOB EQUIPMENT

Danbuoy

Securely stowed on deck and ready to launch

Lifebelt(s)

Securely stowed on deck and ready to launch

All lifebelts have a:
- light
- drogue
- whistle

All buoyant equipment is marked with vessel's name and marine grade fluorescent tape

Throw lines

At least 15m long

Securely stowed on deck and ready to launch

JACKSTAYS

5x19 stainless steel wire, not plastic coated, or webbing with a breaking strength of at least 2,400kg

Fitted port and starboard

Attachment points through bolted with adequate backing pads

When going forward, able to clip into jackstay before leaving cockpit

HARNESS TETHER ANCHOR POINTS

Fitted:
- at all on-deck workstations such as the helm or mast
- around main hatch so that crew clip in before climbing into cockpit or remain clipped in until safely in cabin

Number of anchor points sufficient so that no more than one person is clipped into an anchor point at any time

All anchor points through bolted with adequate backing pads

GRAB RAILS

Securely attached to deck and in good order

LOCKERS

Cockpit lockers closed but unlocked

Cabin lockers open only when in use

BILGE PUMPS

There should be at least two manual bilge pumps:
- one in the cockpit, capable of being operated with all cockpit lockers and hatches closed
- one below decks

Handles to all manual bilge pumps attached by a lanyard to the bilge pump

No bilge pump discharges through the cockpit drains or into the cockpit unless cockpit drains directly outboard

PERSONAL SAFETY

Lifejackets issued and fitted to all crew aboard

All lifejackets have a:
- whistle
- light in working order, strobes preferred
- crotch strap
- sprayhood

All lifejackets are marked with owner's name or vessel's name

All lifejackets checked and in good working order

Exposure suits issued to all aboard

Harnesses and tethers issued to all aboard

All crew have appropriate foul weather clothing

SHORE CONTACTS

Shore contacts informed of plans

FIRST AID

At least one first aider on board

All first aid kits complete and contents up to date

Note made of crew on personal medication

ELECTRICAL

All electrical wiring, AC and DC including junction and fuse boxes, in sound condition

Domestic battery bank fully charged

Engine start battery bank fully charged

All batteries securely fastened down

- Check all instruments on and working properly
- Check all spreader lights working properly
- Check all navigation lights working properly
- Spare navigation lights working properly and are to hand
- Check all domestic lights and appliances
- Chargers for all electronic equipment checked and found to be working properly
- Wind generator output satisfactory
- Solar panel output satisfactory

MECHANICAL

- Engine serviced and in good condition
- Engine starts easily
- Engine mounts in good condition
- Fuel lines in good condition
- Fuel cut off switches/valves in good working order
- Drive train/prop shaft and stern glands in good condition
- Engine exhaust blowers and engine room ventilation in good condition
- Exhaust in good working order
- Oil levels:
  - engine
  - gear box
- Fuel levels:
  - fuel tanks full
  - jerry cans full
- Fuel treatment additives:
  - added to fuel in tanks and cans
  - adequate reserve carried for future refuelling
- Fuel filters:
  - replaced before start of passage
  - adequate spares carried
- Fuel funnel with built-in filter to hand
- Oil filters:
  - replaced before start of passage
  - adequate spares carried
- Spare fuel securely stowed
- Coolant levels checked

ENGINE START SEQUENCE

- Raw seawater seacock open
- Engine started
- Engine warmed up/seawater through exhaust

SUPPLIES

- Food
- Water
- At least 3 litres of drinking water per day for the duration of the passage to be carried for each crew member
- 5 litres of emergency drinking water per crew member to be carried in separate containers
- Fuel:
  - diesel
  - petrol/two-stroke
  - gas
- Cleaning supplies
- Head's supplies

SPARES

- Engine spares:
  - impeller
  - fuel filters
  - fan belts
  - gaskets
- Sail repair kit
- Epoxy/GRP repair kit
- Bilge pump spares
- Spare batteries for flashlights. Consider investing in a 12V charger and using rechargeable batteries

TOOLKITS

- Toolkit electrical
- Toolkit mechanical
- Toolkit bosun

COMMUNICATIONS

SIGNALS

- Fog horn
- Day shapes (ball and cone)
- Torches
- Anchor light
- Signal/high intensity lamp/strobe

RADIOS

- EPIRB(s) checked and working properly
- Fixed VHF checked and working properly
- Handheld VHF(s) checked and working properly

Emergency VHF antenna checked and working properly

SSB radio checked and working properly

Satellite communications checked and working properly

Cellphones checked and working properly

ROUTEING/NAVIGATION

COMPASS

Magnetic marine compass permanently installed with light where it can be easily seen by the helm

Current deviation to hand

Spare compass to hand

PUBLICATIONS

Almanac

Tide tables

Tidal atlas

Admiralty list of lights

Admiralty list of radio signals

Pilots

Charts:
- harbour
- passage
- routeing
- plotting

ROUTE PLANNING

All possible routes identified

Preferred route selected

Limitations to chosen route identified

Waypoints for chosen route identified and noted

Course and distance between waypoints calculated

Estimated time enroute (ETE) between waypoints calculated

Total distance to sail

Total ETE

All clearing bearing and transits en route noted

TIDES

Times of high and low water for all ports/anchorages

Set and drift of tidal streams

Tidal overfalls/gates:
- all relevant tidal overfalls/gates identified
- best times to pass all tidal overfalls and gates noted

TIMINGS

Based on times of high and low water and total ETE calculated:
- estimated time of departure (ETD)
- ETA at each tidal overfall/gate
- ETA at destination

HAZARDS

All hazards along or close to chosen route indentified

Position and identifying marks of all hazards noted

All alternative ports/anchorages identified

Limitations to each alternative port/anchorage noted

Pilotage notes on all alternative ports/anchorages prepared

LIGHTS AND BUOYAGE

All lights and buoys along chosen route identified

Range and characteristic of all lights noted

Expected time when all lights should be picked up noted

PASSAGE PLAN

Departure pilotage to departure point prepared

Passage making between departure point and landfall prepared

Landfall and arrival pilotage prepared

WEATHER

All suitable and appropriate sources of weather forecasts identified and consulted

Weather trends based on forecasts and actual weather over previous few days noted

Latest weather forecast noted

PRE-SAIL CHECKS

All above pre-sail checks carried out, all is on order and vessel is ready to proceed to sea

INDEX

Bold indicates that the topic is covered in some detail, often over several pages